FUNDAMENTAL PRINCIPLES
OF RESTAURANT
COST CONTROL

Contents

Preface

When I enrolled at Florida State University in 1961 to major in hotel and restaurant management, there were very few books available on restaurant cost controls. There was *Profitable Food and Beverage Operation* by Brodner, Carlson, and Maschal; the Horwath and Horwath book titled *Hotel Accounting*, and most memorably, the quintessential cost control book of that time period, *How to Plan and Operate a Restaurant*, written by one of my instructors, the late Peter Dukas. Today, more than a dozen books on the subject of cost controls are in print but only a few have authors who have written about restaurant cost controls from a *first person* perspective.

The Fundamental Principles of Restaurant Cost Control is a book written by a restaurant operator who has also been a student and instructor of restaurant management. Many restaurant managers and owners have had to learn the business through trial and error and are more comfortable with *practice* than *theory*. However, if we always do what we always did, we will always get what we always got. Therefore, new ideas, concepts and theories must be introduced if an independent operator expects to remain in business today competing against the national restaurant chains. This book brings together the author's experience and knowledge as a corporate restaurant administrator, an independent restaurant owner-operator, and as one of the leading academics in the area of restaurant operations.

Operators will surely note the practicality of the cost controls described in this book, used by the author while serving as general manager of Regan's

Restaurants, Inc. Shawnee Mission, Kansas; as owner-operator of Angelo's Restaurants, Inc., Orlando, FL and as professor of hotel and restaurant administration at Florida State and Georgia State Universities.

This book is intended for the independent restaurant operator wanting practical information on food, labor and beverage cost controls as well as individuals thinking about opening a restaurant and chefs and culinarians seeking further insight into practical cost control methods they can utilize in their businesses. As an instructor of cost controls, I have sought to find textbooks that explained cost controls in a practical and realistic manner. This book presents cost control in a practical perspective that every experienced restaurant operator will immediately recognize.

As an independent operator, I realized that my physical presence in my restaurant was not sufficient to control costs. There were too many things that the eye cannot see and the only way they are revealed is by cost control records. Many independent operators do not understand the real purpose of cost controls. Often they believe that because they have friends and family working for them that they would insult them if they instituted cost controls. The most important aspect of cost control is not to detect theft and dishonesty on the part of the employees; its primary purpose is to provide owners and managers with the information it needs to make day-to-day operational decisions and to assess the effectiveness of their decisions.

The amount of knowledge needed by students and practitioners of food service management today is considerably greater than the knowledge needed to be successful yesterday. Operators are no longer afforded a second chance when learning proceeds by trial and error. The high failure rate for new restaurants is well documented. None of those that go out of business *plan to fail;* however, many *fail to plan.* Cost control management is *preventive* first and foremost. If it is always *corrective,* meaning after the fact, cost control systems are lacking and a loss has already incurred.

The concepts, procedures and systems described in this book will provide practical information to the beginning restaurant operator and the experienced operator. Independent operators of restaurants doing less that $1.5 million will find particular application to the examples given.

ACKNOWLEDGMENTS

First, I wish to acknowledge the reviewers of this text: Terence F. McDonough, Erie Community College, Buffalo, NY; and Tom Van Dyke, Indiana University of Pennsylvania; and Neil Marquardt and Barbara Cappuccio at Prentice Hall.

There are several individuals who have had a profound influence on my life, my management style, my teaching philosophy, and my moral and ethical code. I was in introduced to the restaurant business by my step-father Laurence Margarella when I was growing up on the south side of Chicago. While attending Florida State University I was taught by the master of cost controls, Peter Dukas. My mentor in the restaurant business was James P. Regan who believed in me and let me learn from my mistakes. He taught me the importance of being fair and equitable to my employer, my employees, my purveyors and myself. All three of these gentlemen have past on but what they taught me endures.

There are two women who have also had a profound impact on any success I have attained. One is my mother, Diane Margarella who saw to it that I could become the best that I could be, encouraged me to further my education and was the financial support that made Angelo's Restaurants a reality. The other is my wife of 31 years, who has been my biggest booster over the years and has supported me at considerable sacrifice to her own ambitions. Tana, everything I have achieved is because "you have been the wind beneath my wings."

David V. Pavesic

About the Author

Dr. David Pavesic first worked in food service at the age of thirteen as a grill and counterman at an independent drive-in in Chicago, Illinois. His stepfather owned two Italian restaurants on Chicago's south side from 1950 to 1974. There, Dr. Pavesic worked as dishwasher, busboy, waiter, and cook's helper during high school and college. He earned his bachelors and masters degrees in hotel and restaurant management from Florida State and Michigan State.

Dr. Pavesic has consulted for independent restaurants and private clubs in aspects such as layout, menu analysis, cost controls, management, and service personnel training programs. He is a frequent speaker to professional associations, seminars, and university sponsored educational programs.

Dr. Pavesic's industry experience includes three years as general manager of operations for Regan's Restaurants, Inc., Shawnee Mission, Kansas where he was responsible for all phases of unit operation and administration. It is here where he put into practice much of the cost control principles described in this book. He also worked as a college food service director prior to opening his first restaurant, Angelo's Restaurants, Inc. in Orlando, Florida where he served as the chief operating officer. After selling his controlling stock shares he returned to teaching at his undergraduate alma mater, Florida State, where he taught in the department of hotel and restaurant management from 1978 to 1986. He earned his Ph.D. in 1981.

He is currently the senior professor in the Cecil B. Day School of Hospitality Administration at Georgia State University where he teaches courses on restaurant cost controls, food production management, financial analysis, and foodservice management. He also served as program director from 1988 to 1996.

Dr. Pavesic is one of the most prolific authors in hospitality journals and ranks 9th out of 55 of the most cited hospitality faculty (by other authors) and 17th out of the top 100 authors in terms of total publications in the premier hospitality journals. He writes on food cost, menu pricing, equipment layout, labor cost, and menu sales analysis. He is also considered one of the top authorities on hospitality curriculum issues, faculty recruiting, ethics, and industry-education linkages. He is co-author of *Menu Pricing and Strategy, 4th edition.* His research and writing interests are in computer software for menu analysis and design and the history and evolution of commercial food service.

Dr. Pavesic has been happily married for 31 years to his college sweetheart, Tana. They have two grown children; a daughter Polly and son, Pete (who is a sous chef for the Buckhead Life Restaurant Group). They reside in Woodstock, Georgia with their three cats, Truffles, Nicholas, and Lily Belle.

FUNDAMENTAL PRINCIPLES
OF RESTAURANT
COST CONTROL

Chapter One

The Value and Importance of Cost Controls

A cost control program is an essential element of any food-service operation's overall strategic plan. It is not the only element but one of the critical elements necessary for the operation to be able to effectively compete in the marketplace. It has been reported that pretax income in commercial restaurants is down about 4 percent and that operating expenses have increased by 6 percent. Coupled with the rising costs of food and labor, restaurant profitability has been cut significantly.

The difference between financial success and failure in the restaurant business is basically 3 percent of sales. After expenses and taxes are paid, the restaurants showing profits have bottom lines ranging from 0.5 to 3 percent of sales. That small percentage is the difference between going out of business and being a solvent entity.

Much can be done to increase the likelihood that a restaurant will remain solvent when it comes to operational procedures and cost controls. When business is good, even the marginally efficient operations can show a positive cash flow. But when there is heavy competition and demand wanes, only the strong will survive. The "will to survive" is simply not enough. All entrepreneurs do not "plan to fail" when they decide to risk their equity and go into business; however, many of those who are not successful simply "fail to plan."

There is no way around it: Cost control is a *numbers game*. At first glance, paying attention to numbers is viewed as a job for the accountant, controller, or consultant. It involves accounting and that is routine drudgery. However, if you want a detailed assessment of what's going on in your restaurant, you need numbers, lots of numbers. The numbers you collect must be organized, interpreted, and compared. These numbers may represent what happened during a particular meal period, day, week, month, or even year.

The interpretation of the numbers is something you cannot delegate. You have to do it yourself so you can tell others what is going on without having to wait for someone to tell you you have a problem. The numbers are your controls: You review them over and over until their meaning is clear and you have your answers. Comprehension of numbers comes only with constant review, a resulting familiarity from knowing the activities that caused them, and the understanding of what they should be, given the level of business activity.

Eventually you will find yourself looking forward to preparing and reviewing the numbers and calculating the ratios and percentages that reveal the information you need. "The truth is that the drudgery of the numbers will make you free" (Geneen, Harold "A Case for Managing by the Numbers," *Fortune*, Vol. 10, No. 7 pp. 78–81 Oct. 1, 1984). The very fact that you go over the progression of those numbers week after week, month after month, means that you have strengthened your memory and familiarity with them so that you retain a vivid, composite picture of what is going on in your operation. Knowing what happened in the past can provide insight into what is likely to happen in the future.

Understanding the numbers puts you in control. You are aware of significant variances from the standards, which gets you started on what needs to be done either to sustain the gains or to correct the cost overrides. When you have mastered the numbers, you are no longer reading numbers any more than you are reading words when reading a book—you will be reading meanings. Your eyes will be seeing numbers but your mind will be reading the story behind the numbers, such as labor productivity, portion control, purchase prices, marketing promotions, new menu items, and competitive strategy.

CONTROLS ARE PROACTIVE AND PREVENTIVE

The story of Christopher Columbus serves to explain the preventive aspect of cost control. When he set out for the New World, Columbus had no idea how to get there, how long it would take, and what to expect along the way. He had to battle rough seas, going aground on sandbars and coral reefs. When he finally got to where he was going, he didn't know where he was. But like many entrepreneurs attempting to open their own business, Columbus was willing to take the risk. According to government figures, a restaurant investor is given a 1 in 20 chance of getting his money back in five years.

However, today we cannot just set sail in the business world without charts and maps. The competition is too great, and we will perish before we reach our destination. If we were Columbus, we would stay out of dangerous waters and sail around storms that threaten to wreck us. If we cannot avoid certain adverse conditions, we batten down the hatches to minimize loss or dock at a friendly port until danger passes. Such are the economic recessions, inflation, unemployment, interest rates, and tax laws that all businesses must endure. Only those who are prepared will survive the storms. Cost controls are our survival kit. You cannot enter the restaurant business without having a careful plan. Richard Melman, a very successful and innovative restaurateur and president of Lettuce Entertain You, told an auditorium full of people in the food-service industry that 80 percent of the success of any restaurant idea is determined before the doors are opened. The restaurant business is no longer for novices to learn as they go or to proceed on a trial-and-error basis.

One must remove as much of the risk of failure as possible before the ship ever leaves port. With the proper maps, reports, and instruments, you can avoid running aground on a coral reef, know where to stop along the way to get supplies and rest, and, in case of bad weather, make necessary preparations to minimize damage and loss of life. While preplanning is critical, it does not imply that planning ceases once on the way. Cost control is not a one-time program or a pre-opening exercise; it is ongoing and present throughout the life of the business.

If Columbus were a restaurateur today, he would find himself competing against other entrepreneurs who have the latest charts, equipment, and expertise to help their businesses succeed the first time. When things are going right, cash flow is positive, and business is good, cost controls may appear unnecessary. High sales volumes can hide a multitude of cost inefficiencies that become evident during low sales periods. It is much harder to make a profit when sales revenues are low because every dollar of expense takes away from the bottom line.

Marginal operations that show a profit during peak volume periods do not know how much additional profit they could have made had they been more cost-conscious. Too many become "converts" to cost controls after suffering losses and are seeking a way to "heal their wounds." Keep in mind that the *primary purpose* of cost controls is to *maximize profits, not minimize losses*.

Cost control is not a project instituted in response to hard times but a culture ingrained in the everyday practices of a business. As a philosophy, it places a premium on getting the greatest value for the least cost in every aspect of the restaurant's operations.

A large part of what it takes to remain in business today is owed to the ability to keep waste to a minimum and to utilize resources as efficiently as possible. This pertains not only to food and beverage but to also labor, energy, and other operating expenses. When you keep costs under control, you can sell your products and services at a lower price and provide greater price-value to your customers. Even if you charge the going rate in the market, you will make more money than your competitors charging the same price.

Why don't all operators have cost control programs? The answer may be that they are not aware of the waste that is going on around them and therefore do not see a need for it. The truth is that you cannot "see" a lot of the waste with *just* the naked eye. It takes records and reports to see the magnitude of the waste or efficiency that is very likely taking place.

The first step in correcting any problem is to realize that you in fact have one. It is often assumed that there is no problem until something is discovered to be missing or profit margins begin to shrink. By that time, the damage has already been done. Without controls in place to detect variances and shortages, owners and managers remain open to losses. When a loss is discovered, they must then take the appropriate action to limit adverse effects on the financial well-being of the operation. Again, operation success does not happen by chance, but as the result of some very careful advance planning.

DEFINITION OF COST CONTROL

The word *control* is not a particularly friendly and welcome word as it implies "restrictions" and "limits." Its dictionary definition says it is a "process or function" that is used to "regulate, verify, or check" that which is accomplished through some "method, device, or system." Control means to exercise authority over and to restrain.

Every operation, regardless of its size or method of service, should have a cost control system in place. Owners and managers must regularly assemble and review information about the expenses being incurred and the revenues being received. They need to compare the actual results to established standards and budget guidelines.

Over what do we place control in the restaurant business? We place it over all items of income and expense. The major areas are food, beverage, and labor. Consider that the capital costs of building, land, and equipment could exceed several million dollars, but over the life of the restaurant more will be spent on food, beverage, and labor.

PURPOSE OF COST CONTROLS

Regardless of the type of hospitality enterprise you end up working in or operating, cost controls will be a major part of your responsibilities. You may not be purchasing food and beverage, but you will have labor and overhead expenses that must be monitored. Cost controls encompass all areas from back door to front door, from purchasing and checking deliveries to making the bank deposits and paying the bills. These activities are shown in Figure 1.1. All activities in-between must be monitored to some degree. These examples can be generically transferred and applied to all segments of the hospitality industry, and they apply to multi-unit operations as well as single location operations.

Cost control is more than just computing percentages and ratios; it involves making decisions after the information has been compiled and interpreted. Terms like *cost accounting* and *bookkeeping* are not cost control but the means of gathering the information needed for control to take place. Therefore, a more complete definition of cost control can be explained by citing its purposes, which are:

1. To provide management with the information necessary to make day-to-day operational decisions

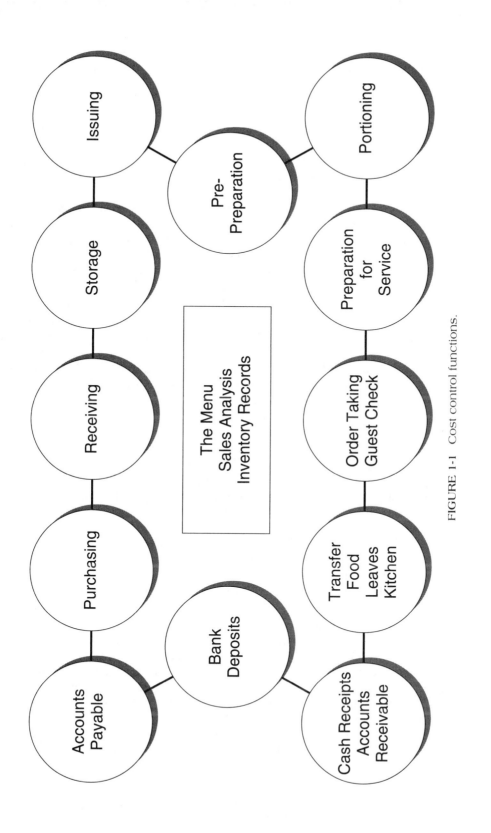

FIGURE 1-1 Cost control functions.

2. To monitor the efficiency of individuals and departments
3. To inform management of what expenses are being incurred, what incomes are being received, and whether they are within standards or budgets
4. To prevent fraud and theft by employees, guests, and purveyors
5. To be the basis for *knowing where the business is going*, not for discovering where it has been
6. To emphasize *prevention* and not correction
7. To *maximize profit* not minimize losses

A key aspect of cost control is *prevention* not correction. Prevention is brought about through *advanced planning*. Correction is after-the-fact; the damage has already been done. If you have read books on the principles of management, you may recall the term *putting out fires*; "fires" are major and minor incidents that management must address. If a large portion of a manager's time is spent dealing with the same problems that occur over and over again, all the manager is doing is "correcting after the fact." If a problem can be prevented from reoccurring, time can be devoted to more important matters.

Another analogy is offered here to make the point that prevention is preferred to correction. All businesses will carry some form of casualty insurance; for example, fire, liability, theft, and robbery. Keep in mind that insurance companies assess the likelihood of a loss occurring and the premium charged reflects that risk. Even so, these companies do much more to reduce the likelihood that they will have to pay a loss claim and, in the event a loss occurs, keep damages to a minimum. They do not simply indemnify the client in the event of a loss. Many companies will inspect your restaurant and recommend measures to reduce the chance of a loss. In some cases, premiums will be reduced when such measures are instituted. Installing burglar alarms, smoke alarms, and certain locks on doors are examples of preventive planning.

PHYSICAL PRESENCE IS NOT SUFFICIENT CONTROL

Some owners or managers assume that, because they are on the premises working during all the hours that the establishment serves food and beverage, no detailed records or system of control needs to be in place. This is not entirely true since theft is only part of the reason for cost controls.

Many independent, family-owned business do not see cost controls as necessary. They view them as a device for theft prevention that would be interpreted as a sign that they are distrustful of family members working for them. They fail to see the main purpose of cost control is that of providing information to management on day-to-day operations. Its ancillary purpose is to detect fraud and theft.

Many operators become converts to cost control only when it is too late. Losses are excessive and they are like a terminal cancer patient: All you can do is make life as comfortable as possible until the inevitable happens. Cost control is the basis for knowing where you're going, not for discovering where you've been. That is the difference between prevention and correction.

COST CONTROL VERSUS COST REDUCTION

Cost control is more than the accumulation and interpretation of information, filling out department reports, taking inventories, costing out recipes, and computing percentages and ratios. It involves interpreting those figures and taking the necessary steps to maintain profitability.

There is a difference between the terms cost *control* and cost *reduction*. Cost *control* is accomplished through the compiling, assembly, and interpretation of data and ratios on revenues and expenses. Armed with the cost control information, we can determine what happened and why. Cost *reduction* is the actual changing of the factors that will influence food, beverage, and labor cost in some manner, which results in the lowering of the ratio. Cost *reduction* is the "action" taken to bring costs within accepted standards.

Cost controls provide owners and managers with the information necessary to determine the efficiency of their operation and the basis for making operational decisions. Cost controls become the "eyes" of the owner, franchisor, or manager when they are not physically present. Keep in mind that many cost inefficiencies are not detectable or preventable simply by one's physical presence in the restaurant. It does not matter how intelligent you are or how many hours you put in each day at the restaurant. No one can possibly see everything that can cause costs to be out of line. Even if it were possible to observe all business activities and transactions, you still could not ascertain on the spot their effect on the financial results.

A national pizza chain utilizes an inventory system that is tied into its menu sales mix. It allows management to detect over-portioning and waste based on standardized quantities for each ingredient used on its pizzas. For example, the system revealed that the use level of mozzarella cheese exceeded standard by approximately 25 pounds over a 30-day period. While initially this seemed to be a significant quantity, it averaged less than 2 grams of cheese per pizza, based on the number of pizzas sold. That kind of variance cannot be detected by simply watching; it takes written cost records of what was purchased and what was sold. Remember, the difference between success and failure in most hospitality enterprises is 3 cents on the dollar!

The further removed the owner or manager is from the actual operation of a restaurant, either in terms of distance or frequency of visitation, the greater the need for proper cost control records. Through required written reports, franchisors of McDonald's, Taco Bell, and Wendy's keep their corporate eye on the thousands of franchisee units across the country from their district and regional offices.

Effective cost control systems must start at the top of the organization. No control program can function well unless management supports, establishes, and enforces its standards and procedures. Employees are quick to notice when standards are not followed and when management fails to act to bring variances from standards into line. Employees seem to deviate from set standards only as much as management allows.

Regardless of the type of restaurant, cost controls will be a major part of management's total responsibilities. Cost controls encompass all areas from the back door to the front, from purchasing to checking deliveries, making bank deposits, paying the bills, and all the activities in-between.

Central to every food or beverage operation are 12 primary function areas (see Figure 1-1). Central to the 12 primary functions are the menu, sales analysis, and inventory records. The menu drives the control process and will be covered in Chapter 5. The menu determines what the customer will buy (the menu sales mix), the specifications for the items purchased, and the quantities held in inventory. These are critical elements of the cost control records.

The steps in the cost control cycle, in sequential order and surrounding the menu, inventory, and menu sales mix records, are:

1. Purchasing
2. Receiving
3. Storage
4. Issuing
5. Prepreparation (i.e., rough prep)
6. Preparation (for service)
7. Portioning
8. Transfer of food from kitchen to dining room
9. Order taking/guest check
10. Cash receipts
11. Bank deposits
12. Accounts payable

Many of the functions overlap and are simultaneously performed. All are interrelated and must be monitored, or you will never uncover the real cause of any variance between actual and standard food cost. Controls for each function area must be operative as soon as the personnel are assigned or have access to the function area. Another way to approach the 12 function areas is the analogy of a chain with each function area being a single "link" in the chain. That chain can only be as strong as its weakest link.

Some owners and managers are very good at controlling costs in one or more function areas while others are ignored. That can leave many holes for losses to occur and go undetected until extensive losses are incurred. The function areas can be separated into two categories, front-of-the-house and back-of-the-house. Basically, this separates the functions of the kitchen (back-of-house) from the dining room (front-of-the-house).

If all the effort is placed on controlling expenses in the kitchen and the dining room is neglected, financial goals may still not be attained and unwarranted pressure placed on those who are not at fault. Closely monitoring recipes, waste, and portioning is for naught when customers are not charged for food served or when sales are underreported. While the emphasis here has been on food cost–related concerns, cost controls are concerned with beverage and labor cost inefficiencies as well as other overhead expenses such as linens, supplies, utilities, and other controllable expenses.

Each of the function areas will be covered more thoroughly later in this text, but a brief summary and description of each function provides an overview of the importance of each area. The starting point of the cost control process actually begins when the menu is planned and designed. The menu will have the greatest influence on the complexity of your cost control procedures. It will impact your labor cost, inventory, equipment needs, and space requirements. Standardized recipes will be prepared for all menu items detailing the steps, ingredients, yields, and portion costs. This information becomes the basis for the detailed cost control and cost reduction methods that will be followed.

Forecasting the sales mix of menu items is the basis for determining purchasing and preparation quantities. Detailed sales records by meal period, day, and week will make forecasting more accurate. A properly designed menu will make the menu sales mix more predictable and allow management to predict sales levels for scheduling staff, determining purchasing quantities, and inventory levels.

The information gathered for cost control purposes is used by many different individuals and function areas. For example, sales analysis data such as customer counts and the mix of menu items sold helps the dining room manager in scheduling servers and bus help. This information tells the person doing the purchasing what and how much to keep in stock, and the kitchen manager how much to prepare. In addition, management interprets the information to schedule advertising promotions and to be able to audit food consumed against food sold.

PURCHASING

The inventory system is a critical component of the purchasing function. Before placing an order with a supplier, you must know what is already on hand, know how much will be used, and allow for a small cushion of inventory so the items will not run out before the next scheduled delivery. Once the owners have established the standardized purchase specifications, the manager basically *orders* the quantities needed from the approved suppliers. Records are kept that indicate all the necessary information to conduct the purchasing function; for example, purveyors, prices, unit of purchase, product specifications, and the like. This information should not be kept only in the mind of the person doing the purchasing but needs to be put down on paper for future reference. You never know when a person may become ill, be transferred to another location, or quit.

In order to accomplish the function of purchasing, information must be obtained on what and how much to purchase. This information is obtained from the menu sales mix analysis. With an estimate of the customer counts expected, order quantities can be accurately estimated.

RECEIVING

The function of the receiving process is to ensure and verify that all merchandise ordered has been received. Inspection is conducted to check for correctness of brands, grades, varieties, quantities, and that prices charged are those that management has approved. Substitutions of brands and grades, damaged products, incorrect prices, or goods that do not meet quality standards need to be noted, returned, or credit taken. Products purchased by weight or count must be checked for correctness.

Merchandise of great monetary value is constantly being purchased by the establishment and adequate security measures should be instituted at the receiving area. In too many instances, this important task is left to employees who do not know what to look for, and the operation is left at the mercy of the delivery man and purveyor. Fortunately, most purveyors are ethical and professional and few purposely will defraud a client. But honest mistakes occur and, if undetected, could cost the operation.

STORAGE

Every food ingredient and supply item must be placed in storage until it is time to use it. The orderly placement of items in storage is essential so that they can be easily found and counted for inventory. The items must be stored properly—for example, proper temperature, ventilation, and free of contamination by chemicals or vermin—so they remain in optimum condition and will not deteriorate. Storage must be secure so expensive items can be safe from theft.

ISSUING

While most restaurants do not have full-time storeroom personnel, procedures for the removal of inventory from storage must be part of the cost control process. Simple locks that limit access to certain storage areas will be a major deterrent to theft and unauthorized entry by personnel. The term *issue* is generally used for taking items out of storage for use. In cases where the chef or cook is preparing food items, he or she will "take" the necessary ingredients from storage themselves. The head bartender will restock the bar with inventory from the liquor storage area. These individuals have the authority to remove items from storage for specific use, and they assume responsibility for the products from that point until they are consumed or sold.

Although there is no physical act performed on the merchandise except to transport it to the appropriate area where it will be processed, consumed, or sold, the function is an extremely important one in all food-service establishments. Without adequate issuing controls, no determination of true costs can be made. The three elements necessary to assess food and beverage cost are (1) beginning inventory, (2) number sold, and (3) ending inventory. You must know how much you had to begin with so you can compare sales figures to what you have left over.

Proper cost allocation to the respective department using the ingredients or supplies must also be noted. For example, food transferred to the bar (e.g., lemons, limes, fruit juice, olives, celery, cherries, and nonalcoholic mixes) are all inventoried as food items. The product used by the bar should be noted and charged against liquor sales and not food cost. Unless issues to the bar are recorded, proper cost allocation will not be possible.

PREPREPARATION

The function of prepreparation is the preliminary processing many food items undergo before they are ready for the final cooking process prior to serving to the customer. This is referred to as "rough" preparation by some culinarians. Examples are vegetable cleaning and cutting, meat cutting, and processing of ingredients for recipes. The procedures followed by the production staff should minimize waste and utilize as many of the byproducts as possible. Excessive trim on vegetables and meats will increase the edible portion cost of the final product.

Standardized recipes must be followed and preparation quantities adjusted according to projected customer counts and the menu sales mix history. Restaurants with fixed or static menus must eliminate leftovers as they have no way to incorporate them into the menu.

PREPARATION

This function refers to the final preparation or "cooking to order" done when the server places the order with the kitchen. The preprepared ingredients are combined or finished off prior to plating for service to the guest. This step is a critical control point in both food cost and quality control. The best ingredients and standardized recipes can be ruined by poor and sloppy final preparation and presentation.

PORTIONING AND TRANSFER (FOOD LEAVES KITCHEN FOR DINING ROOM)

Food cost can be lost with over-portioning of ingredients and accompaniments. Management should regularly monitor final preparation to be sure that quality and portioning standards are being followed. Many restaurants consider this such a critical function that managers are assigned to expedite orders. They will monitor order times, portions, presentation, and food quality with military-like precision.

Excessive leftovers indicate either improper preparation procedures or inaccuracies in the forecasting of the menu sales mix. Over-portioning can impact recipe yields and sales revenue. Food that the guest leaves on the plate can result from poor preparation or sloppy presentation. In every operation the size of the portions must be determined based on the target customer, meal period, and price point. Food cost is not the only basis for determining menu price. What the customer is willing to pay must be taken into account. The question then becomes whether the restaurant can sell the food item at the price the customer is willing to pay and still make an adequate profit.

For example, practically every moderate-price food service operation serves a hamburger of some type. How to prepare it, what size portion to use, and what specific accompaniments are included are variables under the control of the owner and manager when the menu is written. The price to charge will be determined by what the competition charges, the specific check average desired, the competing items on the menu, and many other "indirect" cost factors. This is discussed in greater detail in Chapter 6.

ORDER TAKING/GUEST CHECK

In order for the cost control process to work, every item sold or issued from the kitchen needs to be recorded. That recording can be a simple paper guest check or a point-of-sale computer. Once it is entered into the system, it can be tracked and monitored. Safeguards must be established that make it impossible to get food out of the kitchen or drinks from the bar without having the transaction entered into the system. In the case of a written guest check, a portion of the check is submitted to the kitchen and only items written on the check are prepared. No verbal orders should be accepted for food or beverage orders from anybody, including management and owners.

The guest checks are typically serially numbered and signed out to specific waiters. Unused checks are turned in at the end of the shift and kitchen copies are paired up with the guest copy. Missing checks are noted as are discrepancies between food checks and guest checks, and errors in price extensions and additions. Electronic Point of Sale (P.O.S.) systems like Micros, Squirrel, and Remanco eliminate the need for printed checks and separate all server sales.

CASH RECEIPTS

Whether your operation utilizes a cashier or has the servers carry their own banks, monitoring sales is critically important to cost controls. The amount of food and beverages served by the kitchen and bar will determine the amount of sales receipts that need to be turned in at the end of the shift by servers and bartenders. Under-ringing of checks, overcharging customers, falsification of charge tips, and lost checks must be monitored at the end of each shift. Management must compile all the sales information for each meal period so a historical financial record can be established. It is this historical record that helps management forecast the future.

BANK DEPOSITS AND ACCOUNTS PAYABLE

The revenues must be deposited in a bank account in a timely fashion and charge slips sent to the credit card company for payment. Funds are transferred from these accounts or drawn upon to pay for food, beverage, and labor costs. Proper auditing of these accounts must also be conducted to reduce fraud and theft.

AN ONGOING PROCESS

As mentioned earlier, cost control is not a response that is undertaken after a loss has been uncovered or when revenues and profits have begun to shrink. Cost control is an ongoing process that must be so ingrained in the minds of all employees that it becomes institutionalized and becomes a permanent part of the culture and philosophy of the company. The control philosophy becomes institutionalized when all employees innately place a premium on getting the greatest value for the least cost in every aspect of the company's operations without sacrificing quality or customer service.

Ongoing appraisal is an important part of the control process. A hospitality enterprise must establish goals and have a strategic plan to achieve those goals with the time frame and the budget it has to work with while also maintaining the qualitative standards of performance. Thus, proper control implies the exchange of information for planning, directing, implementation, and appraisal of goals and objectives.

Five elements of a cost control strategy must be present for it to be effective in controlling costs. They are:

1. Advance planning
2. Devices or procedures to aid in the control process

3. Implementation of the program
4. Employee compliance
5. Management appraisal and enforcement

A cost control program cannot be successful unless you have the complete cooperation and participation of all employees and managers. In addition, a cost control program must be assessed against the following questions:

1. Do the cost controls provide *relevant* information?
2. Is the information reported in a *timely* manner?
3. Is the information easily *assembled* and *organized*?
4. Is the information easily *interpreted*?
5. Are the *benefits/savings* greater than the cost of implementing the controls?

When the cost of the controls exceeds the savings made, the control is doing more harm than good. Purchasing a $25,000 point-of-sale system that is not going to be fully utilized is a waste of money. Leasing of automated dispensing equipment that counts draft wine and beer at a cost of $300 a month to save $75 dollars' worth of beverage is not cost-effective.

Although the scope of this book is cost control, control is only one part of the total operational program of a successful business. You may have adequate cost controls and still go out of business. There is another component of operational success. When you see a Burger King or Church's Fried Chicken shut down or sell out, it is likely to have closed for the following reason: *Inadequate sales revenue to retire debt and return a minimum profit*. A business must have adequate sales revenue, which implies a marketing perspective be used along with a cost control program.

Low costs will not make much of a difference without adequate sales volume. There is an old saying in business: "Volume hides a multitude of sins." This basically means that if you have the sales volume, it can make up for cost inefficiencies. However, the time to maximize profit is when business is good, not when it is near the break-even point.

If you were a manager in charge of a business currently returning an average of $1000 profit per week with sales of $10,000 and your boss said that wasn't good enough and expected $1500 profit per week, which strategy would you pursue to increase profit—increase sales or reduce costs? Which do you think is the fastest and easiest way to increase the bottom line?

If you said increase sales, you would have to increase sales by $5000 to realize an additional $500 profit operating the same as you have been in the past. (Currently, a 10 percent bottom line is being earned, $1000/$10,000.) Assuming that profit will continue at the 10 percent of sales ratio, $500 is 10 percent of $5000. Now think of how you would go about increasing sales. You would probably need to advertise and advertising costs money. If you spend $500 on newspaper or radio ads, you will now need to increase business by an additional $5000. What do you think your chances are of doubling sales volume if your business is flat?

Using your personal monthly budget as an example, what would be the fastest way to increase your disposable income—increase your income or cut back on expenses? Clearly, expense reduction remains the fastest way to increase bottom line in business. However, you reach a point where cost/expenses cannot go any lower or you will suffer grave consequences regarding the quality of your food, beverage, and service (or personal lifestyle). In the long run, customers will start going to competitors as they find your prices too high, portions too small, service too slow, and the like. You must never forget that you will incur expenses and need to spend money to make money. Failure to spend enough on remodeling, training, advertising, and quality ingredients may move money to the bottom line faster, but eventually overall business will suffer.

Some operators become too "bottom line oriented" and forget about the qualitative aspects of the business. The brown-edged lettuce that you keep on the salad bar instead of throwing it out, the purchase of lower-quality ingredients to keep food costs low, or failure to *not* charge a guest after a complaint are the little things that can hurt you in the long run. These are pennies; don't be "penny-wise and dollar-foolish" when it comes to controlling cost. The marketing perspective keeps you in touch with the competitive world as a reminder that you cannot forget the importance of food quality and customer service. In the best-selling book, *In Search of Excellence,* the authors reported that in companies that really paid attention to customer service and the quality of their products, their bottom lines had a way of meeting their financial expectations.

THE IMPORTANCE OF STANDARDS

Setting standards is an integral part of any cost control program. What is your definition of a standard? The dictionary says it is simply a measure that establishes a value. Standards establish a minimum acceptable level of performance or results. These values become the yardsticks with which management sets qualitative and quantitative levels of performance for the operation. Actual results are compared to the standards to see if they exceeded or fall below acceptable levels.

When establishing standards, one defines a predetermined point of comparison that will be measured against the actual results achieved and the resources consumed in the process. The difference between resources planned and the actual amounts used is referred to as the variance. Management must reduce or eliminate the negative discrepancies between the predetermined standards and the actual results. A positive variance occurs when performance exceeds that standard. When this occurs, management will praise or reward those responsible. Although standards can show where individuals or departments have not met expectations and corrective action must be taken, they are more important as preventative measures that reduce or eliminate how often corrective action must be taken.

Going back to the principles management, what is the distinction between a formal standard and an informal one? Typically, a formal standard is put in writing while the informal standard is not. However, one could argue that the formal aspect has nothing to do with whether or not it is written but with what is the common everyday practice. The formal standard is the one that management follows on a day to day basis.

Managers employed by corporate chains, are not asked to establish standards; they are responsible for making sure they are followed. Remember that employees will deviate from prescribed standards only as far as management allows. We use terms like *tight ship* and *by the book* to express that things must be done a certain way. Management sets the acceptance level for standards.

Standards become part of the philosophy and culture of a business. Employees should conduct themselves as if they are owners or investors. If this takes place the standards will be upheld by all employees. Both cost and quality standards must be ingrained in employees so they become second nature. This occurs only when employees are thoroughly committed to the values of the company. Setting standards is an important part of cost control. You cannot let employees set standards nor can you openly adopt the standards of another operation and expect to achieve the same results.

Each operation must establish its own standards relative to its financial idiosyncrasies and position in the marketplace. This is necessary because all of the variables that will influence cost standards differ from operation to operation; even within a chain of fast-food outlets. Rent, property taxes, interest rates, amount of debt financing to equity, depreciation schedules, and the like all affect the acceptable cost standards.

Why would two identical McDonald's not necessarily have the same food cost percentages or profit percentages? Ruling out fixed and overhead expenses, differing wage rates, menu prices, purchase prices, waste, and theft, what could be the cause? Consider that one McDonald's does around 23 percent of its total sales volume at breakfast while the other does only 15 percent. The reason they are not the same is because their menu sales mixes are different. Different menu items will have different food costs and gross profits. Breakfast typically runs a lower food cost percentage and lower check average than lunch and dinner sales mixes.

After cost standards are set, one can examine the income statement relative to these standards and break down figures by day, meal period, and department. Cost standards must, however, be determined from observations and calculations occurring under actual operating conditions, not by unrealistic and highly controlled laboratory-like conditions. The danger with such highly controlled conditions that costs will be understated because factors like recipe yields will be overstated and waste understated. Always understate your yields on items requiring portioning unless they are pre-weighed, counted, or pre-portioned. Very few items will result in 100 percent yield, for example, precut steaks should not show any variance between sales and number removed from inventory.

The importance of standards as an integral component of any cost control program can be illustrated by the following five steps:

1. Establish standards of performance and results for all individuals and departments.
2. Charge all individuals to follow established standards to prevent waste and inefficiency.
3. Monitor adherence to standards as a preventive control measure.
4. Compare actual performance and results against established standards.
5. Take timely and appropriate action when deviations from standards are detected. (Dittmer & Griffin, 1994, p. 47.)

The whole aspect of cost control and standards is complicated because a restaurant is essentially a manufacturing operation. It processes raw materials and combines them into end products purchased by the customer. This is further complicated by the fact that we must deal with a perishable product that can be stored or stockpiled for only limited durations. If we overproduce and do not sell out within a given time period, it turns to waste.

Second, products must be produced on demand. Demand is determined by the customer. Third, we must manufacture a variety of products simultaneously on the same production line. In addition, the items produced may change three times during a 24-hour period. Last, controlling quality is a particularly difficult problem because what is produced is also purchased and consumed in the same place at the same time. Therefore, quality control responsibility falls upon the employee closest to the customer.

In a factory, one can inspect what is being produced on the line and reject bad lots or take hours and days to test for quality. In food service, judgments must be made on the spot by the employee. A supervisor cannot inspect every product produced. Therefore, the employee is responsible for the final qualitative check prior to serving food to the customer.

Your job as manager will be to see that your staff is adhering to your standards. If, for example, portioning standards were not being followed, you might implement some of the following cost *reduction* techniques: require the use of measured scoops and ladles; specific sized bowls, cups, and glasses; as well as weighing portions individually; portioning by count; and pre-portioning items in advance.

Cost control is a very basic and fundamental management activity. You have to be able to monitor your costs and recognize when and where costs deviate from standards. Do not lose track of the qualitative and revenue-enhancing aspects when implementing a cost control program. Remember that cost controls are not an end in themselves. Once costs have been contained, the only way to increase bottom line is to increase sales revenue.

The cost control concepts and principles given in this chapter are not by any means limited to commercial restaurant applications. They apply equally to institutional food service and not-for-profit businesses. Although there may be differences in terminology, the principles are basically the same.

Chapter Two

Cost Ratios

Restaurant cost controls require both owner and manager to be on the same page in terms of the meaning and calculation of the numerous ratios that are used to analyze food, beverage, and labor costs. This is absolutely necessary because the terms can have different interpretations depending on the segment of the food-service industry (e.g., fast food, institutional, or commercial table service) and the source of the terminology (e.g., industry trade journal, academic textbook, or public accountant).

In addition, several cost control software packages are now on the market with built-in formulas for calculating ratios and percentages. It is important to review the documentation provided to understand how the ratios are being calculated before you jump to conclusions when a percentage or ratio does not meet your standard. The variance may be due to the way it was calculated and not be a true indication of the cost or profit activity in your restaurant.

The Board of Directors of the National Restaurant Association publishes its *Uniform System of Accounts for Restaurants* (USAR). The USAR establishes a "common language" for the industry that makes it possible to compare ratios and percentages across industry lines and to report industry-wide sales and cost figures to its membership in annual studies and reports. The new seventh edition of the USAR is an essential guide for the restaurant operator on the subject of restaurant accounting.

The emphasis of this chapter will be on operating ratios and the statement of income and retained earnings. The goal is to produce financial statements that are in fact "management tools" and not simply reports for the Internal Revenue Service.

Keep in mind that the mere calculation of the ratios and percentages is not "cost control." The numbers must be interpreted by owners and managers, who will then take appropriate action. When ratios and percentages are not within standards, management will immediately begin their investigation to determine the cause of the variance. Knowledge of food, beverage, and labor cost components is absolutely necessary to reveal the story behind the numbers.

FOOD COST RATIO/PERCENTAGE

This basic ratio is perhaps the most misinterpreted of all the ratios because it can be calculated so many ways. In its simplest calculation it is *food cost* divided by *food sales*. How one arrives at *food cost* is very important. One must ascertain whether the food cost figure is food *sold* or *consumed* as there is a big difference in the food cost percentage between the two.

In addition, for the food cost percentage to be accurate, it is absolutely necessary that a month-end inventory be taken. Without an inventory figure, the food cost percentage shown on an income statement is inaccurate and relatively useless to owners and managers.

I continue to be amazed at the number of restaurant operators who do not take a monthly fiscal inventory. Those who do not very likely do not have their accountant prepare a monthly income statement. If they do, the food cost figure on the statement can only be an estimate of the food cost. It is naive to think that monthly purchases and inventory will even out over the year. The amount of food inventory will vary from month to month even if business volume were the same every month (which it isn't) because the amount on hand on the last day of the month will vary depending on which day of the week the month ends. Think about the inventory on hand on a Friday compared to a Monday or Tuesday.

It is equally important to distinguish the difference between food *consumed* and food *sold*. Remember, all food consumed is not sold. Total food purchases for the month, as indicated from delivery invoices and adjusted for returns and credits, is added to the *beginning inventory* to get *total food available for sale*. Subtracting the month-end food inventory gives you the *cost of food consumed*. Remember, food consumed is all food used, sold, wasted, stolen, or given away to customers (complimentary meals) and employees. *Food sold* is found by deducting known waste, employee meals, complimentary meals, discounts, food transfers to the bar, and any other known food usage for which full price was not received from the total food consumed.

This figure is divided by *food sales*. Most accounting software programs will automatically divide food cost by *total sales* unless you adjust them to do otherwise. If beverage sales are included in the sales figure, it will lower and understate the food cost percentage. Remember the accounting principle that says to match costs with the revenues they produce. Only food sales should be used when calculating food cost ratios.

EXAMPLE

(Calculated from figures shown in Four Faces of Food Cost)
Cost of Food Consumed = $9000/$25,000 = 36%
Cost of Food Sold = $8650/$25,000 = 34.6%

The Four Faces of Food Cost

I Maximum allowable food cost   This is the highest food cost can be and still allow the operation to realize its profit goal. If the month-end food cost percentage exceeds this percentage, profit expectations will not be achieved. It will be different in every operation, including chain operations, because of the financial idiosyncracies of each location. The calculation is as follows:

1. Express labor costs, controllable and noncontrollable overhead expenses, excluding food cost, in dollar amounts. Refer to past accounting periods and year-to-date averages to get accurate and realistic cost estimates.
2. Add the monthly profit goal as either a dollar amount or a percentage of sales.
3. Convert dollar values of expenses to percentages by dividing by food sales for the period used for expenses. *I suggest that you use monthly figures that are neither under- nor overstated. Do not use the highest sales or the lowest sales figures for calculating your operating percentages.* Subtract the total of the percentages from 100 percent. The remainder is your **Maximum Allowable Food Cost Percentage (MFC)**.

EXAMPLE

Assume the following are weighted averages calculated from past accounting periods and represent "conservative" sales revenues and "liberal" expenses. *Resist overstating your sales revenues and understating your expenses. Be conservative with sales projections and liberal with expense estimates.*

Food Sales[1]	$25,000
Overhead[2]	$ 6,900
Payroll[3]	$ 6,000
Minimum Profit[4]	$ 2,000 or 8 percent of sales
Beginning Inventory	$ 5,300
Ending Inventory	$ 4,900
Purchases	$ 8,600
Employee Meals	$ 350
Potential Food Sales[5]	$25,500
Potential Food Cost[6]	$ 8,000
Allowance for Waste[7]	1.5%

Convert to percentages by dividing costs by total sales. Note: If alcoholic beverages were served, expenses would be divided by total sales to calculate percentages. Also, carry out calculations to two decimal places and do not round off.
Labor Cost Percentage: $6000/$25,000 = 24.0%
Overhead Percentage: $6900/$25,000 = 27.6%
Profit Percentage: $2000/$25,000 = 8%
Total: 59.6% (24.0% + 27.6% + 8%)
Maximum Allowable Food Cost = 40.4% (100% − 59.6%)
[1]This restaurant does not serve alcoholic beverages of any kind.
[2]Includes fixed, variable, and controllable expenses; does not include food cost
[3]Includes hourly employees, payroll taxes, and benefits
[4]Profit can be expressed as a dollar value or percent of sales
[5]Based on menu sales mix and listed menu prices
[6]Based on menu sales mix and standardized recipe costs
[7]Management builds in quality control costs and complimentary meals given to customers

II Actual food cost percentage (AFC)   This is the food cost percentage that the restaurant is *actually* running and is found on the monthly income statement. It is calculated by dividing cost of food sold by food sales. Here is a way to tell whether you are calculating cost of food *consumed* or food *sold* percent. If there is a line item on the income statement deducting for *employee meals*, you are calculating cost of food *sold*. If there is no allowance for employee meals, as is the case in most operations, the food cost being expressed is food *consumed*. Cost of food consumed will always be a higher figure than cost of food sold. If inventory is not being taken, the food cost shown on the income statement is basically just an estimate based on purchases and is not accurate.

How can you tell by looking at the financial statements if an operation is taking monthly inventory? One way is to look at the current assets section of the balance sheet. If the operation is not preparing a monthly balance sheet, it is probably not taking monthly inventory, and the food cost shown on the income statement is really an estimate or a total of the invoices for the month. In the current assets section of the balance sheet there should be entries for food inventory, beverage inventory, and supplies inventory. They should be shown separately if the restaurant is following the *Uniform System of Accounts*.

⤳ EXAMPLE

Beginning Inventory	$ 5,300
Add Purchases	$ 8,600
Total Food Available for Sale	$13,900
Less Ending Inventory	$ 4,900
Cost of Food Consumed	$ 9,000
Less Employee Meals	$ 350
Cost of Food Sold	$ 8,650

Actual Food Cost Percentage = 34.6% ($8650/$25,000)

III Potential food cost percentage (PFC)   Potential food cost is also re-ferred to as *theoretical food cost*. This is the lowest your food cost can be because it assumes that all food consumed is sold and that there is zero waste, over-por-tioning, and theft. It is calculated based on the weighted menu sales mix of the number sold of each menu item multiplied by the ideal recipe cost. The weighted cost is divided by the weighted sales (number sold × menu price) of all items on the menu. A complete explanation of the menu sales mix is pro-vided in Chapter 5.

⌒ **EXAMPLE**

Potential Food Cost Percentage = 31.372% ($8000/$25,500)

IV Standard food cost   Because PFC is unrealistically low, it must be tempered with allowances for unavoidable waste, employee meals, and qual-ity control losses to make it a realistic goal for management. This is the food cost percentage that is compared to the AFC and the standard that management must meet.

⌒ **EXAMPLE**

Standard Food Cost = 34.272% (31.372 + 1.5% + 1.4%)

In these four examples, food cost ranged from a high of 40.4 percent (MFC) to a low of 31.372 percent (PFC). The difference between cost of food consumed and food sold was 1.4 percent. You can see then why it is important to clarify how your figures will be calculated if you are seeking to make comparisons to other operations.

Food cost calculations   The calculation of the food cost percentage for an individual menu item is found by dividing the edible portion cost of the entree with all accompaniments by its respective menu price. If the cost of a steak dinner is $5.57 and the menu price is $12.95, the food cost percentage is **43% ($5.57/$12.95)**.

If you are pricing a menu item to achieve a targeted food cost percentage, you simply divide the edible portion cost of the entree and accompaniments by the desired food cost percent expressed as a decimal or **$5.57/.43 = $12.95**.

Food sales   The National Restaurant Association includes revenues de-rived from the sale of food in the restaurant, including the sale of coffee, tea, milk, and fruit juices, which are usually served as part of the meal. If there is no alco-holic beverage service, the soft drink sales would also be included in this category.

Prime Food Cost

Prime food cost was developed first by restaurateur Harry Pope, who realized that marking up food cost only on items made from scratch sometimes under-stated the total cost of producing the item. He decided to include the cost of *di-rect labor* with the food cost. Direct labor is labor incurred because an item is made from scratch on the premises, such as steak cutting and baking pies and breads. The restaurant is incurring additional labor to cut steaks and operate a bake shop. The labor costs associated with the items produced are allocated directly to the items that caused the labor to be incurred. In addition to the raw food cost of the steaks and baked goods, an additional cost for the labor incurred is added to each steak, pie, and loaf of bread. When food cost and direct labor are added together, it is referred to as *prime cost*. This costing perspective is applied to every item on the menu that requires extensive direct labor before it is served to the customer.

Indirect labor is that labor that cannot be charged to any particular menu item and is therefore allocated to each menu item in the form of overhead. Examples are labor for dishwashing, line cooks, bartenders, and waitresses.

Prime Cost

Prime cost, as defined by the National Restaurant Association for purposes of interpreting the figures in the Annual Industry Operations Reports, is the total of the cost of food sold, cost of beverage sold, and the associated payroll costs and employee benefits.

Traditional Labor Cost Ratio

This is the traditional ratio of payroll to *total sales* reported on the income statement. Payroll may include both hourly and management wages, but it is recommended to separate management salaries from the hourly employees. Management salaries and benefits should be carried as administrative expenses and separated from direct controllable expenses. This important distinction needs to be noted when analyzing labor cost percentages. If management salaries are included, the payroll percentage will run 8 to 14 percent higher than the hourly payroll percentage.

> *Note*: The National Restaurant Association includes the *entire* restaurant payroll, including management salaries, hourly wages, extra wages, overtime, vacation pay, and commissions or bonuses paid to employees, when it reports salaries and wages. Employee benefits is reported separately and includes federal retirement (Social Security) tax (FICA), federal and state unemployment taxes, and state health insurance taxes. Other items considered benefits are workers' compensation insurance premiums; welfare plan payments; pension plan payments; accident, health, and life insurance premiums; education benefits; and other fringe benefits employees receive.

Because the traditional labor cost ratio is subject to distortion due to wage and sales fluctuations, it is historical in that it reports what happened in the past, and is nonspecific as to job category, day, and meal period, other ratios must be used to interpret the productivity of employees. The following examples explain those ratios.

EXAMPLE

The following data are used in the calculation of the labor cost ratios.

	UNIT I	UNIT II
Sales	$12,680	$14,000
Payroll	$ 2,220	$ 2,450
Covers	2,400	2,500
Labor Hours	1,065	1,155

Traditional Labor Cost Ratio
Unit I $2220/$12,680 = 17.5%
Unit II $2450/$14,000 = 17.5%

Both units have the same labor cost percentage. *Which unit is using labor more productively?* This requires that the traditional labor cost percentage be supplemented by other ratios.

Sales per labor hour   Some operations determine the number of employees to schedule based on the sales per labor hour. It is calculated by dividing total sales by the number of hours worked or scheduled. If, for example, you were to use $25 per labor hour as a standard, in a time period in which $100 in sales was brought in, up to four employees could be scheduled. If only $75 were forecasted, only three workers would be scheduled.

This calculation is useful only for "variable cost" employees or those employees who are added to the schedule over the "fixed cost" employees as business volume warrants. Fixed cost employees are those who must be scheduled to staff the restaurant during the slowest hours of business, often called the "skeleton crew." Additional employees (variable cost employees) are added to the schedule when business volume exceeds what the fixed cost employees can handle on a qualitative and quantitative basis.

Using sales per labor hour to schedule employees does not work when one figure is used for all meal periods. This methodology was initially used in fast-food operations. However, when breakfast was introduced and the drive-through windows installed, scheduling on the basis of sales per labor hour resulted in severely understaffed operations. Managers soon realized that scheduling had to take into account the number of transactions required to achieve the sales per labor hour they used as a standard.

Breakfast had a much lower average check (fast-food operations use the term "average transaction") than lunch or dinner. When a drive-through window was added it increased the number of transactions per minute and required more employees. Employees are scheduled not by sales, but by customer counts. For that reason, the value of sales per labor hour for scheduling has its shortcomings.

EXAMPLE

Unit I $12,680/1065 = $11.91 sales per labor hour
Unit II $14,000/1155 = $12.12 sales per labor hour

Unit II appears to have an edge on Unit I. However, would your interpretation be influenced by the knowledge that Unit II has a high number of tourists frequenting it and Unit I has strictly a residential clientele? The spending patterns of toursits are much more liberal than local residents eating out on week nights. Thus the check average could be higher in Unit II.

Covers per labor hour   Because sales per labor hour did not always work the way it was intended, a more efficient way to schedule and analyze labor cost needed to be developed. It is not dollars in sales that drives scheduling as much as the number of customers that need to be served. Covers per labor hour is calculated by dividing the number of customers served by the total number of labor hours worked or scheduled. The number of covers per labor hour will be different for each job category.

EXAMPLE

Unit I 2400/1065 = 2.25 covers per labor hour
Unit II 2500/1155 = 2.16 covers per labor hour

While the difference is only decimals, it is significant in terms of productivity. Unit I is better than Unit II in this ratio.

Labor cost per labor hour   This ratio is best compared to past periods. It is calculated by dividing the total hourly payroll (management excluded) by the number of labor hours worked or scheduled. This figure cannot be evaluated based exclusively on a higher or lower number. If higher wages means more experienced and productive employees have been scheduled, overall payroll may still be low because fewer employees need to be scheduled to handle the business. Conversely, lower labor cost per hour may mean less productive employees and payment of minimum wage as a starting rate of pay.

EXAMPLE

Unit I $2220/1065 = $2.08
Unit II $2450/1155 = $2.12

Unit I has a lower cost, which reflects a better operating position than Unit II, if it is assumed that the staffs are comparable in experience and tenure.

Labor cost per cover   Another comparative ratio is calculated by dividing the total hourly payroll by the number of customers served. A lower figure is preferred because it means that the operation is using labor more productively than an operation with a higher labor cost per cover.

EXAMPLE

Unit I $2220/2400 = $.925
Unit II $2450/2500 = $.98

Unit I has a lower labor cost per cover served, indicating that it is again more productive than Unit II. When all the ratios are reviewed and compared, it is clear that Unit I is more productive than Unit II because it has a lower labor cost per labor hour, a higher covers served per labor hour, and a lower labor cost per cover. These interpretations cannot be made from the traditional labor cost percentage.

BEVERAGE COST RATIO

The beverage cost ratio is calculated when alcoholic beverages are sold. It is found by dividing beverage cost by beverage sales (calculated the same way the cost of food consumed is sold, with all the same assumptions regarding the taking of a fiscal inventory). A single beverage cost ratio cannot be given as a standard because the percentage will vary depending on the sales mix of spirits, beer, and wine sold. Restaurants will run a higher beverage cost than lounges with entertainment because more beer and wine will be sold with food. Beer and wine typically will only have a mark up, yielding a cost range from 25 to 50 percent.

Mixed drinks have a much higher markup and therefore correspondingly lower beverage costs, sometimes in single digits. Thus the more mixed drinks that are sold, the lower will be the beverage cost percentage. It is recommended that beverage sales be separated into three categories: beer, wine, and spirits and liqueurs. Inventory should be tallied separately as well to determine the separate beverage cost for each beverage category.

When calculating beverage cost, you consider only beverage sales. However, in a restaurant with both food and beverage sales, a ratio of food and beverage cost to total sales may also be shown on the income statement.

BEVERAGE SALES

The National Restaurant Association includes revenue for the sale of wine, spirits, liqueurs, beer, and ale. Beverage sales *does not include* coffee, tea, milk, or fruit juices, which normally are served with the meals and therefore considered food. Apparently, some operations that serve alcoholic beverages also include the sale of soft drinks in beverage sales. Since the consumption and sale of soft drinks can be significant, the allocation of soft drinks to food or beverage sales will, in most instances, lower the cost of food or beverage sold since the ratio of product cost to selling price of soft drinks is in the single digits.

AVERAGE CHECK

This calculation is more than simply dividing the total food and beverage sales by the total number of covers (customers) served. You can arrive at a check average this way, but it is more important to recognize how this figure compares to the average check you need to achieve your daily sales goals. If you need to get a $10.00 average check and the average is only $8.00, you will have to examine your menu prices. In addition, the check average should be calculated by separate meal periods, especially when different menus are used so it can be of comparative value to the operator. Rules must be established as to how small children and adults who order beverages only are counted or customer counts can distort check averages. Once a policy is made about how customers are counted for purposes of house counts and check averages, it should not be changed or historical comparisons will not be possible. In an inflationary economy or when menu prices are increased, customer counts are the best indication of business growth or decline.

SEAT TURNOVER

Restaurateurs monitor business by another ratio called seat turnover. It is the number of times they can fill an empty chair or booth during a meal period with a different paying customer. Restaurants with low check averages must turn tables frequently in order to achieve the sales volume they need to stay in business. Fast-food restaurants are the prime example of low check averages and high seat turnover. They rely heavily on carryout and drive-through business to increase the number of transactions.

Did you ever notice that the seating in fast-food outlets is not designed for your comfort and that the lighting is very bright? This is done purposely to speed up seat turnover. The calculation for seat turnover is the number of customers (covers) served divided by the number of seats (chairs) in the dining room. The seat turnover is impacted by the type of food served, the type of service, and the meal period. Breakfast and lunch are characteristically quicker turnover meal periods than dinner. The rate of seat turnover and the average check are inversely related. The higher the average check, the slower the seat turnover.

Seat turnover is also impacted by the size of the parties and the allocation of tables for two, four, and six or more. All the tables can be filled; however, if less than 85 percent of the chairs are filled, the restaurant is not optimizing the use of the dining room. The efficiency of the seating of guests is impacted by three factors: the person doing the seating, the size of the parties entering the restaurant, and the allocation of table sizes. An analysis of party size and tables should be examined if long lines and empty chairs are evident. The person doing the seating needs to match parties to tables to get the most people seated as quickly as possible.

INVENTORY TURNOVER

This ratio is used to evaluate the amount of food and beverage inventory relative to monthly consumption levels. The amount of inventory kept on hand varies inversely with the frequency of deliveries and the amount of storage space. Restaurants with limited dry and refrigerated storage have higher inventory turnover ratios than operations with ample storage space. However, the square footage of storage space should never be the determining factor for inventory levels.

Food inventory needs to turn over more frequently than beverage inventory. The biggest reason for this is perishability. However, tying up capital in perishable food inventory or excessive beverage inventory is not putting your cash to its best use. It is much easier to control cash in a bank account than to control perishable food and costly beverage inventory in a restaurant.

Inventory turnover is calculated by dividing the cost of food (or beverage) consumed by the average inventory. Average Inventory is simply beginning inventory plus ending inventory divided by 2. This average is then divided into the cost of food (or beverage) consumed. Using the figures from "The Four Faces of Food Cost" covered earlier, the calculation for food inventory turnover is shown.

⤳ EXAMPLE

Average Inventory = ($5300 + $4900)/2 = $10,200/2 = $5100
Food Inventory Turnover = $9000/$5100 = 1.76 times

The figure of 1.76 times tells us that the inventory turns over in dollar value 1.76 times per month. When this figure is divided into 30 days, it provides another way to examine the dollar value kept in inventory in terms of the number of days of business it should support. In this case, 30/1.76 = 17 days. In a city like Atlanta, where deliveries are at least once a week, this turnover rate appears to be much too low. Given deliveries could come weekly, no more than a 7 to 10 day supply is needed. This would leave the operation in a more liquid cash position. The industry rule of thumb for food inventory is three times a month or a 10-day supply.

With alcoholic beverages the inventory turnover is much lower and is examined from an annual rather than monthly turnover rate. This is necessary because of higher spirit and wine inventories. Some restaurants with extensive wine cellars will have over $100,000 in wine inventory alone. If a restaurant served primarily beer with some wine, the turnover would be higher than where spirits and wine were the primary sellers. Beer is perishable and has a limited shelf life. Wine improves with age, and liquor maintains its quality if unopened and stored at proper temperatures.

RATIO OF FOOD SALES TO BEVERAGE SALES

Food sales are also expressed as a percentage of total sales in operations that serve alcoholic beverages. If total sales were $100,000 per month, food sales were $75,000, and beverage sales were $25,000, the ratio of food to beverage sales would be 75–25, or 75 cents out of every dollar taken in would be for food and 25 cents from beverages.

The industry "rule of thumb" for this ratio has been 75–25. In some operations the ratio is almost 50–50. The greater the percentage of beverage sales, the greater the profit as there is a greater contribution margin from a dollar of beverage sales than in the same amount of food sales.

IMPACT OF THE SALES MIX

While this is not a ratio, it is an important concept that needs to be understood before any critical cost analysis can be conducted. The sales mix is the number sold of each item on the menu. Each item will account for a certain percentage of total items sold and impact the sales and food cost differently. As stated in Chapter One, two McDonald's in the same city will not have the same standard food cost because their menu sales mixes are not the same. Even if we assume that all waste and portioning are equal and that portion costs prices charged are equal, if the sales mix is different, the cost of food consumed and/or sold will be different.

If the sales mix from one restaurant shows a higher percentage of its total sales at breakfast, where food costs are typically lower than with hamburger, it will impact the actual food cost percentage. Subsequently, when variances in food costs between two restaurants occur or when there is a unexpected variance in the month at a single unit, one of the first things to look for are shifts in menu item popularity and the overall menu sales mix.

BREAK-EVEN POINT (BEP)

Break-even (and closing-point) calculations provide owners and managers with another tool to use in financial analysis and forecasting the necessary sales volume to produce desired levels of profit, or the impact on sales of increases and decreases in fixed and variable expenses. In its most basic definition, the break-even point (BEP) is when sales equal expenses and neither a profit nor a loss is incurred. The equation for Break-Even Sales Point is Cost of Sales (Food and Beverage) + Labor Costs + Overhead Cost (Fixed and Variable).

A business may continue to operate indefinitely at break-even if the owner and manager are drawing salaries from the business but when there are investors who expect a return on their money, a profit must be realized. The BEP equation can be modified to include a minimum profit as well as the expenses. The equation for the Break-Even Point in Sales to achieve minimum profit = Cost of Sales + Labor Costs + Overhead Cost + Desired Profit.

Break-even can be expressed in either accounting terms or cash flow terms. Sometimes we can show an "accounting" loss on the income statement, though it is just on paper and not a cash flow loss. A cash flow loss is where the operation must actually reduce its retained earnings to cover expenses in excess of sales.

While break-even analysis is a useful management tool, it must be remembered that the break-even point is "theoretical"—an approximation rather than an absolute figure. The reason for this is that in order for the break-even point to be accurate, the following conditions must exist:

1. Costs/expenses must be expressed as either fixed or variable costs. Fixed costs are expressed in dollar values and variable costs expressed as a percentage of sales. In reality, many costs/expenses are not purely fixed or variable and possess some of each at different sales levels. This alone can affect the break-even calculation significantly.
2. Variable costs must be directly variable to sales. The only truly variable costs on the income statement are food cost and beverage costs. These two costs are always expressed as a percentage of sales. This can occur only if the menu sales mix remains constant from period to period.
3. Fixed costs must remain fixed. While there are more examples of purely fixed costs, several are semi-fixed costs. Utilities, for example, are fixed at the minimum bill, but when the outside temperature reaches 95 degrees and the operation is running at capacity in terms of customer counts, the bill will exceed the minimum due to the volume of activity and the time of year and be a variable cost.

For these reasons the actual break-even point is really not a specific sales point but rather a range of sales that may run $200 to $300 higher or lower. It is more realistically and accurately calculated for the short term, for example, meal periods, day, or week, than for a month or year. The variance from actual break-even will depend on how realistically the costs are expressed as dollars and percentages of sales. Costs that are semi-variable (both variable and fixed properties) and semi-fixed (both fixed and variable properties) need to be correctly estimated for break-even to be precise.

Break-even can be used to determine not only the point where sales and expenses are equal but also for the following:

1. The amount of sales needed to realize a predetermined profit.
2. The impact on break-even if fixed or variable expenses are increased.
3. The impact on break-even if fixed or variable expenses are decreased.
4. The point where it would be better for the operator to close the door for a slow meal period or day because the costs of opening the door are not

being covered. It can also be used to explore the feasibility of expanding operating hours and days.

5. The number of customers that need to be served at a specific check average to achieve a particular sales level.
6. The sales level needed to pay for equipment or remodeling.
7. To determine the purchase or asking price for a business.
8. The impact on break-even if menu prices are increased or decreased (discounted).
9. The number of additional customers that need to be served at discounted prices to break even.
10. The break-even point for a meal period, day of the week, week, month, and year.

CONTRIBUTION MARGIN

Contribution margin is also referred to as "gross profit." It has a different interpretation when used in the context of break-even vis-à-vis menu sales analysis and menu pricing. In the break-even context, contribution margin is what remains after all variable expenses, expressed as a percentage of sales, have been totaled and subtracted from 100 percent. For example, if variable costs of food, beverage, and direct operating expenses totaled 64 percent, the contribution margin would be 100% − 64% = 36%, or .36, when expressed as a decimal.

Another way of describing contribution margin is that it is the excess of revenue (sales) over the variable costs incurred in generating the sales. What remains is the contribution margin, which is used to pay fixed expenses. If there is money left over, a profit is realized.

The contribution margin is a critical element of the break-even calculation. The break-even point can be calculated mathematically by dividing fixed cost (expressed as dollars) by the decimal equivalent of the contribution margin.

$$\text{BEP} = \frac{\text{Fixed Costs Expressed as Dollars}}{100\% - \text{Variable Cost}\%}$$

Contribution margin in the context of menu sales analysis and menu pricing is the difference between the menu price and the raw food cost. For example, if a steak dinner with accompaniments sells for $12.95 and has a raw food cost of $5.57, the contribution margin to cover labor, overhead, and profit is $12.95 − $5.57 = $7.38. Contribution margin in this application is not expressed as a percentage of sales but as a dollar value. Different methods of menu sales analysis look at the individual contribution margin as shown above or the weighted or total contribution margin. If the operation sold 35 steaks per day, the weighted contribution margin from the steak would be $7.38 × 35 = $258.30. Each menu item would be tallied and summed, giving the total weighted contribution margin for the entire menu sales mix.

Break-even is also discussed in some texts as the "cost/volume/profit equation." It is a set of analytical tools that examines the relationships between costs, sales volume, and profit and how these elements impact the break-even point of the operation. It is important to understand the relationship of these elements. For example, the lowering of the contribution margin will increase the sales necessary to break even. The sales must be converted to customer counts with a desired check average to ascertain whether the increase is realistic given the seating capacity of the dining room, the seat turnover, and the competition for business.

On the other hand, an increased contribution margin brought about by increased menu prices or lowered product costs through smaller portions or reduced accompaniments may result in a drop in customer counts. Also, the amount of fixed costs will make a huge difference in break-even and what con-

Table 2.1 THE RESTAURANT INDUSTRY DOLLAR*

	Full Service Restaurants (Average Check Per Person Under $10)	Full Service Restaurants (Average Check Per Person Over $10)	Limited Service Fast Food Restaurants
Where It Came From			
Food Sales	87.2%	76.5%	96.4%
Beverage Sales (alcoholic)	12.8	23.5	3.6
Where It Went**			
Cost of Food Sold	28.2	26.8	31.2
Cost of Beverages Sold	3.5	6.6	0.9
Salaries and Wages	29.9	28.5	24.4
Employee Benefits	3.8	4.4	2.7
Direct Operating Expenses	6.7	7.3	7.4
Music and Entertainment	0.3	0.7	0.1
Marketing	3.5	2.6	5.3
Utility Services	3.0	2.5	2.7
Restaurant Occupancy Costs	5.8	5.3	6.4
Repairs and Maintenance	1.7	2.0	1.6
Depreciation	2.1	2.1	1.7
Other Operating Expense/ (Income)	0.4	(0.2)	(2.1)
General and Administrative	3.3	4.5	5.7
Corporate Overhead	1.8	1.5	1.9
Interest	0.6	0.6	1.0
Other	0.2	0.5	0.1
Income Before Income Tax	5.8%	4.3%	9.0%

*All figures are weighted averages based on 1995 data.
**All amounts are reflected as a percentage of total sales.
Source: Restaurant Industry Operations Report 1996, National Restaurant Association and Deloitte & Touche LLP.

Table 2.2 FULL SERVICE RESTAURANTS (AVERAGE CHECK PER PERSON $10 AND OVER) COST PER DOLLAR OF SALES*

	Total Cost of Sales	Total Payroll and Benefits	Prime Cost
All Restaurants	34.0¢	32.0¢	66.1¢
Type of Establishment			
Food Only	**	**	**
Food and Beverage	34.0¢	32.1¢	66.1¢
Restaurant Location			
Hotel	33.2¢	34.8¢	68.1¢
Shopping Center or Mall	32.5	32.5	64.6
Office Building	31.3	31.0	65.2
Club	36.0	43.2	80.1
Sole Occupant	36.0	30.9	65.7
Other	34.3	33.9	67.8
Profit versus Loss			
Profit	33.5¢	31.9¢	65.6¢
Loss	35.8	37.1	72.6
Meals Served			
Lunch Only	**	**	**
Dinner Only	35.8¢	29.4¢	65.8¢
Breakfast and Lunch Only	**	**	**
Lunch and Dinner Only	33.5	32.3	65.8
Breakfast and Dinner Only	**	**	**
Breakfast, Lunch, and Dinner	34.3	34.6	68.9
Open 24 Hours	**	**	**
Menu Theme			
Steak/Seafood	35.6¢	29.9¢	66.3¢
American (varied)	34.0	33.3	67.3
French/Continental	34.3	31.6	64.2
Italian	31.7	33.9	64.8
Average Check			
$10.00 to $14.99	33.5¢	33.0¢	66.7¢
$15.00 and Over	34.0	31.1	65.1
Affiliation			
Single Unit—Independent	34.8¢	31.5¢	67.1¢
Multi-Unit—Company Operated	32.5	33.0	65.1
Multi-Unit—Franchise Operated	**	**	**
Ownership			
Sole Proprietorship	35.0¢	28.4¢	62.9¢
Partnership	32.0	33.9	65.2
Public Corporation	35.7	25.9	60.8
Private Corporation	34.3	32.7	67.1
Sales Volume			
Under $500,000	36.2¢	30.0¢	66.7¢
$500,000 to $999,999	35.9	32.6	68.1
$1,000,000 to $1,999,999	33.6	33.0	67.4
$2,000,000 and Over	32.3	31.5	63.9

*All amounts are medians.

**Insufficient data.

Source: Restaurant Industry Operations Report 1996, National Restaurant Association and Deloitte & Touche LLP.

Table 2.3 FULL SERVICE RESTAURANTS (AVERAGE CHECK PER PERSON UNDER $10) COST PER DOLLAR OF SALES*

	Total Cost of Sales	Total Payroll and Benefits	Prime Cost
All Restaurants	32.7¢	32.1¢	65.5¢
Type of Establishment			
Food Only	34.2¢	32.6¢	66.6¢
Food and Beverage	32.3	31.8	65.2
Restaurant Location			
Hotel	35.4¢	38.6¢	72.6¢
Shopping Center or Mall	30.0	30.1	60.7
Office Building	**	**	**
Club	**	**	**
Sole Occupant	32.8	32.3	65.7
Other	34.6	33.9	69.0
Profit versus Loss			
Profit	31.5¢	32.0¢	65.2¢
Loss	35.1	37.5	73.4
Meals Served			
Lunch Only	**	**	**
Dinner Only	**	**	**
Breakfast and Lunch Only	**	**	**
Lunch and Dinner Only	32.5¢	30.3¢	63.4¢
Breakfast and Dinner Only	**	**	**
Breakfast, Lunch and Dinner	33.7	34.9	68.3
Open 24 Hours	30.6	32.2	64.1
Menu Theme			
Steak/Seafood	38.3¢	28.8¢	65.3¢
American (varied)	32.2	32.5	66.3
Italian	32.3	29.8	61.6
Mexican	29.8	34.7	65.5
Average Check			
Under $5.00	34.2¢	34.5¢	69.8¢
$5.00 to $9.99	32.6	31.8	64.8
Affiliation			
Single Unit—Independent	34.7¢	32.3¢	66.8¢
Multi-Unit—Company Operated	31.3	34.0	66.8
Multi-Unit—Franchise Operated	27.3	30.2	57.5
Ownership			
Sole Proprietorship	33.6¢	28.2¢	63.0¢
Partnership	33.4	34.0	66.3
Public Corporation	**	**	**
Private Corporation	32.3	32.2	65.1
Sales Volume			
Under $500,000	36.3¢	29.7¢	67.0¢
$500,000 to $999,999	34.0	33.3	67.6
$1,000,000 to $1,999,999	30.9	33.2	65.2
$2,000,000 and Over	27.6	30.1	57.6

*All amounts are medians.

**Insufficient data.

Source: Restaurant Industry Operations Report 1996, National Restaurant Association and Deloitte & Touche LLP.

Table 2.4   LIMITED SERVICE FAST FOOD RESTAURANTS
COST PER DOLLAR OF SALES*

	Total Cost of Sales	Total Payroll and Benefits	Prime Cost
All Restaurants	31.2¢	27.3¢	58.4¢
Type of Establishment			
Food Only	32.9¢	27.1¢	58.6¢
Food and Beverage	29.3	27.5	57.3
Restaurant Location			
Hotel	**	**	**
Shopping Center or Mall	29.6¢	28.3¢	59.3¢
Office Building**	**	**	
Sole Occupant	32.0	27.2	58.1
Other	**	**	**
Profit versus Loss			
Profit	31.1¢	27.2¢	58.3¢
Loss	32.7	32.1	65.5
Meals Served			
Lunch Only	**	**	**
Dinner Only	**	**	**
Breakfast and Lunch Only	**	**	**
Lunch and Dinner Only	30.5¢	27.5¢	58.0¢
Breakfast, Lunch and Dinner	30.4	26.4	62.0
Open 24 Hours	**	**	**
Menu Theme			
Hamburger	32.9¢	25.8¢	57.9¢
Pizza	29.2	28.7	57.8
Sandwiches/Subs/Deli	33.2	27.1	58.8
American	**	**	**
Average Check			
Under $4.00	32.8¢	27.5¢	59.2¢
$4.00 and Over	30.8	27.3	58.0
Affiliation			
Single Unit—Independent	34.0¢	25.9¢	60.4¢
Multi-Unit—Company Operated	30.0	27.5	59.5
Multi-Unit—Franchise Operated	27.7	28.0	56.9
Ownership			
Sole Proprietorship	34.7¢	24.1¢	58.2¢
Partnership	**	**	**
Public Corporation	**	**	**
Private Corporation	30.4	28.3	58.4
Sales Volume			
Under $200,000	**	**	**
$200,000 to $399,999	33.6¢	27.5¢	60.9¢
$400,000 to $599,999	29.8	28.1	58.7
$600,000 and Over	29.3	26.8	55.5

*All amounts are medians.
**Insufficient data.

Source: Restaurant Industry Operations Report 1996, National Restaurant Association and Deloitte & Touche LLP.

Table 2.5 CAFETERIA COST PER DOLLAR OF SALES*

	Total Cost of Sales	Total Payroll and Benefits	Prime Cost
All Restaurants	32.1¢	29.0¢	61.4¢
Type of Establishment			
Food Only	37.1¢	29.0¢	62.8¢
Food and Beverage	**	**	**
Restaurant Location			
Sole Occupant	31.7¢	29.0¢	61.0¢
Other	**	**	**
Profit versus Loss			
Profit	31.8¢	29.0¢	61.0¢
Loss	**	**	**
Meals Served			
Lunch and Dinner Only	31.7¢	29.0¢	61.0¢
Other	**	**	**
Average Check			
Under $5.00	39.2¢	32.3¢	73.0¢
$6.00 and Over	31.7	28.3	60.7
Affiliation			
Single Unit—Independent	**	**	**
Multi-Unit—Company Operated	**	**	**
Multi-Unit—Franchise Operated	**	**	**
Ownership			
Private Corporation	31.7¢	28.9¢	59.9¢
Other	**	**	**
Sales Volume			
Under $750,000	**	**	**
$750,000 and Over	31.8¢	29.0¢	61.2¢

tribution margin is necessary. Each operation must calculate its own break-even point and not attempt to use some rule of thumb or industry average.

CLOSING POINT

Closing point as a very useful variation of break-even analysis is another management financial tool. Closing point was first introduced by Peter Dukas in his book, *Planning for Profits in the Food and Lodging Industry*, Cahners Publishing Co. 1976 pp. 20–22., 1976. Dukas defines closing point as where the sales do not cover the costs incurred in opening the restaurant. Understand that fixed costs continue to be paid regardless of whether the restaurant is open for business or closed.

If a restaurant is opened for a particular meal period as opposed to remaining closed, it will incur expenditures for labor, food, supplies, maintenance, and the variable portion of overhead expenses (e.g., increased utilities).

Rent and debt service continue even if the restaurant does not open for business. Subsequently, if the cost of "opening the doors" are $300 and only $250 in sales is realized, the operator will have an additional $50 in expense that would not have been incurred had the restaurant remained closed.

Closing point is calculated by dividing the costs of opening the restaurant that are best expressed in dollar values (e.g., labor cost) by the contribution margin percentage.

RANGES OF FOOD, BEVERAGE, AND LABOR COST RATIOS

The figures quoted here are those reported in the *Restaurant Industry Operations Report*, 1995, prepared for the National Restaurant Association by Deloitte & Touche LLP. Assumptions are that the figures reported follow the *Uniform System of Accounts for Restaurants*, sixth edition. Keep in mind that these figures will be different for every restaurant, and they include all types of operations ranging from fast food to continental table-service operations, single-unit independents, multi-unit company owned, and multi-unit franchise operated; and with check averages less than $10 and greater than $10, sales volumes less than $500,000; and with ratios to total sales reported in lower, median, and upper quartiles, and by menu theme (e.g., French, Mexican, Steak/Seafood, Italian, and American). Subsequently, comparison to any of these figures by a specific operation is of limited value.

Food Cost Range	26.5–42.5%
Beverage Cost Range	21.0–44.1%
Labor Cost Range	21.9–41.8% (includes benefits)

Tables 2.1 to 2.5 on pages 33–37 are printed with permission of the National Restaurant Association.

Chapter Three

Food Cost Controls

In order to effectively control food cost, you must be able to accomplish four things:

1. Accurately forecast what and how much you are going to sell
2. Purchase and prepare according to sales forecasts
3. Portion effectively
4. Control waste and theft

Before you can correct a problem you need to realize that you in fact have one. If we do not know we have a theft problem, we do not set up a system to stop it. Many of the reasons for high food cost cannot be detected by management unless detailed cost control records are kept. These records are not simply the accounting reports prepared for the company accountant but rather managerial accounting reports that are far more detailed. If you do not have a cost control program that allows you to determine if anything is missing or out of compliance with standards, you are operating in the dark.

When a problem does become evident, it may be too late as serious damage to the financial well-being of the operation may have already occurred. In today's competitive economic environment, one must be able to detect and prevent such losses from occurring.

"Very few operators have a *cost control system*, but most have a *cost accounting* system. The former *controls* costs, the latter *records* costs" (Dukas, *Planning for Profits in the Food and Lodging Industry* 1976, p. 56). It is important to distinguish between these two terms. Accounting records must be kept for tax purposes; cost controls must be kept for operational purposes. Cost control is the accumulation and interpretation of costs that allow management to highlight and pinpoint how, when, and where costs are incurred. Each cost is measured against a budget or standard, and the variance noted.

FOOD COST MYTHS AND MISCONCEPTIONS

Food cost percentage is sometimes misused and its importance both over- and understated. Calculating a monthly food cost is relatively meaningless if one does not take a fiscal inventory at the end of every month. A daily, weekly, or monthly food cost percentage does not inform the operator whether the food cost percentage is good or bad if it is not compared to a realistically determined food cost standard.

Proponents of the contribution margin approach to cost analysis, also known as gross profit return, place little or no importance on the food cost percentage. They are concerned only with the dollar difference between the menu price and the menu item food cost. This approach is also inadequate when used exclusively and without regard for market conditions and competition.

Food cost and contribution margin are *not* mutually exclusive attributes and need be combined for cost analysis. One will keep the other in check. Exclusive reliance on achieving a low food cost percentage can result in lower check averages and lower revenues because low food cost items are typically the lowest priced items on the menu. Ignoring food cost for contribution margin will cause the monthly food cost percentage to increase because high contribution margin items, while the highest priced items on the menu, are typically the highest in food cost as well. In highly competitive markets, the contribution margin approach may not be the correct strategy for building customer counts.

BASICS OF FOOD COST CONTROL

Before these topics are explored, it is necessary to begin with the basics of food cost control. Food-service professionals must have a complete understanding of food cost and contribution margin in order to answer questions such as the following: How does one determine a food cost standard for an operation? What factors influence the food cost percentage? And, how is it calculated? What is a good food cost percentage?

Food cost control begins with the establishment of cost standards. Only after cost standards are set, can you examine managerial cost control reports and financial statements relative to the standards and break down sales and costs by the day, meal period, and department. Cost standards must, however, be determined from observations and calculations occurring under actual operating conditions and not from observations in test kitchens. Costs can sometimes be *understated* because recipe yields in controlled tests are optimized and waste is negligible. These high yields are not likely to occur in an understaffed kitchen that has just been inundated with orders. Therefore, it is more realistic to *understate* your yields on items requiring portioning unless they are pre-weighed, counted, or pre-portioned in advance. Certain items will demand 100 percent yields (e.g., precut steaks), but items like Prime rib will have yields that will vary daily.

The whole aspect of food cost control and cost standards is complicated because a restaurant is essentially a manufacturing operation. It processes raw materials and combines them into an end product purchased by the customer. This is made more complex by the fact that the product is highly perishable and cannot be stockpiled except for limited periods. If we overproduce and do not sell out within a given time period, waste results.

Second, restaurant production is undertaken on demand. Demand is determined by the customer. Third, we must produce a variety of products simultaneously on a single production line. In addition, the menu items produced may change three times during a 24-hour period. Last, controlling quality is particularly difficult because what is purchased is produced and consumed in the same place.

In the traditional production factory, you can inspect what is being produced on the assembly line and reject bad lots, and take hours or even days to test for problems before the product is sold to the customer. In food service, judgments must be made on the spot by hourly employees, not management personnel. Therefore, the last employee to touch the product or place it before the customer must perform the final quality control inspection. In reality, the customer makes the final inspection and has the final say.

THE IMPORTANCE OF STANDARDS

Four main standards that help develop quality, consistency, and low cost are:

1. Standardized purchase specifications
2. Standardized recipes
3. Standardized portions
4. Standardized yields

Standardized Purchase Specifications

Standardized purchase specifications describe in detail the ingredients used in the standardized recipes. Specifications will include, among other things, the brand, size, variety, and grade of recipe components. Purchase specifications serve not only as quality control measures but also as cost control measures.

Both quality and price are agreed upon before purchase is made, making recipe costing consistent from week to week and from unit to unit in multiple location operations.

Specifications also reduce misunderstandings between buyer and purveyor on what to ship and how much to charge. Specifications are an important element in the overall food cost control program. Chapter 9 covers the ordering process and purchase specifications in detail.

Standardized Recipes

Every menu item produced should have a standardized recipe. The recipe becomes the basis for determining the cost of the menu item. In order to assure consistency in quality and cost, purchase specifications are established. In multi-unit operations with the same menu and prices, consistency in cost, quality, and plate presentation are critical. Standardized recipes allow different individuals at remote locations to produce identical products if they use standardized ingredients. If the proper ingredients are used (e.g., brands, varieties, grades, size, etc.) and the recipe followed, a predictable yield and consistent quality will be produced. If portioned properly, it will yield a standard number of orders that when sold at the prescribed menu price will return the desired cost percentage and profits.

A standardized recipe is one that has been customized to a specific restaurant or food-service operation based on the actual ingredients, cooking time, temperature, methodology, and cooking equipment available. It is rare that a recipe can be copied right from another operation or cookbook without some adjustment to the ingredients, equipment, or method. For example, you may decide to use fresh ingredients when the recipe calls for canned, frozen, or dehydrated. Whenever alterations are made to a recipe, you need to check your end product to be sure it results in the quality and quantity you want. The recipe is then checked and rechecked for all factors.

The standardized recipe is the basic component of a food cost control program. If an operator does not know the cost of the ingredients of every item on the menu, objective assessment of the month-end food cost percentage is impossible. The standardized recipe contains the following information:

1. The name of the recipe
2. The yield in number of portions, weight, or volume
3. Ingredient form, quality, and quantity
4. Equipment, utensils, pots, and pans required in preparation
5. Preparation methods, cooking methods, time, temperature, holding procedures, and even how leftovers can be utilized
6. Plate presentation and garnish

There is the assumption that the persons preparing from the standardized recipes have general culinary knowledge and understand the meaning of the terms and instructions used in the written recipe. There is a significant difference between the terms *mix*, *beat*, and *whip*, for example.

The ingredients are typically listed in the order of use. The recipe will state the quantity in terms of measure or weight and not general terms like, "one apple, peeled and cored." What variety of apple and how big of an apple needs to be specified. The correct wording would be more specific, like "one cup of peeled and cored Red Delicious apple, diced."

Accurate measurements are very important to obtaining cost and quality consistency in food production. In food preparation, recipe quantities are expressed in a combination of three ways: *weight*, *volume*, and *count*.

Weight is expressed in grams, ounces, and pounds. *Volume* is expressed in terms of tablespoons, cups, quarts, fluid ounces, and gallons. *Count* refers to the number of individual items, for example, *6 medium whole eggs* or *3 5 × 6 ripe tomatoes*. Quantities need to be expressed in the *largest* full measure. For example, if an original recipe called for 2 tablespoons of peanut oil and the recipe were expanded to a quantity that required 16 tablespoons, convert tablespoons to a larger measure. Since 2 tablespoons are in an ounce, 16 tablespoons equal 8 ounces or 1 cup. That is the quantity used on the expanded recipe.

In the past, chefs have guarded recipes like the combination to a safe containing all the riches of the world. The menu and kitchen do not exist to serve the chef; rather, the kitchen exists to serve what the customers want to eat. Many owners and managers have been "held hostage" by chefs who will not allow recipes to be written for fear that their services will be devalued. However, most American-trained chefs and corporate chefs rely heavily on standardized recipes that they have helped develop. These recipes become property of the restaurant, not the chef.

Food cost control requires that standardized recipes be used as a tool for the chef and management. The written recipe assists with training cooks, educating service staff, and controlling food cost and product quality. Accurate recipe costing and menu pricing demand that standardized recipes be followed.

Standardized recipes are useful in assuring that a menu offered by the restaurant is consistent from one cook to another and from one location to another. Recipes are also the basis for inventory purchase units. This control tool frees management from being dependent on any single individual in the kitchen. Imagine what it would be like to run a restaurant where the menu was completely dependent on existing knowledge at the time of hiring any given chef or cook. With standardized recipes in place, any knowledgeable food preparation worker can follow most recipes and get fairly satisfactory results, and reduce leftovers from over-preparation.

The standardized recipe specifies the type and amount of each ingredient, the rough preparation and cooking procedures, the portion size, and yield. While standardized recipes cannot make chefs out of ordinary cooks, anyone with a basic knowledge of cooking terminology can combine ingredients to produce a consistent chili or spaghetti sauce. There is no "magical" touch that a chef has that turns onions, garlic, olive oil, tomatoes, and spices into a great marinara sauce; however, there is something that my grandmother was never able to show or tell me as to why her homemade buttermilk biscuits were always twice as fluffy as mine. Baking may be an exception because that "special touch" in combining the ingredients listed on the recipe is very critical to producing a fluffy biscuit or flakey pie crust.

When I opened Angelo's Italian Cuisine in Casselberry, Florida, in 1973, I hired a wonderful Italian woman to be my chef. She guarded her recipes as if they were government secrets and she was the only one who made our famous Angelo's sauce. Keep in mind that I was the owner, and I did not know what her recipe was for the sauce. She would prepare a double batch every time she had a day off so we never had to make it. If we ran low, she would come in to make another pot.

She did not get along with my partner and one day he had had enough and fired her. She thought that I would never allow that to happen, but I respected my partner's decision and did not take her back. Needless to say I was beside myself as to how we were going to get the food prepared. We knew the approximate ingredients that went into everything so we wrote them down on 5×7 cards. What resulted was that both my partner and I and three other employees all could make the sauce, as well as all the other items that had previously been made only by my chef. We were liberated and I cannot express how much more independent we felt about running the restaurant. My restaurant operated for eleven years and was voted the favorite Italian restaurant in Orlando for three years running without having a chef. I still have those recipe cards in my files. They are stained with tomato sauce and olive oil and remain a symbol of my independence from my temperamental chef.

I do not recommend that you wait until your chef quits or is fired to develop your standardized recipe file. Start with whatever recipes you are now using and begin with the most popular menu items. Weigh and measure quantities that may be currently added by the "handful" or "pinch." Quantities prepared should be based on storage life and sales demand. However, I noted when making homemade Italian sausage and meatballs that the steps of "get ready" and "clean up" took the same amount of time whether we made 25 or 50 pounds. Consequently, there are optimum batch sizes that should be prepared and the product kept frozen until needed or in vacuum tight packaging.

One thing I recommend be included on your recipes is a list of the pans and utensils needed to prepare the item. The old *mise en place*, "everything ready," is essential in quantity food production. The purpose of this book is not to detail the steps in standardizing a recipe. There are many wonderful books available and I will defer to culinary experts at Johnson and Wales University and the Culinary Institute of America on this subject.

PRODUCTION CONTROL AND LEFTOVERS

For production control, only enough food to meet the demand for the day is prepared with the objective of *eliminating* leftovers completely. A leftover is defined as any prepared food that cannot be sold the next day in its original form at its original price. Most commercial restaurant menus are fixed or static in that they offer the same items every day with the exception of two or three seasonal changes. Consequently, they do not have an outlet on their menu for "daily specials." Besides, what kind of customer acceptance would you expect for items that are put on the menu driven exclusively by foods that are left over? Even employees will balk at eating items that are made from leftovers.

Whenever leftovers are incorporated into the menu, food costs are likely to increase rather than decrease. This is true because additional ingredients must typically be added to create the "new" menu item and it will be priced considerably lower than what the primary leftover ingredient would have returned had it sold in its original form. Consider the leftover Prime rib that is made into beef stroganoff or beef burgundy. As a luncheon special it will have to be priced under $7 when it would have originally been priced at twice that amount. Consider, too, the additional ingredients and labor required to offer the item all reduce the profit return.

When chefs are asked if they had their choice of not having to deal with leftovers versus having to work them into the menu, the majority would elect not to have to work with them. Incorporating leftovers into the menu can cause standardized recipes to be altered. Whether it is the homemade vegetable soup that suddenly incorporates an additional vegetable ingredient or changing the lineup of a menu to incorporate yesterday's roast chicken, compromises are made. In the case of the soup, the customer will notice that there is inconsistency in the ingredients, and the food cost will be higher because the additional cost is not reflected in the price.

Now there are some who in reading this section are thinking, "How can he say that food cost would be increased by using leftovers?" If the alternative to using leftovers is throwing it away as waste then yes, using leftovers will lower food cost. However, the cost will still be higher than if the food were sold in its original form at the original menu price. There are exceptions that have been brought to my attention by chefs over the years. One is BBQ ribs of beef made from the leftover bones from a 107 Rib. Since the cost of the bone is figured in when the Prime rib is sold, the leftover ribs basically contain only the cost of the BBQ sauce and accompaniments. The other exception is leftover food from a buffet or banquet that has been paid for with the guarantee. If a restaurant put these items out for sale in the restaurant, they would have basically zero food cost. There may be several other "extended" dishes like stew, goulashes, and casseroles that are expanded with the use of rice or noodles that can return a low food cost. However, they will not bring in the gross profit that the original item would have, and very few contemporary restaurants have menus that will permit the addition of such daily specials.

Even in an institutional operation such as school or hospital food service, having to incorporate leftovers into the menu disrupts the menu cycle that has been balanced in terms of taste, texture, preparation method, and variety. Most food service contractors must adhere to specific menu parameters requiring a certain number of entrees, salads, vegetables, and desserts. Further, the requirements may call for entrees that offer one beef, fowl, poultry, and fish item.

Trying to incorporate yesterday's leftover roast chicken may require that two extended dishes be offered instead of one, and now the production manager has to move the turkey that was purchased for that day to another menu. Consequently, a domino effect of changes on future menus occurs.

This is why operators will design menus and preparation methods that will eliminate leftovers completely. The first step in eliminating leftovers is accurate forecasting of customer counts. If the same menu is placed before guests day after day, a predictable menu sales mix will result. From sales histories management can make predictions on how much to purchase and prepare. Standardized recipes and portioning result in standardized yields so we can prepare the optimum amounts.

How do restaurants like Applebee's, Chili's, Houston's, and Outback Steak Houses keep leftovers to a minimum? Remember, a leftover is a prepared item that cannot be sold the next day at its original price. Uncooked steaks are not leftovers because they can be sold the next day. These are restaurants whose menus cannot incorporate leftovers in the form of daily specials. They do not have the expertise in their kitchens to entrust that a cook will be able to prepare and cost out a dish made of leftovers.

The most effective way to eliminate leftovers is to *cook to order*. If an item is refrigerated until it is cooked for service, there are no leftovers. Many menu items do not lend themselves to be cooked to order, for example, Prime rib, BBQ ribs, and chicken. These items need to be partially cooked and finished off on the charbroiler or in a convection oven. To reduce leftovers of these items (if the item is more than three days old it will not be served to a paying guest and is therefore a leftover), they are cooked in small batches in quantities based on the menu sales mix and forecasted customer counts.

If quantities required are large or the cooking times extended, cooking to order is not practical. In such cases cooking small batches frequently will keep leftovers and waste to a minimum. Another way leftovers are reduced is through the use of technology in the cooking equipment. Equipment such as convection steamers allow individual orders of fresh vegetables to be cooked in a matter of minutes. The new combi-convection-steam ovens can cook half inch pork chops in 12 minutes. Quartz ovens and broilers, and clamshell broilers can take frozen items to table-ready in minutes. There is no reason to have leftover baked potatoes, french fries, and baked bread and biscuits if management watches production quantities based on customer forecasts. If there are some leftovers, they will be minimal and can be discarded as quality control waste.

PORTIONING STANDARDS

When food cost percentages exceed standards, one must examine the elements that can cause the variance. You will want to refer to the list of "100 Reasons for High Food Cost" at the end of this chapter. However, management can observe many things on the job that will indicate that cost standards are out line or compliance. For example, over- and under-portioning can be a cause of high food costs and low price-value perceptions of customers, even when standardized recipes are being followed.

Some of the things that signal to management that portioning standards may need to be reevaluated follow:

1. Not using measuring tools to portion food (e.g., scoops, ladles, scales).
2. Lack of size standards for serving bowls, plates, cups, and glasses. It is impossible to put more than 10 ounces of juice in a 10-ounce glass.
3. No portion markers used to cut pies and cakes. Management would notice miscut pieces being served or wasted. Remember, the profit comes from selling the last two pieces, not the first ones.
4. Customer comments to servers and cashiers about portions being too small or large.
5. Amount of plate waste or lack thereof. Check the bus tubs and soiled dish table. Are certain menu items seen coming back? It may be due to taste as well as portion. Are plates completely empty (portions too small)?
6. Return trips to salad bar to fill up.
7. Sales of side orders and appetizers.
8. Sales of desserts.
9. Use of doggie bags.
10. Production yields, number sold, and leftovers do not add up.

THE FOUR FACES OF FOOD COST

You may have *cost control* systems in place that will help you detect such occurrences. The *cost reduction* response is the *action* taken to bring costs within standards. For example, strict compliance to serving food with measures, scoops, and ladles will be enforced. Specific employees will be responsible for marking and portioning cakes and pies. Numbers sold of certain menu items will be tallied and compared to production quantities and leftovers.

Food cost is not a one-dimensional concept or calculation. It cannot be accurately and completely analyzed from just a single percentage. In order to fully understand and appreciate the relevance that food cost percentage has in the financial results of any food-service operation, one must approach food cost from not one, but four difference perspectives. In its most basic and fundamental presentation, food cost is expressed as a percentage of total food sales.

Food cost is calculated by dividing the food expense by the food revenue. Typically you will see the formula:

$$\frac{\text{Total Food Cost}}{\text{Total Food Sales}} = \text{Food Cost \%}$$

This calculation is for the overall food cost percentage for all food sales, as is shown on the monthly income statement.

It can also be calculated for individual menu items by the formula:

$$\frac{\text{Menu Item Food Cost}}{\text{Menu Item Price}} = \text{Menu Item Food Cost \%}$$

The food cost referred to in the formula is the "raw food cost" of preparing the menu item or items. The cost is worked up from the standardized recipe and is called the "standardized cost."

The food cost of any given menu item is going to be influenced by three factors under management's control and responsibility. They are not the only factors that influence food cost percentage, as we will see, but we must start with these three:

1. The "as purchased" price of the ingredients (quality)
2. The portion size (quantity)
3. The menu price charged

By altering any one of these three variables, you can change the food cost percentage. However, once the quality, quantity, and price have been established and the menus printed, these are not sufficient in themselves to guarantee that the food cost goals will be achieved. In order for that to occur, management sees to it that the standards are adhered to in purchasing specifications, standardized recipes, and standardized portions. In addition, waste and theft must be controlled and guests charged and revenue collected.

Now the food cost figure that appears on the income statement example (see Table 3-1) is shown as an "absolute" or dollar value and as a "relative" value or percentage of food sales. Where do we get the figures for the food cost on the income statement? It starts with the assumption that a complete and accurate inventory is taken at least monthly of all food cost related items.

Table 3-1 INCOME STATEMENT, ANGELO'S RESTAURANTS, INC. ANYMONTH, 199X

	$	%
Food Sales	$36,700	72.386
Beverage Sales	14,000	27.613
Total Sales	$50,700	100.00
Cost of Sales		
Food Cost (Consumed)	$15,500	42.234
Less Employee Meals, and food consumed and not sold	$ 1,510	4.114
Food Cost (Sold)	$13,990	38.119
Beverage Cost	2,940	21.000
Cost of Goods Sold	$16,930	33.39

The following steps are recommended by the National Restaurant Association in the sixth edition of the *Uniform System of Accounts for Restaurants*. The separation of food cost into the cost of food served to customers and that eaten by employees as part of their employment benefits is a critically important step. This separation indicates more clearly the direct relation of menu prices to food costs and distinguishes between cost of food *consumed* and cost of food *sold*. Please refer to Tables 3-2 and 3-3.

Where does the figure for purchases come from? It is the total of all invoices for food received during the month whether they have been paid or not. Let's add some numbers to see how the numbers used in the example were derived.

Let's look closely at the important differences between the cost of food consumed and the cost of food sold percentages.

$$\text{Cost of Food Consumed } \frac{15{,}500}{36{,}700} = 42.23\%$$

$$\text{Cost of Food Sold } \frac{13{,}990}{36{,}700} = 38.12\%$$

The difference of 4.11% represents $1508 in inventory that was consumed and not sold. The point is, you need to know which of these two food costs is being reflected on the income statement. How can you tell? The first thing I look for is employee meals. If an allowance for employee meals is shown somewhere on the statement, it is as close as you're going to get to cost of food sold. Inquire as to whether the accounting systems follow the Uniform System of Accounts for Restaurants. If they do, employee meals are deducted from cost of food consumed. However, unless the restaurant tracks employee meals, the figure it reports as employee meals may be just an estimate and not an actual cost. Many restaurants give their employees a "free" meal and do not calculate the actual cost of what employees eat.

Since 1967, when restaurants came under the jurisdiction of the Fair Labor Standards Act and were required to pay the federal minimum wage, the cost of

Table 3-2

	Beginning Inventory (Which Is the Ending inventory for the Previous Month)
+	Food Purchases for the Month
=	Total Food Available for Sale
−	Ending Food Inventory (Taken last day of the month)
=	Cost of Food *Consumed*
−	Employee Meals
−	Food Transfers to Bar
−	Discounts and Complimentary Meals
+	Beverage Transfers to Kitchen
=	Cost of Food Sold

Table 3-3

	Beginning Inventory Food	5,800
+	Food Purchases	15,000
=	Total Food Available for Sale	20,800
−	Ending Food Inventory	5,300
=	Cost of Food Consumed	15,500
−	Employee Meals	(1,100)
−	Food Transfers to Bar	(450)
−	Discounts and Complimetary Meals	0
+	Beverage Transfers to Kitchen	40
=	Cost of Food Sold	13,990

employee meals took on a new aspect of importance. Under the Wage and Hour Law, an employer can take a credit against the minimum wage for the *cost* of meals given to employees without charge. If an operator takes a meal credit against the minimum wage, it must be able to show the *true and accurate costs* of the meals eaten by employees.

The meal credits are them prorated on an hourly basis for the hours worked. Different meal credits will be determined based on the time of day and type of meal eaten. For example, the *reasonable cost* of a breakfast meal will be lower than that of a lunch or dinner meal. An example should clarify how the meal credit is used.

Assume the employee is paid $4.75 per hour and works an average of 8 hours per day. The total daily wage rate would therefore be $4.75 × 8 hours or $38.00. Assume further that the employee is given a free meal with a reasonable cost of $2.00. A credit against the hourly wage can be claimed in the amount of $.25 per hour ($2/8 hr). Therefore, the hourly wage would be reduced from $4.75 to $4.50. In addition, if the employee is given a 30-minute break to eat, the employee will be paid only for a total of 7.5 hours, and the payroll savings would total $4.25 per employee per day. When you have a crew of 25 employees, the savings can be significant. In this simple example, over the year this would amount to a reduction in payroll of $38,781!

How could you monitor food consumed but not sold, such as employee meals, discounts, and complimentary meals? You could have employees write checks for their food. In fact, if the policy is that a check must be presented for a customer's meal, employees should be required to follow the same procedure and not be allowed to order employee meals verbally. Once they are written, you can collect them and estimate what employee meals are costing you.

What about discounted and complimentary meals? Again, all complimentary meals should be separated and tallied at the end of the month. Most restaurants attach coupons to guest checks to determine how the promotion is proceeding and have actual records of the cost of the discounted food. "Known" waste can be recorded as well. At the end of the night, the kitchen prepares a list of food that is being discarded, and management checks it and signs off. Waste forms are part of the daily reports at McDonald's and Wendy's. With all known employee meals, discounts, complimentary meals, and waste recorded, food cost percentage shown on the income statement becomes a more accurate figure as to what is being controlled or not controlled by management and employees.

The calculation of a food cost percentage is a simple mathematical calculation. The determination of a food cost standard for any given food-service operation is not quite so simple. What percentage should a food cost be? Can individual operators use industry averages or some universal rule of thumb to establish a food cost percentage for their particular operation? The answer is a resounding NO!

Operators *cannot* arbitrarily select another's food cost percentage to use as a standard for their operation. National restaurant chains are becoming more sophisticated in establishing standard costs because a single food cost standard cannot be assigned to all locations. Although standardization in menu offerings, purchasing, preparation, portioning, and pricing are assumed, identical food cost percentages are not likely to occur. They will not be identical even if waste, theft, and over-portioning were assumed to be equal. Even if two operations achieved identical food cost percentages, their bottom line profits may differ significantly. The point is that there are too many operational and financial variables that make it impossible for one's food cost percentage to be exactly applicable to any other operation.

Among the influencing variables, aside from waste, theft, and inconsistencies in following recipes, specifications for ingredients, and portioning, the *menu* will have the greatest impact on food costs. The menu affects the purchase requirements, storage space and temperature, equipment and utensil needs, and the number and skill levels of employees. The menu must utilize employees productively and satisfy the customers. The reason for the variance in food cost percentages is twofold: (1) differences in the ratio of sales by meal periods, that is, breakfast, lunch, dinner; and (2) the *sales mix* of individual menu items.

As is often the case in restaurant chains serving three meal periods (e.g., Denny's and Shoney's), the units with the greatest percentage of total sales being accounted for during breakfast hours will likely achieve a lower food cost percentage than those with lower breakfast volumes. Even chain restaurants with static daily menus or single meal periods will not sell individual menu items in the same proportion. (This is referred to as the *menu sales mix*.)

Each operation, whether chain or independent, must establish its own standard food cost. The menu sales mix cannot be absolutely controlled so variances in food costs will occur. Many managers and operators express food cost in a *single* percentage and do not know how to develop their own standard food cost. In order to completely comprehend food cost, it must be expressed and analyzed from the four perspectives listed in Table 3-4.

Table 3-4 THE FOUR FACES OF FOOD COST

Food Cost	Origin
1. Maximum Allowable Food Cost (MFC)	calculated from operating budget
2. Actual Food Cost (AFC)	shown on income statement
3. Potential Food Cost (PFC)	determined by sales mix
4. Standard Food Cost (SFC)	PFC + allowances

Maximum Allowable Food Cost Percentage

The first and most important of the four faces of food cost is the *maximum allowable food cost* (MFC). It answers the question, "What food cost percentage does the operation need if it expects to achieve its minimum profit objectives?" Although the name may be new, the methodology as to how it is derived is not. It was first presented by the Texas Restaurant Association in the early 1960s. The MFC can be calculated from historical accounting records or from proforma figures if opening a new restaurant. Every restaurant will have a different and unique MFC due to different overhead expenses, depreciation schedules, interest rates, taxes, labor rates, and insurance expenses, all of which will impact the bottom line. These costs will in turn influence the actual maximum allowable food cost percentage needed to achieve the restaurant's minimum profit objectives.

The procedure for calculating the MFC is as follows:

If using historical financial statements, select a representative accounting period not biased by high or low extremes in revenues or expenses. In most cases, year-to-date or weighted average figures will prove to be more representative and reliable. Express all expenses first in dollar values that accurately reflect the expenses incurred. If using proforma figures, be liberal with estimating expenses and conservative with revenues.

Express payroll and related expenses separately from other fixed and variable expenses. *Exclude* any food cost in this calculation because we will calculate it *after* we have determined all other costs and added a minimum profit. Included here would be advertising, utilities, supplies, repairs, and maintenance, depreciation, rent, interest, and so forth. After listing all overhead expenses, add in an amount for the *minimum* profit you are willing to accept for investing your time and money.

Convert each of the dollar figures to percentages by dividing by the total sales for the period of time reflected in your expense and profit figures. For example, if all expenses and profit were expressed as monthly, divide by a month's sales. After converting the dollars to percentages, sum the percentages and subtract from 100 percent. Note that there is no allowance for food cost and what you have calculated is *total costs plus profit,* but *without* food cost. Therefore, the difference between the sum of the percentages and 100 percent is the maximum allowable food cost.

The name comes from the value of the calculation. It tells you the *highest* your monthly food cost can go and still allow you to achieve your *minimum* profit expectations. It represents a "high water mark" for your food cost. You should establish menu prices to achieve food cost below this percentage.

For the sake of example, assume that labor cost is $12,500, overhead (fixed and variable expenses) is $11,500, and minimum profit is $4,000 per month. If sales were $50,000, then labor would be 25 percent, overhead 23 percent, and profit 8 percent. See Table 3-5. The total percentage of expenses and profit *without food cost* is 56 percent. That means that the *maximum allowable food cost* is 44 percent.

Actual Food Cost Percentage

The second food cost, *actual food cost* (AFC) percentage, is frequently discussed between managers and operators and is reported on the monthly income statement. If the operation follows the *Uniform System of Accounts for Restaurants*, sixth edition, the percentage shown will be *cost of food sold* because it will *deduct* the cost of employee meals, food transfers, allowances for discounts and complimentary meals, and recorded waste. If the Uniform System is not followed, the income statement will reflect the *cost of food consumed*. The AFC indicates *what the food cost is currently running* but is really of little value unless the operator knows what the food cost *should be* running. Again, for the sake of example, assume for comparison that the AFC for the month was 42.5 percent. This formula is Cost of Food *sold* divided by *food* sales.

While the AFC food is lower than the MFC by 1.5 percent and profit is increased from 8 to 9.5 percent, one still cannot evaluate this as good or bad based on these two food cost percentages. MFC is a value arrived at from financial statements and sets the upper limits of food cost, and AFC tells us what we ran during the most recent accounting period. In order to make a judgment as to the food cost efficiency, one must establish a benchmark value or standard for comparison. Before one can arrive at the standard food cost, the menu sales mix must be examined.

Potential Food Cost

From the menu sales mix we can calculate the third food cost, referred to as *potential food cost* (PFC). Sometimes called "standard food cost" or "theoretical

Table 3-5 MAXIMUM ALLOWABLE
FOOD COST

Sales	$50,000	
Labor	$12,500	25%
Overhead	$11,500	23%
Minimum Profit	$ 4,000	8%
25% + 23% + 8% = 56%		
100% − 56% = 44% MFC		

food cost" in the literature, it is influenced by the actual menu sales mix. This food cost percentage utilizes the menu sales analysis and the recipe cost of each item on the menu. The calculation of the PFC reflects the fact that the most popular items will have the greatest effect on the resulting food cost percentage. The number sold of each individual menu item is multiplied by its respective food cost and menu price. The total *weighted* food cost for the menu sales mix is divided by the total *weighted sales*. The PFC is calculated from only the *cost of food sold*. It indicates what the food cost would be in a perfectly run operation where all food consumed was sold, and where there was zero waste and perfect portioning given the existing menu sales mix. It is the lowest food cost can ever go and is not an achievable percentage in 99 percent of food-service operations. This is why it is a "theoretical" percentage. In actual practice, revenue is not received for all food consumed, and this fact alone will cause AFC to always be higher than PFC. The example in Table 3-6 demonstrates this concept.

Note in the example menu sales mix that none of the five menu items actually has a food cost percentage equal to the PFC of 38.03 percent. Three items have food cost greater than the PFC. If the sales mix were to shift away from items 1, 2, and 3 to items 4 and 5, the PFC would be lowered.

Although every operation will have its own specific *potential food cost*, one cannot assume that achieving the PFC will automatically achieve the budgetary profit objectives. In situations where an existing restaurant's sales mix was examined, the PFC exceeded the MFC. This restaurant had a existing overhead and labor expenses that required food cost to be unrealistically low for the segment of the market it sought to attract. While nothing could be done in the short run to lower property taxes, interest, and insurance, labor cost and other controllable overhead were brought into line to bring the operation closer to break-even.

Table 3-6 COMPUTING POTENTIAL FOOD COST

Menu Item	Food Cost	Menu Price	Number Sold	Weighted Cost	Weighted Sales	Food Cost Percent
1	$2.25	$4.95	115	$258.75	$569.25	45.45
2	1.43	3.65	269	384.67	981.85	39.17
3						
4	.74	2.75	100	74.00	275.00	26.90
5	.80	2.70	154	123.20	415.80	29.62
Totals			768	$1082.42	$2846.40	38.03 (PFC)

Formulas

(1) Item food cost × number sold = "item" weighted food cost

(2) The total of the weighted food cost for *all* menu items = "total" weighted food cost

(3) Number sold × menu price = "item" weighted sales

(4) The total of the weighted sales for *all* menu items = "total" weighted sales

(5) Total weighted food cost *divided by* total weighted sales = POTENTIAL FOOD COST PERCENTAGE ($1082.42/$2846.40 = 38.030%)

Since the potential food cost of 38.03 percent is an unobtainable benchmark for food cost, it must be "adjusted" to reflect employee meals, unavoidable waste, quality control standards, and other "known" situations where food is *consumed* and not *sold*. If employees are given a free meal, this can consume an additional percent or two of food cost. A guest satisfaction guarantee policy could add an additional percent to food cost when meals are discounted or given as complimentary by management. In addition, restaurants like Houston's have very high quality control standards that may find management discarding up to $100 in raw food cost per day. Such standards need to be reflected in adjusting the PFC upward to arrive at an obtainable food cost standard.

Standard Food Cost Percentage

The tolerance that management adds to the potential food cost is how one arrives at the fourth and final food cost percentage, *standard food cost* (SFC). This percentage is compared to the monthly actual food cost found on the income statement. Therefore, with all "known" and controllable contingencies accounted for by management, the difference between standard food cost and actual food cost percentages must represent "avoidable" waste and loss that should have been controlled by management. An acceptable variance between PFC and SFC ranges between 0.25 percent to 3 percent of food sales.

The exact percentage, determined by management studies, will be influenced by the ratio of convenience foods to scratch foods, employee meal policy, quality control standards, discounts, waste reports, and the like, which will differ from operation to operation. The more convenience foods and the more limited the menu, the smaller the tolerance between AFC and SFC. In our example, management set the tolerance for unavoidable waste at approximately 2.5 percent, making the standard food cost 40.5 percent. Table 3-7 shows the percentages for all four faces of food cost.

The AFC is 2 percent greater than the SFC, indicating that more food was consumed than the sales mix indicated. Although the AFC is below the MFC and minimum profit objectives are being exceeded, they are not being optimized. The reason for this sizable difference needs to be investigated. It may be caused by any number of things ranging from incorrect extension of inventory to under-ringing of guest checks. Both the cost and revenue sides must be examined to determine the cause.

Table 3-7 THE FOUR FACES
OF FOOD COST

Maximum Allowable	44.0%
Actual Food Cost	42.5%
Potential Food Cost	38.03%
Standard Food Cost	40.5%

The concept of food cost must be examined from multiple perspectives in order to understand the total impact it has on operating profit. The four faces of food cost must be individually calculated for each operation because no two operations will be identical in all contributing variables. Maximum allowable food cost determines whether the potential food cost for the menu sales mix will allow profit objectives to be realized. The PFC must be adjusted with allowances to arrive at the standard food cost, which is the "realistic" food cost objective. The actual food cost taken from the income statement should not exceed the SFC. When it does, losses being incurred are exceeding allowances set by management.

The most important aspect of operational analysis is being able to interpret the figures on departmental cost reports. You need to know what the numbers are telling you. Once a variance from standard cost has occurred, examination of the probable causes must be undertaken. The simple calculation of a food cost ratio or percentage is only the beginning of the investigation process. Knowing how to interpret a ration requires knowing all the possible reasons for the cost control variance. Only then can a remedy be prescribed.

In order to control food costs effectively, one must be familiar with the numerous causes of high food cost. One needs to start the process by examining the largest or most frequently occurring costs first. A small cost variance that occurs frequently can add up to a sizable cost variance if left unchecked. Keep in mind that cost control covers more than just the back-of-the-house. The cause of the higher than standard cost could result from activity taking place outside the kitchen. The following list of over 100 reasons is by no means exhaustive and complete, but it will provide you with areas to begin your investigation.

Remember, a restaurant exists to sell food to customers. Any control measure that reduces sales volume or costs more than the resulting savings is counterproductive. Also, controls put in place for the convenience of the operation that are not "customer-friendly" are also counterproductive.

ONE HUNDRED REASONS FOR HIGH FOOD COSTS

MENU

Poor forecasting of business volume
Menu offerings that do not appeal to clientele
Poor menu design for cost control
Too many items on the menu
Monotonous menu choices
No balance between high and low food cost menu items
Poor promotion of low cost items

Improper pricing of menu items
Failure to adjust prices when food costs increase

PURCHASING

Excessive inventory of perishable items
No competitive purchasing policy
No detailed specifications
Poor relationships with suppliers
Use of fixed versus flexible standing orders
Not monitoring markets for supply and price
Graft between buyer and purveyors
No regular and organized inventory procedures
No formal written inventory records
Overbuying
Par stock levels too high—slow inventory turnover
Ficticious company invoices being sent for payment
Reprocessing of paid invoices for payment
Failure to take discounts for early payment

RECEIVING

Theft by delivery person
Failure to check invoices for correct prices, quantity, quality
No system to assure proper credit for returned merchandise
No weighing items purchased by weight
Failure to adhere to purchase specifications
Signing invoices without checking deliveries
No backup record of purchases to compare to delivery invoice
Acceptance of less than complete shipments with "full" billing and failing
to receive back-ordered items

STORAGE

Improper storage temperature of perishable items
Failure to rotate inventory (FIFO)
Failure to properly cover supplies
Poor sanitation of storage areas
No periodic report of dead stock or inventory turnover
Spoilage due to vermin

No daily inspection of perishable foods
No locks on storage areas
Unorganized storage areas
No limited access to storage areas
No written record of issues
No "forced issues" of dead stock

PAPER CONTROLS

No serially numbered guest checks
No audit of cash register readings
No control of voids and payouts
No reconciling of kitchen checks with guest checks
No reconciliation of statements to invoices
No record of reported waste and spoilage

PREPARATION/PROCESSING

Excessive trim waste on meats and vegetables
Inability to incorporate trim/by-products into production items
Overproduction
Failure to follow standardized recipes
Failure to follow standardized cooking techniques
Not cooking in small batches
Inadequate or improper processing equipment and utensils
Preparing too much food in advance
Failure to check portioning standards
Overreliance on value-added (convenience) products
Overcooking foods and resulting low yields
No production/menu mix history to guide production amounts
Oversized portions
Using more costly varieties/grades than needed for intended use
Excessive use of high cost convenience foods

SERVICES

No standardized dishes, bowls, cups, and so on for plating
Failure to use measured portioning tools, for example, scoops, scales, ladles
Food issued from kitchen without written checks
No recording of waste and returned items

Carelessness, spillage, waste

Failure to adhere to portioning standards

Standard portions too large

Inadequate customer counts for food bars/buffets

SALES

Server theft

Cashier theft

Customer walkouts

Improper recording of items on guest check

Inaccurate price extensions on guest checks

Errors in addition on guest checks

Intentional or accidental omission of items from check

Poor menu design to promote low-cost high-profit items

Lack of internal selling by servers

No calculators provided for servers to total checks

No records of past sales for use in forecasting business

No monitoring of complimentary meals and discount coupons

No monitoring of voids and overrings

Failure to charge for add-on items, for example, coffee, tea, blue cheese

High incidence of bad checks and invalid credit cards being accepted

Missing guest checks

Failure to reconcile kitchen requisitions with guest checks

No record of mistakes and returned food orders

Ability of servers to get food from kitchen without recording sale

Resetting cash register readings

Under-ringing of guest checks

Guest checks not serially numbered and assigned to servers

OTHER

No allowance taken for employee meals

No monitoring of employee meals

Failure to adhere to control rules and policies

Collusion between receiving and purchasing agents

Theft by delivery person

Errors made by accounts payable bookkeeper

Failure to deduct food transfers to bar

THE FALLACY OF GROSS PROFIT: THE IMPACT ON BOTTOM LINE

Ever since the introduction of menu engineering sales analysis (Smith and Kasavana, 1982), the consideration of food cost percentage has been deemphasized and overlooked. Advocates of the gross profit approach (also called contribution margin) treat food cost and gross profit as mutually exclusive, often citing that "You bank *dollars* not percentages."

Treating food cost percentage and gross profit in this way can sometimes lead to a false sense of "profitability" that does not translate to the bottom line unless a number of other variables fall into place. The truth is that in most cases, the examples provided to show the benefits of high gross profits over low food cost percentage will reveal some very startling evidence that indicates the gross profit scenarios sometimes return less gross profit per dollar of food cost and require more sales to achieve the "dollars" they put in the bank.

While gross profit is important, completely ignoring food cost can lead to reduced profits and is not always practical. The same is true for food cost; a goal of achieving *the lowest overall food cost percentage* can sacrifice revenue and profit. *Typically, items with low food cost are the lowest priced items on the menu. A menu sales mix made up of primarily low food cost items will result in a lower check average, and unless customer count increases, overall revenue will be lower as well.*

A balanced menu sales mix will contain both items with low food costs and items with high gross profits. The cost/margin analysis (Pavesic, 1983) seeks to identify items on the menu that are both low in food cost and high in contribution margin. On the other hand, reliance on selling only items with high individual gross profit (menu price less raw food costs) will result in a higher overall food cost because the high gross profit items on the menu have higher food costs (e.g., steaks, seafood, Prime rib) and are often the highest priced items on the menu.

The gross profit method of pricing works best in operations like country clubs and destination restaurants with long waiting lines. However, in competitive markets, reliance on gross profit pricing may result in declining customer counts. In other words, if price inelasticity exists, gross profit pricing seems to work best. However, most operations are in markets where price elasticity exists and higher prices can mean reduced demand. Therefore, those relying on gross profit pricing will not see an increase in the bottom line return unless customer counts hold steady and fixed cost percentages decline more than food cost percentage increases due to higher sales levels.

The examples that follow will demonstrate this theory using the figures previously offered as examples showing that the gross profit approach is superior to the food cost approach. The results show that the *financial efficiency* is lower with gross profit pricing examples and the increases in cost are far greater than the additional dollars returned from the effort.

A *middle ground* position is recommended and the *cost/margin analysis* provides an alternative that combines food cost and gross profit. Cost/margin *op-*

timizes both food cost and contribution margin and is not subject to the biases of a reliance on a single measure.

We start with the premise that sales increases must occur for gross profit to offset the increased food cost percentages. While fixed costs (e.g., rent, loan payments, insurance, overhead) remain stable in dollar amounts from month to month, the percentage of overall sales they account for will vary inversely with sales. Consequently, higher sales will result in lower fixed cost percentages and reduced sales will cause fixed cost percentages to increase.

Menu sales mix "A" in Table 3-8 shows the overall results when a "low food cost" is achieved while sales mix "B" shown in Table 3-9 is offered to show the results that occur from a sales shift to higher gross profit items with higher food costs. Sales mix B was presented at a past NRA seminar as an example of an "improved" financial performance over sales mix A.

Table 3-8 MENU SALES MIX "A"

Menu Item	Number Sold	Menu Price	Food Cost	Food Cost Percent	Item Gross Profit	Weighted Gross Profit
Lobster	42	$28.50	$14.90	52.3%	$13.60	$571.20
NY Strip	74	$16.50	$7.40	44.8%	$9.10	$673.40
Prime Rib	143	$17.25	$7.25	42.0%	$10.00	$1430.00
Chop Steak	88	$8.95	$2.75	30.7%	$6.20	$545.60
Pasta	72	$7.50	$1.80	24.0%	$5.70	$410.40
Grilled Fish	96	$7.95	$2.40	30.2%	$5.55	$532.80
Totals	515					$4,163.40

Total Weekly Sales: $6975.55; Total Weekly Food Cost: $2812.15; Food Cost %: 40.3%

Table 3-9 MENU SALES MIX "B"

Menu Item	Number Sold	Menu Price	Food Cost	Food Cost Percent	Item Gross Profit	Weighted Gross Profit
Lobster	62	$27.00	$14.90	55.2%	$12.10	$750.20
NY Strip	101	$15.50	$7.40	47.7%	$8.10	$818.10
Prime Rib	180	$16.25	$7.25	44.6%	$9.00	$1620.00
Chop Steak	54	$9.95	$2.75	27.6%	$7.20	$388.80
Pasta	52	$8.50	$1.80	21.2%	$6.70	$348.40
Grilled Fish	66	$8.95	$6.55	26.8%	$6.55	$432.30
Total	515					$4357.80

Total Weekly Sales: $7734.50; Total Weekly Food Cost: $3376.70; Food Cost % 43.7%
Example used at NRA Seminar on "Your Menu Is Like a Supermarket," Educational Foundation, National Restaurant Association, 1996.

Sales mix B shows 10.9 percent more in sales revenue, or $758.95, over sales mix A. However, in realizing that sales increase, it consumed $564.55 in additional food cost. This is 20 percent more than in sales mix A. Sales mix B realized a 4.7 percent increase in overall gross profit, or $194.40 over what was achieved in sales mix A.

When you analyze these changes some rather startling percentages jump out. Consider that the additional sales of $758.95 used an additional $564.55 in food inventory. The food cost to sales ratio is 74.38 percent! How comfortable are you offering items for sale on your menu that would result in a 74 percent food cost? This occurred because the sales increase was 10.9 percent while the increase in food cost was 20 percent, resulting in an increase in overall gross profit of only 4.7 percent.

Proponents of the gross profit approach would focus on the additional $194.40 in gross profit and not call your attention to the fact that the actual food cost percentage increased from 40.3 to 43.7 percent! We do not have the complete income statement to be able to determine what happened to the overall bottom line profit dollars and percentages. It is unlikely that a sales increase of 11 percent lowered fixed cost percentages to offset the 3.4 percent increase in food cost.

In the examples provided to show the advantages of gross profit over food cost percentage, the customer counts remain the same in both scenarios, an unrealistic assumption that will not hold true in highly competitive markets. Also, the sales mix cannot be "manipulated" perfectly. Techniques of menu design can increase the likelihood that certain items will be read and improve the chance that they will be selected by the patron. However, other forces in the marketplace influence the customer traffic on any given day or meal period. Menu pricing is only one aspect of the total operating picture that impacts the overall menu sales mix.

If this does not have you questioning the soundness of ignoring food cost for gross profit pricing, consider the following financial results. Sales mix A returned $1.48 in gross profit for every dollar of food cost expended ($4163.40/$2812.15) while sales mix B returned only $1.31 ($4357.80/$3316.70). Sales mix B had to generate $1.77 in sales to return $1 of gross profit ($7734.50/$4357.80) while sales mix A needed only $1.67 to return $1 of gross profit ($6975.55/$4163.40).

The purpose of this explanation is to tell restauranteurs not to completely abandon their low food cost philosophy for the gross profit approach. It is not for everyone. In fact, most operators in competitive markets where demand and price elasticity are at work need to keep food cost percentages within standards of acceptance and not forsake it for gross profit. The author recommends considering a middle-of-the-road approach, similar to that of the cost/margin analysis (Pavesic, 1983). Cost/margin is covered in complete detail in Chapter 5.

Chapter Four

Yield Cost Analysis

In Chapter 3 a restaurant was compared to a factory where raw materials are transformed into the final product consumed by the customer within minutes of completion. The production process is guided by the standardized recipe, which if followed will result in quality and quantity standards being achieved. In order to calculate the *plate cost* (also called *edible portion cost*, or *EP*), you must first determine the cost of your ingredients. The data required for this calculation are (1) the purchase price of the ingredients and (2) the edible yield.

YIELD TERMINOLOGY

There are several terms used in yield cost analysis with which you should be familiar.

As-purchased (AP) weight: The weight of the product as delivered to the restaurant by the purveyor including bones, fat, and unusable trim.

Edible portion (EP) weight: The amount (weight or volume) that is available to be portioned after loss in carving or shrinkage in cooking. This is also referred to as *as-served* and *plate cost*. No further losses will occur due to trimming or shrinkage in cooking.

Waste: The amount of unusable product that is lost due to processing, cooking, and portioning or by-products for which there is no salable value.

Usable trim: By-products that result from processing or cooking that can be sold as other menu items to recover all or part of their cost. For example, trim resulting from cutting steaks in the restaurant that is used for ground beef, sirloin tips, or stew are usable trim. They are costed as *equivalent products* that can be purchased from suppliers; for example, the market price for ground beef, sirloin tips, and stew meat.

Yield: The yield is the net weight or volume of food after it has been processed and made ready to serve. This refers to the yield from a ham or turkey that has been weighed after cooking, but *before* portioning.

Standard yield: The yield that results from following the standardized recipe and standardized portioning procedures. It is the amount of usable product available for portioning after all processing and cooking have been completed. The yield percentage is calculated by dividing the as-purchased weight by the standard yield.

Standard portion: The size of the portion indicated on the standardized recipe and the basis for determining the plated portion cost of the menu item.

YIELD FACTORS

The following discussion of yield cost factors offers an extremely practical procedure for costing out items that involve trim losses, cooking shrinkage, or usable trim. One very valuable tool accompanying these calculations is the *portion divider*, which makes determining order quantities of items with trim and shrink simple and accurate to estimate. Once the as purchased price has been determined, portion costs can quickly be calculated whenever market prices fluctuate.

The calculations are relatively easy to do when you are dealing with any food item that only has to be portioned prior to plating. Such items are often referred to as *convenience foods*. A convenience food, however, is any food item purchased with some preparation labor already performed on it. Some or all of the production steps to bring the particular product to that level of readiness are performed *outside* the restaurant by the processor. A frozen Sarah Lee muffin and pre-mixed cookie dough are easy to cost out and are examples of "convenience foods."

Would you classify raw fresh chicken cut into eight pieces a convenience food? According to the definition given earlier, it is because it eliminates the need for the restaurant to cut up the chicken after it has been delivered. Yes, it will cost a few cents more per pound than you would pay if it were purchased whole, but consider the labor-intensive task of cutting hundreds of chickens if you were a KFC or Popeye's chicken franchisee. Think of the money these restaurants save on equipment and space by purchasing pre-cut chicken, not to mention the reduced number of workers' compensation claims for employees who would likely cut themselves performing this duty. Other examples of convenience foods are frozen french fries, precut steaks, pre-pattied hamburgers, bottled salad dressing, and shredded cabbage.

CALCULATING PLATE COST

Calculating the plate cost for a convenience food is not difficult. In the case of pre-mixed cookie dough, if one 24-ounce package costs $2.50 per pound, the cost of 24 ounces would be $3.75. If the portion size is 0.75 ounce of dough for each cookie, you should get 32 cookies from each package (24/0.75 = 32). Therefore, the food cost per cookie is approximately $.12 ($3.75/32 = $.12). If you sell them for $.39 each, the food cost percentage is 30.7% ($.12/$.39 = 30.77%). This calculation is easy because there is no waste or loss in processing.

If you knew that the food cost for making the cookies from scratch was approximately 25 percent lower than the purchased dough, would you make them yourself? By using the pre-mixed dough, the restaurant eliminates having to purchase the preparation equipment, raw ingredients, and the labor cost of a baker to prepare the cookies. The price paid for these ready-made products or ingredients raises the food cost over what they would be if made from scratch on the premises, but the operation simplifies its purchasing, can hire less skilled employees at lower wages, and does not have to carry large inventories of ingredients that complicate the purchasing and storage functions.

COSTING CONVENIENCE FOODS

With most convenience foods, all you have to do to determine portion costs is to simply count, weigh, or measure the size of the portion to determine how many orders you can get. You divide the number of servable portions into the as purchased price to get the portion cost. However, even with convenience foods, an allowance for normal waste due to portioning must be factored in the cost of each portion. This may be as little as one portion per case or as much as 2 percent of possible yield.

In the case of the cookies, what if you discovered that you were getting only 28 and not 32 cookies out of each 24-ounce package of dough? If you get only 28 cookies at $.39, your food cost per cookie increases from $.12 to approximately $.14 or 35.9 percent. The total revenue from a package of dough drops from $12.48 to $10.92 (28 × $.39 = $10.92). You did not just increase your cost per cookie by $.02; you reduced sales revenue by $1.56.

Some allowance for waste must be made even with raw cookie dough. It should be very minimal if the dough is weighed or portioned with a measured scoop. Most convenience foods would have minimal or no allowances for waste (e.g., pre-portioned steaks, pre-portioned desserts like pie and cheesecake).

Portion cost calculations are not this simple when it come to items *made from scratch* in the kitchen. When you cut your own steaks, bake your own pies, make your own gravies and soups, the costing out of the recipe and servable portions requires much more than dividing portions into as-purchase prices. Whenever you process, trim, cook, or otherwise perform any preparation step on a menu item, you will end up with less weight, count, or volume of product to serve than when you started. Therefore, the cost per pound, per ounce, or per piece will be greater than when you started. Because of this loss, the cost per servable pound will be greater than the cost per pound as purchased. The greater the trim loss, cooking shrinkage, and portioning loss, the higher the cost per servable pound relative to the purchase price per pound.

A calculation of the actual portion cost for every menu item must be made. Although this may be done only a few times during the year, the fluctuating market costs of the ingredients requires that menu prices be updated and adjusted. With the system that is explained in this chapter, this process is reduced to a simple yet accurate bookkeeping adjustment. Efficient cost controls demand such data be part of the overall cost control program. Without such records, costs cannot be accurately determined.

The cost of the edible portion is rarely calculated from the invoice price, referred to as the *as-purchased price (AP) per pound or unit*. Determination of portion costs for items like frozen french fries that are packed six-pound bags to a case at a cost of $15 a case is a simple calculation of the cost per pound divided by the portions per pound. If the portion's size is 5 ounces, the portion cost for the french fries is $.16 ($15/30 lb = $.50/lb; 16 oz/5 oz = 3.2 portions per pound; $.50/3.2 portions/lb = $.16. That food cost may actually be understated because it assumes you will get 3.2 portions per pound. If you get only 3 portions per pound (allowing for over-portioning and a waste factor), the true portion cost is $.50/3, or $.17. An additional cost of $.03 to $.05 per portion should be added for the the frying oil and the catsup typically served with the fries.

Another example of a convenience product would be ready-made cheesecakes purchased from a specialty baker. All the operator has to do is cut the cake into portions and serve. The same applies to all ready-to-eat pies and cakes. If the cost of the cheesecake is $15.00 and 12 servings are cut, the cost per slice is $1.25. One important thing to keep in mind is that the profit is in the last three or four pieces that are sold! Some operators will pre-plate each piece and wrap it to insure proper portioning and yields.

It is always a good idea to calculate portion costs on less than 100 percent yields, even with convenience foods. Doing so, you build in a cushion for error and quality control. There will always be a questionable item that should not be served. Do not allow food cost decisions to be counter-productive to quality control standards. When in doubt, throw it out. Build quality control losses into your food cost! This is applicable to both convenience and scratch prepared foods.

COSTING ITEMS MADE FROM SCRATCH

Most menu items contain ingredients that require trimming, processing, and preliminary cooking that will result in shrinkage of some kind. Consequently, whenever the weight or volume of cooked product is less than the AP weight or volume, the EP cost will be higher than the AP price. This requires that *yield cost analysis* be conducted on these menu items to determine their true cost per portion.

The buyer for a food-service operation uses yields to help determine quantities to be purchased and kept on hand to meet production needs. For example, if cutting yield tests for a whole salmon weighing 20 pounds as purchased produce 16 pounds of steaks or fillets, only 80 percent of the original as-purchased weight will be usable. This has significant implications on the plate cost of each portion and order quantities.

Over time, the chef or owner will discover the optimum size to purchase that results in the highest yield and least amount of waste. Thus, purchase specifications are developed that indicate the minimum and maximum weight of a single fish and even the specific variety of salmon.

Certain cuts of meat will have both trim loss and shrinkage during cooking. Yields must be measured and portion cost determined after cooking. The amount of product that remains after processing, cooking, and portioning is called the *yield*. The ratio of the *edible portions* to the original weight is called *yield percentage*.

Yield tests do not have to be taken every time the product is prepared. If standardized purchase specifications, standardized recipes, and standardized portioning are followed, you can assume that the yields, and therefore portion costs, should remain consistent over time. The only variable that will change the portion cost is the price paid to the purveyor.

Yield tests should represent a weighted average of several tests, not just a single test. Operations where standardized recipes and purchase specifications are inconsistently applied will have a variance in food cost that will fluctuate from day to day and month to month. Close adherence to standards assures that variances will be minimal and that costs will be consistent over time.

In cooking from scratch, there are two primary steps in making an item ready for sale. They are (1) prepreparation (that is, *rough preparation*), which includes such steps as butchering, vegetable cleaning, processing foods such as slicing meats, boning fish, cleaning shrimp, peeling and chopping vegetables, making salad dressings, and the like; and (2) preparation, which is taking the partially processed ingredients and completing the cooking or combining with other preprepped ingredients in advance of serving the item to the customer.

Owners, managers, and chefs need to have at their disposal the most accurate portion costs for all the major entrees and accompaniments on their menus. In addition, they need to monitor the purchase prices of key ingredients so they can adjust menu prices when necessary. The calculations and formulas that follow can simply, quickly, and accurately translate increases in *as-purchased prices* to update portion costs. In addition, once yields have been standardized, quantities to order for busy periods and special parties can also be determined quickly, easily, and accurately.

The accuracy of your costs and quantities is dependent upon diligent adherence to standardized purchase specifications, recipes, and portioning. If you have tight standards and follow them religiously, your costs will be consistent and accurate, and they will not have to be recalculated unless you change any of the three standards. Without consistent standards you cannot accurately determine purchase quantities and food costs.

COSTING AN OVEN-READY PRIME RIB WITHOUT USABLE TRIM

In the example that follows, you need to focus on the *methods described* and not the actual numbers derived. The prices and yields are not necessarily representative of what you would achieve with a like product nor are they presented as industry standards. Further, assume that the final figures given are the result of a weighted average of dozens of yield tests, not a single one. As I was told by a statistics instructor many years ago, "If you want to claim a valid and reliable conclusion from a test, your sample is critical." Therefore, the greater the number of yield tests you conduct under all kinds of conditions and employees, the more representative your standard of actual yields will be .

Further, after testing different grades, weights, and brands of products, you discover that certain ones produce better yields. Thus you will establish a purchase specification for the ingredients, and will accept no substitutions at any price. In the following example, it is assumed that the quality and yield grade that give the best product, the best cooking method and temperature, and the best portion procedures have been determined in this manner.

With such standards in place, cost and yield predictions on Prime rib becomes more accurate. As a result of this consistency, you will be able to calculate several numerical constants to quickly determine the *cost per servable pound, cost per portion, and the amount to purchase*. To demonstrate these factors, two yield tests will be conducted to explain how to determine these same factors for your own use.

In the first yield test, we will be using a product that has only servable product and waste. Waste has no value and the more waste you have from cooking shrinkage or carving loss, the smaller will be your standard yield, the fewer salable portions you will get, and the greater will be your cost per servable pound.

All weights less than a pound are expressed as decimal fractions to eliminate the necessity to convert pounds to ounces in the math required. For example, 4 ounces is a quarter of a pound or 0.25 pound. Eight ounces is a half a pound or 0.5 pound, and so on. To convert ounces into decimal equivalents, simply divide the number of ounces by 16, the number of ounces in a pound.

The first test will be on a 109 oven-ready Prime rib. It is a USDA Choice, yield grade 3. Yield grade is an indication of the ratio of lean to fat. A yield grade of one (1) will weigh under 17 pounds as purchased and have less fat and marbling. A yield grade 5 will weigh 25 pounds as-purchased weight. This yield grade is an important addition to your purchase specifications when purchasing primal beef cuts. Purchase specifications require it to weigh between 19 and 22 pounds.

The Institutional Meat Purchasing Specifications (IMPS) number 109 is a standard of identity that translates into a very specific description of this cut of beef. IMPS describe products customarily purchased in the food service industry. Refer to *The Meat Buyers Guide* published by the National Association of Meat Purveyors. The USDA specifications say that a 109 rib . . .

is prepared from a 7 rib primal rib (no. 103) by a straight cut across the ribs at a fixed point measured three inches from the extreme outer tip of the rib eye muscle at the 12th rib and continuing in a straight line through a fixed point 4 inches from the extreme outer tip of the rib eye muscle at the sixth rib. The chine bone is removed. . . .

I believe the point is made.

The original as-purchased weight is 20.25 pounds. See Table 4-1. Since the rib is *oven ready* there is no trimming before cooking. It goes right into the oven and is roasted at the prescribed temperature until the desired internal temperature is reached; a timer is also set. Remember, cooking at high temperatures increases shrinkage. The new cook-and-hold low temperature roasting cabinets reduce shrinkage from 25 percent to less than 10 percent. That translates to an additional 15 percent yield. In the case of this rib, it would have meant an additional 3.0375 pounds of rib to sell. This yield test is not using such an oven. The cook-and-hold oven cooks at 250 degrees for about 6 to 8 hours, depending on the degree of doneness sought. An additional advantage of the cook-and-hold oven is that the meat is cooked to the same degree of doneness throughout instead of well done on the end cuts and rare in the middle.

The weight of the cooked rib is 16.375 lb or 16 lb 6 oz. That means we had cooking shrinkage of 3.875 lb or 3 lb 14 oz. This is 19.136 percent of the original as-purchased weight. After it sits for about 20 minutes, it is cut into portions. If the entire rib were portioned at one time, as might be the case if it were for a banquet, the yield will be higher than if it were portioned for à la carte dining room service. Typically, Prime rib is sold in two or three sized cuts, all cut from the same rib. This would increase the likelihood of over-portioning and waste from miscut portions that could not be served to customers. Thus this yield test would be more appropriate for a banquet situation.

Table 4-1 STANDARD YIELD CALCULATIONS

Item: Oven-Ready Rib, IMPS 1110R (109) Grade Choice, Yield 3
As-Purchased Price/lb: $3.43
As-Purchased Weight: 20.25 lb Total Cost: $69.46
SUMMARY OF YIELD TEST RESULTS (The figures represent the weighted average yield determined from several similar yield tests.)

	Decimal Weight	**Lb and Oz**	**% of Total Weight**
Loss in Cooking	3.875 lb	3 lb 14 oz	19.136%
Loss in Carving	5.1875 lb	5 lb 3 oz	25.617%
Total Loss (Waste)	9.0625 lb	9 lb 1 oz	44.753%
Servable Weight	*11.1875 lb*	*11 lb 3 oz*	55.246%

1. Percentage of Servable Weight
   Formula: $\dfrac{\text{Servable Weight}}{\text{As-Purchased Weight}}$ $\quad \dfrac{11.1875}{20.25} = 55.246\%$

2. Cost per Servable Pound
   Formula: $\dfrac{\text{As-Purchased Price/lb}}{\text{\% of Servable Weight}}$ $\quad \dfrac{\$3.43}{0.55246} = \$6.21$

3. Cost Factor per Servable Pound
   Formula: $\dfrac{\text{Cost per Servable Pound}}{\text{As-Purchased Price/lb}}$ $\quad \dfrac{\$6.21}{\$3.43} = 1.810$

4. Cost per Portion (Assume 8 oz portions or 2 per lb)
   Formula: $\dfrac{\text{Cost per Servable Pound}}{\text{No. of Portions per lb}}$ $\quad \dfrac{\$6.21}{2} = \$3.11$

5. Portion Cost Multiplier
   Formula: $\dfrac{\text{Cost Factor per Servable/lb}}{\text{Portions per lb}}$ $\quad \dfrac{1.810}{2} = .905$

6. Portion Divider for 8-oz Portion
   Formula: % of Servable Wgt × No. Portions/lb $\quad$ .55246(2) = 1.104

7. Number of Pounds to Purchase
   (Assume 100 eight-oz portions)
   Formula: $\dfrac{\text{No. of Portions Needed}}{\text{Portion Divider}}$ $\quad \dfrac{100}{1.104} = 9.0576 \text{ lbs*}$

*Since each rib will weigh between 19 and 21 lbs, 5 ribs are needed.

This is a caution to you when conducting yield tests in controlled environments and extrapolating to costs that would occur in a table-service restaurant. There are many distractions in an actual restaurant kitchen, and the fast pace does not offer the time and attention often given in a test kitchen. Under such controlled conditions, most yields will be greater than will occur in the actual operation. Therefore, if costs and prices are determined by unrealistically high yields, the food cost goals will not be achievable in the individual units serving the public.

Out of the original 20.25 lb purchased, the combined shrinkage and carving loss was 9.0625 lb, or 9 lb 1 oz. This is 44.67 percent of the original as-purchased weight. Keep in mind that the results are approximate yields on what you can expect on *all the ribs* when purchasing and cooking specifications remain the same. If a restaurant does not adhere to such standards, any given rib will vary to greater extent from the average of the yield test figures.

The percentage of servable weight is 55.25 percent of the original as-purchased quantity. Since there is only salable product and waste, the cost per *servable pound* of the 11.1875 lb of servable Prime rib cannot be $3.43. Remember, the total cost of the rib as purchased was $69.46. We cannot assign any value to the cooking shrinkage or trim loss. Therefore, we have to recover the total cost of the rib from the amount we have to sell.

There are two ways to calculate the cost per servable pound. The first is to divide the total as-purchased price, $69.46, by the servable weight, 11.1875 pounds. The result is $6.21 per pound. However, there is a better method that incorporates the yield percentage. Simply divide the as-purchased price per pound by the percentage of servable yield, or $3.43/0.5525. You will get the lost per servable pound of $6.21.

The second method is better because you can estimate your yield percentage easier than you can calculate the actual pounds and ounces of servable product. Servable yield is what determines your cost per servable pound. In this case, there is an increase of $2.78 per pound, or over $.17 per ounce from purchase to the plate.

This makes a significant difference when computing actual food costs. Remember, the figures here are really the weighted average of many such cooking and carving tests, and you can expect that any given rib you roast and carve will have some yield if you uphold your purchase and preparation standards. For this reason, we can calculate a *constant value* that will allow you to quickly determine the cost per servable pound regardless of the as-purchased price per pound.

The cost factor for converting any as-purchased price per pound to the cost per servable pound is found by dividing the cost per servable pound, $6.21, by the as-purchased price per pound, $3.43. $6.31/$3.43 = 1.81. The cost factor per servable pound, 1.81, has no value like dollars or pounds; it is just a mathematical constant. It will remain constant as long as all the variables remain constant, for example, purchase specifications, cooking methods, and carving procedures. With this factor, you can convert any as-purchased price per pound to your cost per servable pound by multiplying the cost factor, 1.81, times any as-purchased price per pound that you are quoted by your meat purveyor. As proof, you multiply $3.43 × 1.81 = $6.21. If the market price increases to $3.50, the new cost per servable pound would be $6.34 ($3.50 × 1.81). This is a valid factor based on the average yields.

Once the cost per servable pound is calculated, it is simple to determine your portion costs. Simply divide the cost per servable pound by the number of portions per pound. In this example, we are serving only 8-ounce portions, or two portions per pound. Therefore, $6.21/2 = $3.11 per portion. You would add the food cost of the salad, bread and butter, potato, vegetable, and condiments to get your total plate cost.

Since most restaurants offering Prime rib serve more than one size portion, you will find it useful to be able to convert any as-purchased price per pound directly to a portion cost. This is accomplished quickly and accurately with the use of what is called the *portion cost multiplier*. This constant is calculated by dividing the number of portions per pound into the cost factor per servable pound, or $1.81/2 = .905$.

With the portion cost multiplier, you convert the as-purchased price per pound to your portion cost by multiplying it by the as-purchased price per pound. In this example, $\$3.43 \times .905 = \$3.11$. If the price increases to $\$3.50$, your new portion cost for 8 ounces is $\$3.50 \times .905 = \$3.17$.

There is one more of these constant factors that I think you will find particularly helpful, especially if you are purchasing for banquets or institutional food service operations. This factor is called the *portion divider*, and it tells you how many pounds of product you need to purchase to serve a specified number of portions. For the sake of example, assume you are going to serve an 8-ounce Prime rib to 100 people. How many ribs do you need to purchase?

The quickest way to do it is with the portion divider. It is derived by multiplying the percentage of servable weight by the number of portions per pound, or $.5525 \times 2 = 1.105$. To use the portion divider, divide it into the number of covers you need to serve, or $100/1.105$, and it gives you 90.5 pounds. You don't call up your meat purveyor and order 90.5 pounds of 109 ribs. Since the average weight of the ribs will be between 19 and 22 pounds, you will need to order a minimum of 5 ribs. If this were a banquet, you would have a built-in allowance for additions, and if they are under guarantee, you will still charge for the full 5 ribs.

> Proof
> As-Purchased Weight   90.5 lb
> Less Waste of 44.75%   (40.5) lb
> Servable Weight   50 lb
> 50 lb × 16 oz = 800 oz
> 800 oz/ 8-oz portions = 100 portions

What you would normally do is calculate a different portion multiplier for each size portion you serve. If you served a 10-ounce portion, there would be 1.6 portions per pound. $.5525 \times 1.6 = .884$. $100/.884 = 113.12$ lbs, or six 109 ribs.

The application of utilizing the percent of servable yield to other products that do not have usable trim is extensive. Assume you have a delicatessen or sandwich shop that uses precooked meats for your sandwiches. In this example, we are testing the various forms of corned beef. You sell reubens and corned beef sandwiches and your portion size is 4 ounces. (The following example is adapted from C. Levinson, *Food and Beverage Operation*, Prentice Hall pp. 188-189, 1989.)

The corned beef products we are testing are:

	Waste or Shrink
Raw Corned Rounds	25%
Raw Corned Briskets	50%
Cooked Corned Rounds	5%
Cooked Corned Briskets	10%

This same test could be done with roast beef, turkey breast, and ham, as they are all similar in the ways they can be purchased. The percent of servable weight for each of the corned beef products would be 75 percent, 50 percent, 95 percent, and 90 percent, respectively. We will compute the portion divider by multiplying the percentage of servable weight by the number of portions per pound, in this case, four. The portion dividers are:

Raw Rounds	$0.75 \times 4 = 3.0$
Raw Briskets	$0.50 \times 4 = 2.0$
Cooked Rounds	$0.95 \times 4 = 3.8$
Cooked Briskets	$0.90 \times 4 = 3.6$

Assume the following are as-purchased prices per pound:

Raw Rounds	$1.45
Raw Briskets	$1.05
Cooked Rounds	$1.95
Cooked Briskets	$2.25

The cost per servable pound can be computed by dividing the as-purchased price per pound by the percentage of servable weight.

Raw Rounds	$1.45/0.75 = $1.93 lb
Raw Briskets	$1.05/0.50 = $2.10 lb
Cooked Rounds	$1.95/0.95 = $2.05 lb
Cooked Briskets	$2.25/0.90 = $2.50 lb

Another method of calculating the portion cost is to divide the original as-purchased price per pound by each respective portion divider.

Raw Rounds	$1.45/3 = $.49
Raw Briskets	$1.05/2 = $.54
Cooked Rounds	$1.95/3.8 = $.52
Cooked Briskets	$2.25/3.6 = $.62

Raw rounds end up being the lowest cost per portion, but selecting them assumes that you have the equipment and personnel to properly cook them.

There is labor cost that must be considered. Other considerations that may override cost are the taste preference of your clientele and your quality standards. It may be that only corned beef brisket will meet customer expectations. Therefore, your decision on which one to use cannot be based only on cost. Quality and customer preferences are sometimes more important than food costs in the selection process.

To determine how much to purchase for 700 sandwiches, divide the number of covers by the portion divider. Using cooked briskets, we would need at least 195 pounds (700/3.6 = 195).

COSTING A PRIME RIB WITH USABLE TRIM

In the previous examples, there were only two end products to deal with, servable portions and waste. This example considers *usable trim* as an additional end product of in-house butchering of meat.

This example simulates a butchering and cooking test on a Primal rib, IMPS 103. To elect for this alternative, you would need to have the skilled labor to do the meat cutting, have a meat saw, and have a menu that allows you to sell the resulting usable by-products. If the restaurant has a fixed or static menu, it will not be able to incorporate short ribs, stew meat, or ground beef into the menu. The breakdown of the rib is shown in Table 4-2.

The breakdown of the rib yields are: waste trim (fat, gristle, bone), cap meat, short ribs, and ground beef trimmings. Each of these by-products is col-

Table 4-2 YIELD TEST WITH USABLE TRIM

Item: 103 Primal Rib	As-Purchased Weight: 33 lbs
Grade Choice, Yield 2	As-Purchased Price/lb: $2.75
Total Cost: $90.75	

	Weight	Market Value
Usable Trim		
Cap Meat	1.55 lb	$4.40
Short Ribs	3.25 lb	$9.07
Ground Beef	1.25 lb	$1.25
Total	6.05 lb	$15.02
Waste	3.3 lb	0
Total Trim	9.35 lb	
Weight of Oven-Ready Rib	23.65 lb	

Total: *As-Purchased Price* less the market value of the usable trim equals the cost that needs to be recovered from the oven-ready rib. $90.75 − $15.02 = $75.73 or $3.20/lb ($75.48/23.65 lb)

lected in a separate pan for weighing prior to determining its market value. The industry standard for determining the value of usable trim is to assign a market value based on what it would cost to purchase these items from a supplier. You would simply ask your supplier to obtain prices on such trim or similar items. Fat and bone, although sold to rendering companies, is not given a value. Total value of all usable trim in this test comes to $15.02, and the breakdown is shown in Table 4-3.

The calculations follow simple word problems such as "If one pound costs $2.25, how much does 0.75 of a pound cost?" The value of the usable trim is *deducted* from the total as-purchased price of the rib ($90.75 – $15.02). The difference of $75.73 is the amount you need to recover from the sale of the Prime rib. The cost of the usable trim will be recovered from the sale of the menu items in which they are used. Of course, the assumption is that you have an outlet for these items; that is, daily luncheon specials or a special of the day.

The butchering test has converted the 103 rib into a 109 rib like the one purchased oven ready in the first cooking and carving yield test. This one is a little larger as it weighs 23.625 pounds or 23 pounds, 10 ounces. This costs out to $3.21 per pound. This is compared to the $3.43 paid for the 109 oven-ready

Table 4-3 BUTCHERING YIELD TEST

Item: 103 Primal Rib Grade USDA Choice, Yield 2
Total Cost: $90.75
As-Purchased Weight: 33.0 lb   As-Purchased Price/lb: $2.75/lb

Description	Lb	Oz	Decimal	%	Value
103 Rib	33	0	33.0	100	$90.75
Waste/Trim	3	5	3.3125	10	0
Usable Raw Weight	29	11	29.6875	90	$90.75
Usable Trim					
Cap Meat	1	9	1.5625	4.73	$4.70[1]
Short Ribs	3	4	3.25	9.84	$9.07[2]
Hamburger	1	4	1.25	3.79	$1.25[3]
Total	6	1	6.0625	18.36%	$15.02
Oven-ready Rib	23	10	23.625	71.59%	$75.73[4]
Shrink/Carving Loss	9	10	9.625	29.17%	0
Servable Weight	14	0	14.0	42.42%	$75.73
Cost per Servable Pound					$5.41[5]

Market Value of Usable Trim
[1]Cap Meat $3.03/lb
[2]Short Ribs $2.79/lb
[3]HB Trim $1.00/lb
[4]$90.75 – $15.02 = $75.73 Cost per pound at oven-ready stage $75.73/23.625 or $3.21
[5]$75.73/14 lb = $5.41 lb

Table 4-4 COMPARISON OF YIELDS

	109 Oven-Ready Rib	103 Primal Rib
AP Price/lb	$3.43	$2.75
Oven Ready		
Cost Per/lb	$3.43	$3.21
% Servable Weight	55.24%	59.26%
Cost/Servable lb	$6.21	$5.41
Equivalent Market		
Cost	$81.12*	$75.73**

Cost saving of 103 rib is $5.39 plus the $15.02 of usable trim.
*23.65 lb @ $3.43
**23.65 lb @ $3.21
Special Note: Whenever there is usable trim, you cannot calculate the cost per servable pound by dividing the percentage of servable weight into the as-purchased price per pound. The reason is that the resulting cost does not take usable trim into account; it assumes all trim is waste. All other constant factors still apply.

rib. However, we must consider that you have to pay a skilled meat cutter and invest in additional equipment that will add to labor and overhead costs.

The cooked rib is carved to determine the yield of edible portions. After cooking and portioning, there is 14 pounds of servable product. The total cost is still $75.73, so the cost per servable pound is $5.41, which is less than the $6.21 of the 109 rib in the previous example. This would be the way to go if you had the skilled labor, space, equipment, and ability to sell the usable trim. If you use the trim in employee meals, it would reduce only your cost of providing employee meals.

You can calculate the constant cost factors. The first is the cost factor per servable pound, which is the cost per servable pound divided by the as-purchased price per pound ($5.41/$2.75 = 1.967). This factor converts the AP price per pound into the cost per servable pound by multiplying it by the market price per pound ($2.75 × 1.967 = $5.41). The portion cost is calculated by dividing the cost per servable pound by the number of portions per pound; in this case $5.41/2 (8 oz) = $2.71.

You calculate the portion cost multiplier by dividing the cost factor per servable pound by the number of portions per pound, (1.967/2 = 0.9835). The portion cost multiplier converts the AP price per pound into the portion cost ($2.75 × 0.9835 = $2.71).

The portion divider is calculated by multiplying the percentage of servable weight by the number of portions per pound, or 0.4242 × 2 = 0.8484. This factor is used to determine how many pounds to purchase by dividing it into the number of covers, or 100/0.8484 = 117.87 pounds. You can proof your calculations with 117.87 lb × 0.4242 = 50 lb. With two portions per pound, you would get 100 portions.

An example using steaks instead of Prime rib will review all the yield calculations. As in any yield test, the less waste one has, the greater the yield and the smaller the difference between the as-purchased price per pound and the cost per servable pound. The only way waste can be recovered is by charging it to the cost of the salable cuts. If waste and trim are excessive, cost will be high and will be reflected in the menu prices charged.

As in the previous examples, the first step is to weigh out the usable trim, assign a market value, and then subtract it from the total AP price. In this case, the value of the 19 eight-ounce steaks is $22.96. See Table 4-5.

Since the 19 steaks weighed 9.75 pounds, divide the weight of the steaks into $22.96 to get the cost per servable pound, or $2.36. With two steaks per pound, the portion cost is $1.18 ($2.36/2). However, that is an average cost knowing that steaks may be over or undercut in successive yield tests. Therefore, the assumption is that they will even out over the long run and $1.18 per steak is a representative cost. In this yield test, the 19 steaks weighed 156 ounces, not 152 ounces. Therefore, the cost per steak was actually $1.21. In another yield test, 19 steaks may weigh only 149 ounces and would carry an actual cost less than $1.18. The more consistent we are in our purchase specifications and cutting efficiency, the smaller such variances will be.

You can now calculate the constant cost factors. The cost factor per servable pound is $2.36/$2.05 = 1.151. To convert any AP price per pound, multi-

Table 4-5 STEAK YIELD TEST

Item: USDA Choice Top Sirloin Butt IMPS No. 184
Weight: 11.75 lb As-Purchased Price per lb: $2.05 Total Cost: $24.09

	Yield	Value
Waste Trim	1.125 lb	0
Stew Meat @ $1.29 lb	0.875 lb	$ 1.13
Steaks 19 @ 8 oz each	9.75 lb	$22.96
Totals	11.75 lb	$24.09
Cost per Servable lb	$24.09 − $1.13 = $22.96/9.75 lb = $2.36/lb	
Cost per Portion @ 2 steaks per lb	= $2.36/2 = $1.18	
Cost per Portion for 19 steaks	= $22.96/19 = $1.21	
Reason for difference:	19 × 8 oz (avg) = 152 oz	
	19 @ 9.75 = 156 oz (actual)	
Portion Cost Multiplier	1.151/2 = 0.5756	
	$2.05 × 0.5756 = $1.18	
Portion Divider	% of Servable Weight = 9.75 lb/11.75 lb = 82.98%	
	0.8298 × 2 = 1.659	
	100 covers/1.659 = 60.28 lb	
Proof	60.28 lb × 0.8298 = 50 lb = 100 8-oz steaks	

ply it by the cost factor, $2.05 × 1.151 = $2.36. The portion cost multiplier, which allows you to convert the AP price per pound directly to your portion cost, is 1.151/2 = 0.5756. Proof: .5756 × $2.05 = $1.18.

The Portion Divider is 9.75 lb/11.75 lb = 0.8298 × 2 = 1.659. 100 covers/ 1.659 = 60.28 lbs. Proof: 60.28 lbs × 0.8298 = 50 lb, or 100 8-ounce steaks. Obviously, if the average top sirloin butt weighs close to 12 pounds, you will have to purchase 5 top butts.

Since our tests are based on standardized purchase specifications, standardized recipes, and cutting procedures, we can assume these yields will represent actual yields on all like items in the future. So, with a card file of cost factors and your calculator, you can quickly and accurately determine portion costs and purchase quantities. When your menu is being updated, a quick check of market prices will tell you which items may need to be increased when you reprint the menu.

Buyers have the option of purchasing cuts of meat in different forms. They may purchase a rib that is oven ready and merely has to be placed in the oven and cooked, or they may elect to purchase the item fully cooked and processed or do the butchering on a primal cut. The purveyor charges different prices at each stage of the processing. Buyers, therefore, must be able to calculate their servable yields so they can compare prices at different stages of product preparation.

COSTING A DELUXE HAMBURGER PLATTER

Yields need to be known for all food items, not just the entree. Consider the ingredients and accompaniments that go into the common hamburger platter. The menu description says "A quarter pound of grilled lean ground sirloin, served on sesame seed bun, with lettuce, tomato, onion, and pickle accompanied by a side of french fries and cole slaw."

Let's look at the list of items and their respective AP costs.

Ground sirloin at $2.24/lb
Sesame bun at $.98 per dozen
Lettuce at $13 for a case of 24 heads
Tomato at $7.50 for a lug of 5 × 6 size
Onion at $8.50 for 50 lb
Pickle at $4.50 gallon
French fries at $.50 lb
Homemade cole slaw consisting of shredded cabbage at $.40 lb, shredded carrots at $.59 lb, and dressing at $4.50 gallon
Condiments of mayonnaise, mustard, catsup

Costs based on repeated yield tests and allowance for waste are as follows:

Cost ground sirloin: $2.24/4 = *$.56* for a quarter pound pattie.

Bun: $.98/12 = *$.09* (round up to next penny)

Lettuce: (yield 20 portions per head) $31/24 = $.55 head/20 = *$.03*

Tomato: $7.50/30 = $.25 each/5 portions per tomato = *$.05*

Onion: 50 lb yields 45 lb edible product. Cost per servable pound = $8.50/45 = $.19 lb; portion 2 oz = *$.03*

Pickle: $4.50/75 portions = *$.06*

French fries: *$.20* ($.17 + $.03)

Cole slaw: Recipe for 10 pounds of slaw; 8 lb at $.40 = $3.20; 1 lb shredded carrots at $.59; 1.5 cups of cole slaw dressing (1.5 cups = 12 ounces; 128 oz (1 gallon)/12 = 10.7 portions/gallon; $4.50/10.7 = $.42. Total cost of 10-lb batch = $3.20 + $.59 + $.42 = $4.21 or $.43 lb, or *$.08* for 3 ounces.

Condiments: Catsup at $17.00 for 24/14 oz bottles = $.71 bottle, or $.05 oz = *$.10*; Mustard at $8.00 for 24 8-oz jars = $.34 jar, or $.04 oz = *$.04*; Mayonnaise at $3.50 gallon, or $.03 oz = *$.03*.

Total cost of the hamburger platter is $1.27. The yields would basically stay the same on all items, and the only adjustment in cost would come from price increases on the ingredients. Yields on each item would be recorded for reference each time items containing them are placed on the menu.

Chapter Five

Menu Sales Mix Analysis

THE RESTAURANT CONCEPT, LOCATION, AND MENU

The menu is the starting point of all planning and design of a food-service operation. If you have a specific operational or menu concept in mind, the location must be selected with care to be sure customer traffic will support the concept. Granted, destination restaurants will draw customers from more distant points than family and fast-food operations; the fact remains that a major part of the success of the restaurant will rest upon its location. You may design a wonderful menu in terms of offerings, ingredients, and preparation methods and still not be financially successful if the restaurant is not in the right location.

On the other hand, if you have a specific location in mind to build a restaurant, you need to be very flexible on the restaurant concept and menu. If the location and customer traffic favor a family restaurant or cafeteria, a white tablecloth operation with a fresh seafood menu may not be successful. The rule therefore is if you have a specific concept and menu in mind, you must be flexible on the location. If you have already picked out the location, you must be flexible on the concept and menu.

THE MENU DETERMINES EQUIPMENT NEEDS

Once the concept has been determined, the equipment selection and kitchen space requirements are specifically designed around the menu. The kitchen of a food-service establishment is designed after the menu has been written and the recipes determined for all items. Once the kitchen is installed, the equipment becomes a limiting factor in future menu decisions. The kitchen equipment package and layout will impact what the operation can prepare. Certain kitchens are more flexible than others and can adapt quickly to menu changes. However, in the highly specialized fast-food industry with limited menus and equipment packages, the addition of new menu items is difficult. Space has been reduced to a minimum, and new pieces of equipment are difficult or impossible to add without major renovation.

There is no universal equipment package that can be suggested by food-service consultants unless they see a menu complete with recipes and forecasted volumes of product that will need to be prepared within specified time periods. However, certain "essential" pieces of equipment are likely to be found in just about any food-service operation, such as refrigerators, ice machines, work tables, dishwasher and dish tables, open top ranges, and deck ovens. However, the real challenge is to make the right decision concerning what size (capacity) and how many of each piece of equipment are needed.

The selection of specific pieces of equipment requires knowledge of the type of equipment best for the job to be done. In selecting a piece of equipment to cook steak, for example, you have to choose among charbroilers, infrared broilers, quartz broilers, whether the heat source is above or below the cooking grates, and whether it is gas or electric. Once this decision is reached, the selection of a manufacturer and model must be made from an extensive list. There are approximately 24 different manufacturers that produce broilers and, to complicate the decision even further, they will probably show you several models with various options and features. In short, a broiler is not just a broiler, and you will find that to be the case with deep fryers, griddles, and even reach-in refrigerators.

Another consideration is the size or capacity of the equipment. Deep fryers, for example, are available from 7.5-pound fat capacity up to hundreds of pounds. The size and capacity of a fryer needed by a small neighborhood bar selling breaded mushrooms as snacks is considerably different from that of a high-volume seafood or chicken restaurant. Consider the "downtime" that all equipment eventually requires for maintenance and repair. You can still "limp" along with one of two ovens, but business may come to a standstill if your single piece breaks down in the middle of the dinner rush.

Since you will have a choice of several manufacturers for the equipment, the one you select will be determined by considerations **other** than price. Reliability, reputation, and service record are more important than just the lowest price when it comes to commercial cooking equipment. Shop for the lowest price only after you have determined the best equipment for your menu needs. If you are unable to conduct such a study on your own, seek out information from local equipment distributors. Many have kitchen design consultants who can help you write your equipment specifications.

Such decisions cannot be made without a detailed chart or spreadsheet that "tracks" each menu item from the delivery of ingredients to final warewashing and storage of flatware and kitchen utensils. The correct number and size of kitchen equipment, utensils, pots and pans, china, glassware, and silver cannot be accurately determined by simple rules of thumb. You will find that someone has tried to simplify the selection of such based on the number of seats, beds, meal periods, or even the total number of patrons to be fed. Rest assured that they will not be accurate for all applications.

In order to determine the optimum number and capacities for each piece of equipment, utensil, and storage area, such intervening variables as the state of the raw ingredients upon delivery, storage temperature required, delivery frequencies from distributors, product perishability, preparation methods, product service presentation, and even final warewashing must be examined. You must start with the detailed recipes and service specifications for each item on the menu. Therefore, the menu planning team needs to consist of food production and dining room service representatives.

What you must ultimately do is visualize the delivery, processing, preparation for service, presentation to the guest—tabletop arrangement included—and the warewashing of all pots, pans, utensils, and flatware. You cannot do this without being familiar with the preparation and service of the food items. This requires consultation with the food and beverage manager, chef, maître d', and equipment distributor. This is too important a task to be left for rules of thumb.

The menu preparation methods determine the type of equipment needed. The quantities prepared of each item determine the size or capacity of the equipment, and the peak production demands will influence the number of pieces and specific sizes needed. In addition, budget and space restraints will further limit your choices. Rarely does one have an unlimited budget and complete flexibility in selecting and arranging kitchen equipment. Plumbing, ventilation, and building codes will restrict placement in many situations, particularly when you are occupying a leased building or one that has already been wired, plumbed, and vented.

The best example of this equipment planning process can be better understood if you contemplate the following. Each of us has some food item we like to prepare. For those who have a tough time combining dry cereal and milk, seeking the counsel of your mother or grandmother will be required. However, for those who are "kitchen crusaders" and are at home with fresh ingredients and sharp knives, this will be a simple exercise. Remember, if you have never made the dish, you will not be able to "visualize" the preparation from start to finish.

Assume you are asked by friends who are planning a party to cook the main course at their apartment or home. You will be required to bring all the necessary pots, pans, and utensils. You want to be sure that the kitchen you are going to use is equipped with the essentials such as sinks, refrigeration, ovens, and range top so you will assume that you have nothing to work with. This is what it is like when you are planning a new kitchen from the ground up. Unless you specify it in your list of equipment, you will not have it available.

Whether your specialty is Texas-style chili with beans, lasagna, chicken Divan, or Chinese sweet and sour pork, you will need to be as specific as you can in stating quantities of ingredients and preparation methods. For example,

Equipment Menu Item	Top Sirloin Steak	Shrimp Scampi	Fried Catfish	BBQ Ribs	Eggplant Parmesan
Primary Storage	Walk-in refrigerator	Walk-in freezer	Walk-in freezer	Walk-in refrigerator	Walk-in refrigerator
Primary Cooking and Processing	Slicer	Sink and range (gas)	Sink	Deck oven	Range (gas), slicer
Secondary Storage	Reach-in refrigerator (line)	Reach-in refrigerator (line)	Reach-in refrigerator (line)	Reach-in refrigerator (line)	Reach-in refrigerator (line)
Secondary Cooking and Storage	Charbroiler	Salamander broiler	Deep fryer	Charbroiler	Salamander broiler
Utensils	9-inch clam tongs; SS spatula; 14-inch slicer (knife); cutting board	14-inch colander	9-inch clam tongs	14-inch slicer; 9-inch cleaver; cutting board	9-inch tongs
Landing Areas	Cutting table	Countertop	Breading table	Cutting table	Breading table
Pots and Pans	SS full size 2.5-inch pan	18 × 24 sheet pans	SS full size 2.5-inch pan; SS full size 6-inch pan	SS full size 2.5-inch pan; 18 × 24 sheet pans	15-inch iron skillet; 2.5-inch fill perforated SS pan; SS full size 2.5-inch pan
China and Flatware	10-inch pewter plate	5.5 oz casserole; 9.5-inch round dinner plate	1.5-inch oval platter	10-inch pewter plate	5.5 oz round casserole; 9.5-inch round dinner plate
Silverware	Standard place setting plus steak knife	Standard place setting plus serving spoon	Standard place setting	Standard place setting	Standard place setting plus serving spoon
Glassware	Standard water glass	Standard water glass	Standard water glass	Standard water glass	Standard water glass
Sanitation	Standard dish and pot washing	Standard dish and pot washing	Standard dish and pot washing	Standard dish and pot washing	Filter cone holder
Auxiliary Equipment	Platform scale; dollie, portion scale	Platform scale	Platform scale	Platform scale; dollie	N/A
Quantities and Time Period	40 lb/day, 120 covers	15 lb/day, 25 covers	10 lb/day, 15 covers	30 lb/day, 15 covers	Half case/day, 40 covers

FIGURE 5-1 Equipment matrix

one "scoop" of mashed potatoes is too vague. Instead, state no. 12 scoop, 4-ounce ladle with 9-inch handle, 4-1/2 inch flexible spatula, 5-quart saucepan.

In a food-service operation, this exercise would be conducted for every appetizer, entree, side dish, vegetable, and dessert and repeated for each meal period. Once all the recipes have been written, the results are then converted to an equipment matrix or spreadsheet. See Figure 5-1.

You must go through this process mentally, and then on paper, to determine quantities and sizes of pots and pans, refrigeration, and freezer space as well as the number of burners on a range top or wells in a steam table. The planning process considers even auxiliary equipment such as scales, trash receptacles, can openers, cutting boards, dollies, and heat lamps. The more detail, the better the matrix.

From the matrix you begin to prepare the item specifications in advance of obtaining price quotations or bids from distributors or manufacturers. New projects seeking financing cannot afford to underestimate their capital requirements, and lending institutions want documentation that shows system and planning went into the design process. Visit distributor showrooms, equipment shows, and new installations, if possible. Talk to service people about maintenance records of certain manufacturers, and ask chefs and managers for their opinions on equipment and manufacturers.

THE ROLE OF THE MODERN MENU

Adapted with permission from *"Introduction to Hotel & Restaurant Management, 5th Ed,* 1988 Kendall-Hunt Publishing Co. The menu concept should evolve over time with serious thought given to each item served. The personality of a restaurant is a direct result of the menu offerings. The menu concept will entail decisions on the kind of food and beverage served, the preparation methods, the type of service, and the theme and decor package. You must expand your definition of a menu. It is an oversimplification to consider it a mere list of what the restaurant or food-service operation has to offer. Too often menus have been considered simple bills of fare without any consideration for the way the menu can affect the revenue and operational efficiency of the establishment.

You must start with the assumption that the items have been selected with customer preferences in mind and possibly even after some rather detailed market studies have been undertaken. Menus that are driven by factors other than customer preferences and consider only the personal likes and dislikes of an owner, manager, and chef will not serve the operation well.

The menu should not attempt to be all things to all people. Although you may try, you cannot cater to everyone's tastes. There has never been a restaurant that successfully appealed to every customer and offered items from eggs and bacon and fast-food fare to gourmet French and continental cuisine on a single menu. If you try, you may become known for variety, but without any menu identity or house specialties, nothing is done particularly well. Therefore, menus must emphasize what your staff does well and what the majority of your clientele want to eat.

A menu will be impacted by the skills levels and availability of the food preparation staff. This is not meant to imply that the menu is employee driven. The fast-food segment of the food-service industry is noted for its limited and simple menu offerings. This has allowed such operations as McDonald's, Wendy's, and Burger King to employ unskilled employees. However, the expanding tastes of today's more sophisticated customer are requiring even fast-food operators to expand their menu and include more elaborate menu items. Arby's, for example, has broken the $3 price range for sandwiches. It has offered a roast chicken club that combines sliced chicken breast, crisp bacon, lettuce, tomato, and mayonnaise on a grilled poppy seed roll. Arby's new sandwich offerings are a sharp contrast to the simple sliced roast beef sandwich on which it started.

In this chapter you will discover that the menu is a major communication device that projects the personality and concept of a restaurant; it is an important cost control tool and an internal merchandising tool.

Imagine you are planning to dine out at a new restaurant for the first time. You have not been inside or even seen its exterior. However, a copy of the menu is handed to you. When you pick up and look at a menu, images should begin to form in your subconscious in regard to the food, decor, prices, and ambiance of the food-service operation. When you actually see the restaurant and step inside, you will compare your perceptions derived from the menu to the actual theme and decor. A well-designed menu will project an accurate identity and personality of the establishment without the customer ever having set foot in the establishment. You begin to formulate expectations based on advertisements on television or in the newspaper and from word of mouth among friends and business associates.

Heretofore, the independent restaurant operator knew many of his or her customers. The owner greeted, seated, and even personally prepared the food for customers. The menu design wasn't considered important in projecting the personality of the restaurant because the owner was present in the establishment. This type of personal attention exists today primarily in owner-operated establishments. In Los Angeles, the personalities of individuals like Wolfgang Puck and Michael McCarthy are now personified in the menu and decor, as they have opened multiple locations and their physical presence is not possible.

In Chicago, Richard Melman, president and co-founder of Lettuce Entertain You Enterprises Inc., spreads his genius and innovations in restaurant concepts. His latest breakthrough concepts are Maggiano's Little Italy and The Corner Bakery, recently acquired by restaurant powerhouse Brinker International. As is the case with all corporate chain restaurants, the personality of the restaurant rests not so much with the unit manager but with the company's corporate image. The personality of the chain is represented in the menu and decor of the restaurant. Independently owned and operated restaurants have an added advantage when the owner or manager personally interacts with the customers.

The reality is, however, that as one expands to two, three, and more units, the personality of any one individual becomes diluted and ceases to be the main identity or personality of the restaurant. According to the National Restaurant Association, 80 percent of the 500,000 plus commercial restaurants in existence today are independently owned and operated and they account for approximately only 20 percent of the 2 billion annual commercial food sales each year. Corporate national and regional chain operations with absentee owners transact the remaining 80 percent. The top 100 chains account for close to 50 percent of the food and beverage sales annually.

In corporately owned restaurants, the personality of a manager, maître d', or chef is not the primary vehicle for establishing and maintaining the personality or image of the restaurant concept. The menu plays the most significant role in establishing the public image and personality because managers, chefs, and maître d's are often transferred. The menu, through the image it communicates, remains the most permanent link between the operation and the dining public.

When a friend suggests that you try a new restaurant, don't you usually inquire about the kind of food served there? This does not mean that the personality of an owner, chef, manager, or maître d' has little to do with the success of a given restaurant, but, given the high turnover of personnel and normal promotions and transfers that take place, it would be somewhat impractical to try to sustain a restaurant's popularity on the strength of the personality and physical presence of any individual. Relying exclusively on that aspect holds the operation hostage. It is because of this that the menu needs to be well planned and designed from the outset. Chain restaurants have obviously used their menus to project their personalities to the public in an effective manner.

To demonstrate how the visual impact of a menu can paint certain images in your mind and form expectations, consider the following. Picture in your mind's eye a large black leatherette menu cover with a gold cord around the fold. Does it elicit feelings of formality, double-digit prices, white tablecloths, French or continental food, and waiters in tuxedos?

Country Pride Restaurants are clearly family restaurants with prices and menu items families would appreciate. Their menu design projects that image. The surprising incongruity of it is that you will not find these restaurants in shopping centers. Country Pride is owned by Truck Stops of America, and its restaurants are found on interstates with truckers as the major customer base.

The menu is also an integral cost control tool. The menu determines the degree of sophistication and detail of your cost control system. Cost control does not just involve methods to control waste and theft. The ultimate purpose of cost control is to provide management with the information it needs to make decisions concerning day-to-day operations. The menu will influence which items sell and impact your overall food cost percentage, contribution margin (gross profit), the average check, and total food and beverage revenue. Achieving food cost percentage and gross profit objectives does not happen by accident. It is built into the menu design from the very beginning.

The menu may just be the most important internal advertising tool used to direct customers to make their selections when they order in the restaurant.

Not only can it influence what customers will order but how much will ultimately be spent. The menu can determine not only the volume of business you will do, but strongly influence the ultimate success or failure of the restaurant. Using forecasted customer counts and average check targets, the menu design can directly influence sales revenue. Management is constantly forecasting business volume and relating this knowledge to decisions on how much to buy, store, and prepare as well as how many employees to schedule. The menu will have a bearing on every one of these decisions.

A properly designed menu can direct the attention of the diner to specific items and increase the likelihood that those items will be ordered more frequently than random chance consideration. Although the customer's selection cannot be "controlled," it can be "directed." The profit picture brightens, the food cost improves, and the check average increases when the customer chooses an item that contributes positively toward these ends.

The menu is the only piece of printed material used by a restaurant that the customer will positively pick up and read. Because it impacts in so many areas and has a significant influence on the success or failure of a restaurant, it deserves to be given the attention, planning, and financial consideration reserved for matters requiring major investment consideration. More money will be spent on real estate construction, equipment, and furnishings, but nothing is more important than the menu when it comes to the overall success or failure of a restaurant concept. To make a profit, you have to plan for a profit. There is no room for guesswork when it comes to the menu. A poorly planned and designed menu not only can increase you food costs but also add to your payroll, complicate your purchasing, upset the flow of work in the kitchen, destroy your service, drive away customers, and reduce your sales revenue.

THE EVOLVING MENU

The competitive nature of the food-service market for the dining public's business and the changing tastes of more adventuresome palates, dictate that menus change frequently to reflect the trendy preferences that will attract new clientele and keep the regulars coming back for more. With the high cost of commercial real estate, construction, and leases in prime locations, building space must be kept to a minimum without sacrificing production efficiency or customer service aspects. The fact that menus will "evolve" over time requires kitchen design and equipment packages to conserve space and be versatile to allow quick adaptation to achieve production flexibility without expensive renovation costs and premature replacement of under-depreciated equipment.

As a case in point, Burger King was very slow to enter the breakfast market pioneered by McDonald's and Hardee's. The major reason cited was the lack of a griddle to cook eggs and pancakes. Remember that Burger King uses a flame broiler, which does not lend itself to cook scrambled eggs. However, because of its desire to serve breakfast items, Burger King enlisted the help of the AMF Wyott Company to design a griddle that would allow conversion of deep fryers into griddles during the breakfast hours. The fryers would be set at 375 degrees and fry oil was pumped through the griddles that were placed in the fryers. The oil heated the griddle surface to 350 degrees, and Burger King was able to cook eggs and other breakfast items requiring a griddle.

Such flexibility can be achieved if kitchens are well planned and equipped. Every square foot of kitchen space must be productive space and utilize equipment selected for its versatility, ease of operation, sanitation, maintenance, and energy efficiency. The more uses a piece of equipment has, the greater the ability to add new menu items in response to changing customer preferences. Some of the most versatile pieces of equipment are the tilting skillet, which can be used to fry, braise, grill, saute, and stew items; the infrared hotel broiler, which is the workhorse of the classical hotel kitchens for steaks, chops, fish, and poultry; the steam-jacketed kettle; the griddle; the salamander broiler or its variation called a cheese melter; and, perhaps the most versatile, the open burner gas range. It is recommended that equipment be installed on casters for ease of movement within a bank of equipment and have the gas and electricity brought to the equipment on flexible quick-disconnect hoses and receptacles.

New menu items must be evaluated as to how they will impact the kitchen and service staff. You must determine how a new item will flow through the kitchen from the time it enters the back door through storage, issuing, preparation, cooking to order, service, and dishwashing. You must be conscious of overloading particular stations or individuals with items requiring complicated processing, which can reduce efficiency. However, one word of caution: If an item is desired by the customers but requires more than the average processing and preparation, you should examine ways in which the item could be turned out more quickly and efficiently. This usually requires some preprocessing, partial assembly, and workstation rearranging.

Because the tastes of the dining public have become more adventuresome, menu offerings are being expanded. This is taking place even in the fast-food segment previously noted for its limited menu offerings in terms of both ingredients and preparation methods. You might think that there is a greater need for efficient equipment selection and layout in operations with extensive menus, scratch preparation, and finesse in plate presentation than in limited menus, particularly fast-food operations. However, just the opposite is true. The extensive menu food-service operation like most hotel kitchen and fine dining restaurants, is a "craftman's workshop" with all sorts of specialty tools and equipment. It has order and system to be sure, but the high check average and the lower seat turnover allow time for chefs to "personalize" each dish. Mass production is not practiced.

Contrast this to the "assembly line" fast-food or limited menu operations. Speed in preparation of menu items is critical in serving large numbers of customers in relatively short periods of time. The check average is low so the number of transactions must be high to achieve revenue objectives. Therefore, the high volume–low check average operations are hurt more by inefficient kitchen layouts than are the fine dining restaurants.

GOALS OF AN EFFECTIVE MENU

The goals of an effective menu can be summarized in five statements. An effective menu is one that:

1. Emphasizes what the clientele wants and what the restaurant prepares and serves best;
2. Is an effective communication, merchandising, and cost control tool;
3. Obtains the necessary check average for sales and profit considerations;
4. Utilizes staff and equipment in a productive and efficient manner;
5. Makes forecasting sales more consistent and accurate for purposes of purchasing, preparation, and scheduling.

A menu can be written on a continuum ranging from what can be described as "limited" to "extensive" in the number of selections. The aspect of limited versus extensive menus can be examined for two perspectives:

1. The actual number of items listed on the menu, referred to as "variety";
2. The number of ways a product is prepared or presented.

The most simplified and limited menu in terms of both parameters is best exemplified by the menus of fast-food operations. There has been considerable broadening of the menu variety in some fast-food operations while others have held fast to doing only a few items. KFC, long noted for its "We Do Chicken Right" strategy, has expanded the number of ways it prepares chicken. It used to be that the Colonel's recipe was the only way it was sold, and now you can get extra crispy, spicy, chicken nuggets, hot wings, and roast chicken.

From the limited/limited menu, we progress to a limited/extensive menu; that is, limited in variety but prepared and presented in an extensive number of ways. Examples of such a menu would be in restaurants like Red Lobster. They offer fish, shrimp, and other seafood prepared by frying, broiling, baking, and steaming with a variety of accompaniments such as vegetables, rice, pasta, and potatoes. Also, restaurants like Chili's and Le Peep demonstrate how variety in preparation can broaden an otherwise limited selection of items.

The next progression in menu item development would be the menu that offers an extensive variety of items prepared or presented in a limited number of ways. The best examples are coffee shop and family restaurants like Denny's, Shoney's, and International House of Pancakes, as well as restaurants like Bennigan's and Ruby Tuesday.

The fourth and final menu category is the operation with a menu that is extensive in both variety and preparation methods. Usually, fine dining French and continental restaurants with certified chefs and large kitchens are in this category, as are many hotel restaurants and private clubs. However, after seeing menus like those used by the popular TGI Friday and Houlihan's restaurant chains, I would have to categorize menus like theirs as extensive in both the number of items and the preparation and presentation.

Menus expand to broaden the customer base and to appeal to more people. However, if operators had their druthers, they would probably want to limit their menus for some very logical reasons. Limited menus require less equipment and space than extensive menus. Preparation of items can be simplified and speeded up, which is clearly what fast-food operations consider as most important. With simple menus, less skilled employees are needed, and with the labor crisis what it is, many operators believe that the answer lies in hiring "alternative labor sources" such as the handicapped, mentally retarded, elderly, and disadvantaged. Such labor sources are sure to move menus toward the limited end of the continuum. Inventory and storage space is minimized with limited menus, cost controls are less complicated, and quality control is easier. In addition, overall operating costs are lower than in full menu operations.

However, proponents of extensive menus believe that to be competitive and financially successful, a restaurant must offer variety. You cannot limit menu offerings for operational cost reasons and disregard the competitive repercussions of such reasoning. Extensive menus have their advantages as well. An extensive menu will appeal to a broader range (base) of customers. Extensive menus appeal to first-time customers more than limited menus. Some believe that patrons are more likely to try a new and unfamiliar restaurant if the menu offers a wide range of choices. In addition, regular customers will not become bored with the menu and are more likely then to return more often.

Restaurants with extensive menu offerings are more responsive to customers' changing tastes as they can add new items easily because of their extensive inventories of ingredients. Therefore, new items will appear more often and more quickly than in operations with limited menus. This menu flexibility has a built-in competitive benefit that creates product differentiation and allows the operator to charge higher prices for unique items. Clearly, the advantages of the extensive menus are driven by marketing-oriented reasons rather than the cost-oriented perspective of the limited menu advocates.

The advantages of one are the disadvantages of the other. Most operators will try to strike a balance between the two extremes and emphasize the positive aspects of limited and extensive menus. Figure 5-2 shows in matrix form the four categories of extensive/limited menus by the number of menu items and the variety of preparation methods.

Extensive menus require more equipment and more kitchen and storage space for ingredients. Equipment needs will be more specialized, and skills of kitchen workers will need to be at a higher level. It is more difficult to maintain quality control and waste is greater. The inherent danger in the attempt to provide variety is that the identity of the operation is lost. You must have some signature menu items that will build the restaurant's identity and reputation. Remember, you cannot be all things to all people. Ingredients must be utilized in

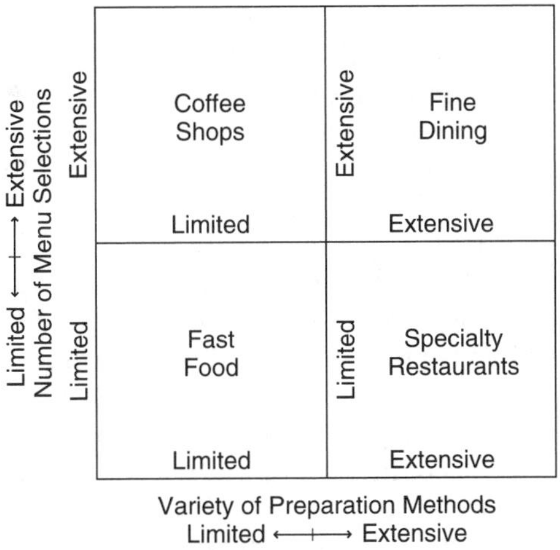

FIGURE 5-2 Limited and extensive menus.

(Figure 5-2 shows a 2×2 grid. Vertical axis: Number of Menu Selections, Limited ←→ Extensive. Horizontal axis: Variety of Preparation Methods, Limited ←→ Extensive. Upper left: Coffee Shops (Limited). Upper right: Fine Dining (Extensive). Lower left: Fast Food (Limited). Lower right: Specialty Restaurants (Extensive).)

more than one dish, and "daily specials" need to be used to work off excessive inventories of perishable ingredients. Record keeping must be more sophisticated as well.

Extensive menus are certainly more costly to produce than limited menus and, therefore, will be priced accordingly. However, the truly adventuresome diners are willing to pay for their sophisticated tastes. This means operators catering to this market can change a premium for increased variety and unique menu items.

Regardless of these factors, an optimum number can be given as to the extensiveness of entree selections. Twenty to 24 entrees is a number that can provide variety and be efficiently managed. Studies have shown that if you take a sales analysis and count the number of each entree sold for a period of 30 days or more, that approximately 60 to 75 percent of the items sold will be concentrated among the same 8–12 menu items. This means that of the total entrees sold, these 8 to 12 of them will make up the majority of items sold. This will be the case whether there are 60 entrees or 20 entrees. You can see that offering more than 24 entrees is of little value.

TYPES OF MENU FORMATS AND ITEM LISTINGS

The frequency of menu changes and the format for listing entree accompaniments will vary among various food-service operations. To begin with, there are three basic types of menu formats used in menu design. The one you use will depend on the type of food-service operation and your target market. They are (1) static or nonchanging menu format; (2) cyclical menu format; and (3) static and cycle, combination format. Some consider a fourth category, called market format.

Commercial food-service establishments, particularly the larger chains, primarily use the static or fixed menu format. Essentially the menu items stay the same from day to day, and changes are made only to delete slow sellers and add new or seasonal items. Their menu selections are therefore carefully selected and monitored for popularity with their customers. Much product research goes into testing and developing new and unique items that will provide product distinctiveness over their competition.

However, with the intense competition for the public's dining dollars, no operation, whether chain or independent, can expect to sustain a product or price advantage over the long run. The reason is that if someone develops a popular new item, others will follow to negate the advantage. Consider when the very popular fajitas were first introduced. Fajitas were likely copied from an independently operated Mexican restaurant and now is served in just about every type of operation from table service to fast food. The higher check restaurants have even upgraded the traditional ingredients by substituting chicken or beef with shrimp. This is why it is almost imperative to have new products being tested so you can introduce at least four or five a year in the hopes that you may discover a new food trend. Remember, for multi-unit operations the menu, not a manager or chef, is the key element in maintaining the image of the concept with the dining public.

There are some fairly obvious operational benefits of a limited or static menu, especially from a cost and quality control perspective. That is why they are so widely used. Fixed menu can be effectively used in establishments whose target market is large in numbers and diverse in customers or where frequency of visitations is no greater than three or four times per month.

Remember, a static menu is not necessarily a limited menu in both number of items and preparation methods. Fast-food operation menus are static and limited but almost all table service chains, from family restaurants like Bob Evan's, Shoney's, and Denny's to the "fern bars" (noted for their abundance of hanging plants) like Bennigan's, Houlihan's, and Ruby Tuesday are static yet extensive in the number of items or preparation methods.

Static menus have many of the advantages of limited menus and some further distinctions are worth mentioning. Leftovers are virtually eliminated because almost all the cooking is done to order. The forecasting of purchase and preparation quantities is easier and more accurate. Generally, the same percentage of items sold will prevail night after night. The costs of menu printing and production cost are reduced. Imagine the cost of changing menus for a chain Bennigan's or IHOP nationwide. The cost could easily reach five figures when you consider production costs, printing, and paper. With static menus the kitchen personnel become specialists in preparation, and quality control is more easily accomplished.

The reciprocal of the static menu is the cyclical or changing menu. A cycle menu is an organized schedule for presenting different preplanned menus in a set pattern over a specified number of days. It is used primarily for food-service operations that often cater to a "captive clientele"; that is, students, either elementary, high school, or college, and hospitals, industrial plants, or large office complexes feeding employees who cannot leave the premises to eat.

Cycle menus are usually designed to provide nutritionally balanced offerings as well as variety in food groups, preparation methods, and plate presentations. Although primarily used in the institutional segment food service, they have been adapted and used in commercial food-service operations. They offer variety to regular clientele who visit the restaurant two or more times in a week, usually at lunchtime, which by the way is the most frequent meal eaten out by Americans. If a menu remains static, regular clientele could become tired and bored with the menu selections. To alleviate this, a cycle of daily specials is prepared to supplement the regular static menu. However, purely cyclical menus are not practical or necessary for most commercial operations.

Many menus will be a combination of the static and cycle menus for certain meal periods and days of the week. These "specials" are advertised through menu clip-ons, blackboards, table tents, and back-lit menu signs. They were once referred to as "blue plate specials" and offered the clientele a form of table d'hôte menu at a very reasonable price. They also allowed the food-service operator to serve the lunch clientele faster and more efficiently than cooking to order from the regular menu.

A la carte prices each course or menu item separately. Fast food restaurants traditionally have priced each sandwich, drink, and accompaniment separately allowing the customer to exercise control over how much they spend. However, more and more fast food operations are offering *value meals*. The price is reduced if one purchases the "bundled" menu items. The purpose is to increase the average check or transaction per person and is fundamentally a form of table d hote pricing.

Table d' hôte pricing, in the classical sense, includes all courses at one price. Because more items are included, the price charged will reflect that fact. Over the years inflation pushed up prices making *table d' hôte* menus seem out of reach for most of the dining public. In addition, customers became more concerned with how many calories they were consuming and the nutritional values of foods. Table d' hôte menus were seen as expensive and offered more food than one really needed or wanted to consume.

Today's menus use a pricing format that is a combination of à la carte and modified table d'hôte. Luncheon and dinner specials are likely to be priced table d'hôte, while the regular luncheon and dinner entrees will be served with one side dish and bread and butter only. Most commercial restaurants include salad and bread with dinner and charge extra for potato or vegetable. Quincy's Family Steak Houses includes the potato but not the salad in the price of the steak. Apparently the strategy is that more people are likely to purchase an additional à la carte salad than potato and therefore increase the likelihood of building their check average.

PSYCHOLOGY OF MENU DESIGN

Remember that a menu is more than just a list of what the restaurant has for sale, and the way a menu is designed is as important as the items it lists. A menu must be designed to allow an operation, whether it be a commercial table-service restaurant, private club, or fast-food operation, to achieve its sales goals, keep its costs in line, and return a desired profit. This does not happen by accident—it must be planned for ahead of time.

When certain practices are incorporated into graphic design and layout of a menu, they can actually "influence" the menu selections of the guests. This is accomplished through techniques referred to as menu psychology. The influence is not subversive or subliminal in any way. The truth is that any given menu design or format will produce a predictable sales mix of menu items if used week after week without change.

The well-designed menu can help management sell certain items more often than if the items were "randomly" placed on a menu. If management were given their druthers of indicating which items they would prefer to sell more than others, their decisions would differ based on the criteria they deemed most important. Specific items might be singled out for emphasis for a number of reasons. When such items are emphasized, they will sell more of those items than if they had just randomly placed them on the menu. Menu psychology techniques cannot make unpopular items popular or make liver and onions outsell southern fried chicken or sirloin steak. However, they will allow an operator to sell more liver than would otherwise be sold if left to random chance.

A well-designed menu can make things a lot easier for the operator. It can help keep costs in line and even help distribute the workload in the kitchen. Think about the advantages of such a menu: You can influence the minimum amounts a customer will spend so you can realize the check average you need to achieve your daily sales projections based on seating, customer counts, and hours of operation. Being able to guide a customer's selection will improve the accuracy of sales forecasts, purchase and preparation quantities, and even labor scheduling.

The menu is also important in projecting the image or personality of a restaurant. Depending on the type of operation, the menu can be the main communication link between the customer and the restaurant. It is especially important in the moderate-priced table-service operations where management or chef personalities are not visible or well known to the restaurant patrons. The old saying, "You can't judge a book by it cover," should not apply to menu covers. The menu cover should project an accurate image of what to expect in terms of decor, degree of formality, price range, and in some cases type of food served. If a menu cover leaves one with vague or incorrect expectations, it is not doing its job.

The most important aspect of menu psychology is to design the menu in such a way to get the customers' attention and influence their decision to select certain items over others. Generally, you want to emphasize items that have low food cost, have high gross profit, help increase the average check, are easy to prepare, or are combinations of these criteria. You don't want to leave this to chance or have the printer or graphic artist pick the items for emphasis.

The concept of "menu psychology" was first introduced to the industry through menu seminars conducted by two educators and consultants. Jack Miller, author of several books including *Menu Pricing and Strategy*, and long-time instructor in the hospitality program at St. Louis Community College, and his colleague, Joe Gregg, were the ones who popularized the concept of menu psychology. They were strongly influenced by the writings of the late Albin Seaberg, author of the book *Menu Design*.

The techniques of menu psychology are most applicable to the printed menu; however, some of the theory works with verbal menus. The material presented herein is limited to printed menus since it is far and away the most universal method of displaying food and beverage offerings. I recommend that verbal menus be used to "supplement" printed menus and do not approve the use of complete verbal menus for a number of reasons.

Verbal menus take away time from customer service. The time spent on recitation and question-and-answer follow-up may consume an extra 15 minutes of order-taking time, time that could be put to more direct customer service. The majority of servers do not do an adequate job when it comes to describing and explaining the menu. The presentation may range from monotone and indifference to speeding through the spiel to get on to more pressing matters. Customers don't pay absolute attention and are reluctant to ask for items to be repeated. A printed menu is paced for all customers to reread as often as necessary.

Verbal descriptions have a place and serve an important purpose in upselling guests. Verbal up-selling can reinforce the printed menu for even greater emphasis. Verbal menus are not an alternative to printed menus. A well-known west coast restaurant relegated its verbal recitations to the slag heap of gastronomic history. After going back to printed menus, it found that the sale of its daily specials increased, and the waiters were free to lavish even a greater level of service on their parties.

What are the specific menu psychology techniques employed in the design and production of a menu? Some involve such elements as the print style and size, the paper and ink color, the texture and finish of the paper, graphic design, artwork, and illustrations. Actually, anything used to direct the reader's attention to certain parts of the menu to increase the likelihood of certain items being selected more than just randomly is a technique of menu psychology.

The menu should "showcase" those items you want to sell the most for whatever reason. Once you get the customer's attention, you increase the chances of certain items being selected. Many menus are expensive pieces of artwork, graphic designs, paper, and even leather. Some are printed in full color, which is very costly. Yet some elaborate menus that win awards do very little to improve the operation's menu sales mix.

Menu psychology techniques are borrowed from the retailing industry, which has used window, counter, and mannequin displays to boost sales of specific items. The menu is to a restaurant what a merchandise display is to a major department store. You want the customer to see all the things you have for sale. When Houlihan's redesigned their original menu several years ago, the company felt that the design on the old menu, which lumped all types of items next to one another on the same foldout page, was contributing to customers ordering only appetizers and not dinner items. The new menu was designed to lead the customer from the high-margin specialty drinks on the cover to the appetizers on the first page to the complete dinners inside.

In a student study of a menu from Bennigan's, over three fourths of all menu items sold were either snacks or appetizers. It is of interest to note that both companies used multiple-page menus where dinner entrees were listed on the back pages. Apparently customers didn't page through to the end, which may have contributed to the resulting sales mix. A recent Gallup survey studied the time customers spend reading a menu and found the average time to be 109 seconds. Customers become impatient if they have to read more than 6 pages.

Since menu psychology techniques are designed to get the patrons' attention, it is important to understand the way a customer typically looks at or "sights in" on the menu content. Studies have monitored the eye movement across a page. Through the use of laser beam technology, a device is attached to the forehead of a subject, allows the eye movement to be recorded. This has been referred to in a number of books and articles as "gaze motion" or "eye tracking." Figure 5-3 shows random eye movement across a plain three-panel menu. Note that the eye first focuses on the center and passes over that point at least two more times. This finding has resulted in the center panel being the prime menu sales area.

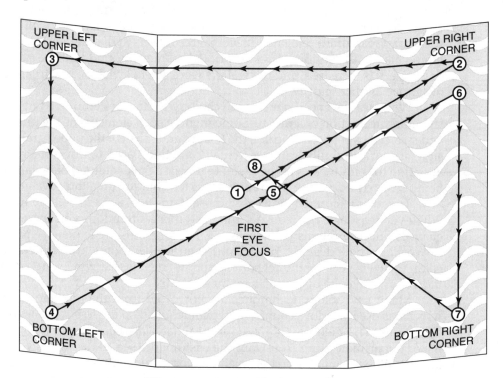

Eye movement across the three-fold menu.

FIGURE 5-3 Eye movement chart.

It must be noted that eye movement is not static. Studies have not indicated whether graphics, photographs, color, or typefaces were used to "draw" the eye. Menu psychology can create "eye magnets" that will alter random eye movement and direct it to an area of emphasis. The areas of emphasis would be used to list the items that the operator wishes to promote the most. Since the first grade when we were taught to read, we learned to begin reading at the upper left side of a page. This is the most natural reflex when one's eyes are not directed anywhere in particular. After a quick scan of the page, we begin serious reading at the upper left.

Another important menu psychology technique that should be used to compliment gaze motion is called the principle of primacy and recency. This psychological phenomenon explains why people are more likely to remember or recall the first or last thing they see or hear. This is put to use in menu design along with gaze motion in the following way. If the menu is designed to draw the eye to a certain panel or section on a page, since it is the first place the eye focuses, place the items you want to sell in that location. The fact that it is the first or last thing customers read increases the chance of those items being ordered by more than random chance.

Menu psychology is not designed to make people buy items they do not want any more than counter and window displays do in department store windows. They do, however, make the customer give them a little extra thought, which will pay off with some when it comes to their purchase decision. I would recommend that in operations where the menu is verbally presented, that the order in which the items are given can impact the guest selection. Again, the first and last items mentioned should be the ones the management prefers to sell.

This is taken one step further when putting menu items in a list format on a printed menu, chalkboard, menu board, or drive-through menu. Try to remember the first item on the drive-through menu at McDonald's. It is not the regular hamburger. It will likely be their "feature" sandwich and one they are using in their national advertising. It will be followed by the Big Mac and Quarter Pounder. McDonald's wants to sell more of those items so they are the first ones the customer will read. Notice how some fast-food operations are listing their drink prices from large to small instead of the other way. They want to sell more large sizes.

If you have ten or more items you want to list in a particular section of the menu, primacy and recency suggests that to divide the items into two lists so you can better merchandise the items you want to sell. The items in the middle of the lists are somewhat lost, and this is where you can "hide" high-cost or labor-intensive items. You see, primacy and recency can work in reverse to de-emphasize selected items. Remember, all we are doing is trying to increase the odds that certain items will be ordered more often than random chance would permit. If an item is remembered, it may be selected more often.

In some cases, in an attempt to "catch the eye," menu design ends up fighting itself by confusing the customer. When you overuse graphics, artwork, or lettering, a cluttered and disorganized menu results, forcing the reader to return to the upper left-hand corner. Very few commercial restaurant or club menus effectively use gaze motion and primacy and recency to full advantage.

Customers will react to the physical form of the menu, its shape, paper texture, size, cover material, and color. The customer begins to interpret the message the menu is trying to convey. This is where one can judge the effectiveness of the menu design. Does it clearly indicate which items the operation specializes in and does the menu project the correct image?

Since the menu plays such an essential role in determining whether a restaurant realizes its cost, revenue, and profit objectives, the resulting menu sales mix must be examined to see how it helps or hinders the restaurant from reaching its financial goals. The *menu sales mix* is the number sold of each menu item.

While the selection process can never be completely controlled through menu design, it can be greatly improved, even on menus offering multiple selections of appetizers, entrees, and desserts. When the same menu is used week after week, a predictable sales mix will result, allowing management to accurately forecast how much to order and prepare in advance.*

COST/MARGIN MENU SALES MIX ANALYSIS

Operators have long sought a method for analyzing their sales mix to determine the impact each menu item has on resulting sales, costs, and profits. It is common practice to adjust menu prices and food costs when profit projections are not realized. It is shortsighted to conclude that lost sales revenues and profit are due solely to poor purchasing, over-portioning, rising costs, and excessive waste.

Operators who have costs and waste under control must look to the menu sales mix as a possible cause of high costs and reduced profits. Certain items on the menu need to be aggressively promoted while others need to be de-emphasized or dropped from the menu. The categorization of each menu item will greatly affect the ultimate strategy used by management to improve the sales mix.

Heretofore, menu sales analysis has used *either* food cost percentage or item contribution margin (selling price minus food cost) to define an optimum sales mix. Both perspectives use the number sold (popularity) of each menu item to determine its respective impact on cost and gross profit.

Those utilizing the food cost perspective have reasoned that it is better to sell the popular low food cost menu items. Each menu item is classified according to its popularity and food cost percentage. An item is either popular

---

*Author's Note: For a complete explanation of menu psychology and design, I recommend Menu Pricing and Strategy, 4th edition, by Jack Miller and David Pavesic (Van Nostrand-Reinhold Publishers, 1996).

and high cost, popular and low cost, not popular and high cost, or not popular and low cost.

The shortcoming of this perspective is that if you promote the menu items with the lowest food cost percentages, you will sacrifice revenue because the lowest food cost items are also the lowest priced items on the menu, for example, chicken and pasta. Therefore, your average check will fall, and unless you increase your customer counts, overall revenue will not be optimized. Lower sales will cause fixed cost percentages to increase (fixed cost percentages react inversely to sales revenue increases or decreases) and cancel out any lowering of the food cost percentage.

Proponents of the contribution margin or gross profit perspective completely ignore food cost percentages and concentrate on the amount of dollars a menu item contributes to profitability. Here, menu items are classified into four categories according to their popularity and item contribution margin (menu price minus food cost). Menu items are either popular and high in contribution margin, popular and low in contribution margin, not popular and high in contribution margin, or not popular and low in contribution margin.

Concentrating only on item contribution margins and ignoring food cost percentage results in a higher food cost percentage. This occurs because the items with the highest item contribution margins are the items with the highest food cost percentages on the menu, for example, steaks and seafood. While this works well in exclusive restaurants and country clubs where demand is price inelastic, it will be ineffective when used in competitive markets on menu items with market-driven prices.

When price elasticity exists, promoting the highest priced items on the menu will cause demand to drop even though the average check may increase. If customer counts are already flat or declining, this pricing philosophy will not be effective. (See Chapter 3 and the section titled, The Fallacy of Gross Profit: The Impact on the Bottom Line.)

Both the food cost perspective, referred to as the Miller Methodology, and the contribution margin approach, also known as *menu engineering,* are heavily biased to either food cost or individual contribution margin. They treat their respective perspectives as being mutually exclusive when, in fact, both food cost and contribution margin must be optimized in a menu sales mix.

A third approach combines the elements of both food cost percentage and total contribution margin and reduces the biases that are inherent in the Miller and Menu Engineering methods. The premise is that *the true optimum menu sales mix is one that simultaneously optimizes (not maximizes) total dollar contribution margin and total sales revenue while keeping the food cost percentage as low as possible.*

The methodology used to accomplish this is called *cost/margin analysis;* the name reflects both food cost and contribution margin criteria in its analysis. Every item on the menu is examined from three, not just two, perspectives. Using the criteria of popularity (number sold) of each menu item, the item food cost percentage, and the *weighted* contribution margin (total gross profit) for each menu item, menu items are grouped into one of eight categories instead of four.

The eight classifications of menu items afforded by the cost/margin analysis provide a greater in-depth perspective of the impact individual menu items have on the total sales mix. (See Table 5-1.) The items that need to be emphasized are those that have a high sales volume (popular), are low in food cost, and return a high *weighted* contribution margin.

Menu items with high individual contribution margins but are unpopular, will have less impact on the total gross profit than popular items with moderate to low individual contribution margins. High-volume items with moderate to low individual contribution margins will put more *dollars* into the cash register than low-volume items with high individual contribution margins. This is why the *weighted contribution margin* (individual contribution margin times the number sold) is a more relevant criterion on which to assess the sales mix potential of promoting certain menu items.

In Table 5-2 we have seven menu items in the sales mix. When items are ranked by *individual contribution margin,* the lobster tail is the top-ranked item and one that would be targeted for promotion. Because it is the highest priced item on the menu, it is more difficult to increase its sales. It is one of the two least popular items on the menu, and in spite of the $10.45 contribution margin contributes only $627 in weighted or total contribution margin. The chicken breast, the menu item with the lowest individual contribution margin of $5.90, is the top-selling item on the menu and brings in the highest gross profit dollars of $1652. This demonstrates that a popular lower food cost menu item with a lower individual contribution margin can bring in more gross profit dollars than an unpopular high food, high individual contribution margin item.

The data needed to conduct cost/margin analysis are the same data needed for the Miller and menu engineering analysis:

1. The number sold of each menu item
2. The food cost of each menu item
3. The menu price of each item

Table 5-1   COST/MARGIN MENU ITEM CLASSIFICATIONS

Sales Volume	Food Cost %	Weighted Contribution Margin
High (popular)	Low	Low
High	Low	High
High	High	High
High	High	Low
Low (not popular)	High	High
Low	High	Low
Low	Low	High
Low	Low	Low

Table 5-2 RANKINGS OF MENU ITEMS BY INDIVIDUAL AND WEIGHTED CONTRIBUTION MARGINS

Menu Item	No. Sold	Menu Price	Food Cost/$	Food Cost%	Individual Contribution Margin	Individual CM Rank	Weighted Contribution Margin	Weighted CM Rank
Sirloin Steak	240	$9.95	$3.95	39.7	$6.00	6	$1440.00	3
King Crab	50	$15.95	$6.00	37.6	$9.95	2	$497.50	7
Lobster Tail	60	$18.45	$8.00	43.4	$10.45	1	$627.00	5
Prime Rib	180	$14.50	$5.50	37.9	$9.00	3	$1620.00	2
Whitefish	80	$8.75	$2.50	28.6	$6.25	5	$500.00	6
NY Strip	150	$12.45	$5.75	46.2	$6.70	4	$1005.00	4
Chicken Breast	280	$8.50	$2.60	30.6	$5.90	7	$1652.00	1

In the example that follows, taken from a popular fern bar restaurant chain, the menu items were classified into the following four categories:

1. Appetizers
2. Snacks
3. Entrees
4. Desserts

A total of 72 different menu items were identified and tallied. The sales figures, food costs, and number sold were provided by the management of the unit. The grouping of menu items was also that of unit management. (See Tables 5-3 through 5-6.)

Lotus 123 software was employed to generate the multi-column spreadsheets and graphs that follow. Menu item sales are tallied, and each menu item is classified as popular or unpopular according to the calculation suggested by Kasavana and Smith (1982) in their *Menu Engineering* methodology. The formula is:

1.00/number of menu items × .7 (constant) × sum of all items sold

Substituting data from Table 5-7, which summarizes totals from Tables 5-5 and 5-6:

$$(1.00/72) \ (.70) \ (19,098) = 185.68$$

The value 185.68 is interpreted as any menu item that sells more than 186 orders a month is considered popular (high volume), while any item that sells 186 or fewer a month is considered unpopular (low volume). Individual menu items can be identified by reading down the "No. Sold" column on Tables 5-3 to 5-6. Note that snacks account for 22 of the 43 items considered "high volume." Appetizers account for 11 while entrees have 8 and desserts only 2 items that sold more than 186 orders.

The cutoff point that separates high food cost percentage from low is the *potential food cost percentage (PFC)* for the entire sales mix. The calculation is:

$$\frac{\text{Weighted (or total) Food Cost}}{\text{Weighted (or total) Food Sales}} = \frac{\$29,521.63}{\$81,666.30} = 36.15\%$$

Items that run a food cost percentage less than or equal to 36.15 percent are classified as low in food cost, while menu items over that amount are considered high food cost. The menu had 36 of 72 tracked items at or below this percentage. Sixteen low-cost menu items were snacks, 13 were appetizers, 5 were entrees, and 2 were desserts.

Similarly, menu items are classified as high or low in weighted (or total) contribution margin according to the quantitative values calculated by the formula shown on page 107.

Table 5-3 COST/MARGIN ANALYSIS—APPETIZERS

Item Name	No. Sold	Menu Price	Raw Food Cost	Sup. Food Cost	Total Food Cost	Item Cont. Mar.	Wgted. Food Cost	Wgted. Cont. Mar.	Wgted. Sales	% Item f.c.	% Total Sales	% Total f.c.	% Items Sold	% Wgted. CM	Sales Vol. Class	Food Cost Class	CM Class	Problem	Standard	Sleeper	Prime
0 mid point	185.68					2.73		724.23		36.15											
1 Onion Soup	507	1.95	0.42		0.42	1.53	212.94	775.71	988.65	21.54	4.81	3.33	8.10	5.48	1	0	1	0	0	0	1
2 BOWL SOUP	290	1.85	0.10		0.10	1.75	29.00	507.50	536.50	5.41	2.61	0.45	4.64	3.59	1	0	0	0	0	1	0
3 Spin/Sal	349	1.95	0.30		0.30	1.65	104.70	575.85	680.55	15.38	3.31	1.64	5.58	4.07	1	0	0	0	0	1	0
4 Batter	286	3.75	1.09		1.09	2.66	311.74	760.76	1072.50	29.07	5.22	4.87	4.57	5.38	1	0	1	0	1	0	1
5 Fr Cheese	1602	2.95	1.14		1.14	1.81	1826.28	2899.62	4725.90	38.64	22.99	28.54	25.61	20.49	1	1	1	0	1	0	0
6 Fr Mush	257	2.95	0.87		0.87	2.08	223.59	534.56	758.15	29.49	3.69	3.49	4.11	3.78	1	0	0	0	0	1	0
7 Zucc	289	2.95	0.66		0.66	2.29	190.74	661.81	852.55	22.37	4.15	2.98	4.62	4.68	1	0	1	0	0	1	0
8 Guac	170	2.95	0.69		0.69	2.26	117.30	384.20	501.50	23.39	2.44	1.83	2.72	2.71	0	0	0	0	0	1	0
9 Fing App	383	3.75	1.32		1.32	2.43	505.56	930.69	1436.25	35.20	6.99	7.90	6.12	6.58	1	1	1	0	0	0	1
10 Skins BC	551	4.45	1.90		1.90	2.55	1046.90	1405.05	2451.95	42.70	11.93	16.36	8.81	9.93	1	1	1	1	1	0	0
11 Skins Combo	175	4.45	1.81		1.81	2.64	316.75	462.00	778.75	40.67	3.79	4.95	2.80	3.26	0	1	0	1	0	0	0
12 Skins Chili	29	4.45	1.86		1.86	2.59	53.94	75.11	129.05	41.80	0.63	0.84	0.46	0.53	0	1	1	1	0	0	0
13 Nacho 1	585	3.95	1.02		1.02	2.93	596.70	1714.05	2310.75	25.82	11.24	9.32	9.35	12.11	1	0	1	0	0	0	1
14 Nacho 2	129	4.25	1.34		1.34	2.91	172.86	375.39	548.25	31.53	2.67	2.70	2.06	2.65	0	0	0	0	0	1	0
15 Nacho 3	386	4.95	1.19		1.19	3.76	459.34	1451.36	1910.70	24.04	9.30	7.18	6.17	10.25	1	0	1	0	0	1	1
16 Nacho 4	130	4.95	1.60		1.60	3.35	208.00	435.50	643.50	32.32	3.13	3.25	2.08	3.08	0	0	0	0	0	1	0
17 Fr Fries	138	1.65	0.17		0.17	1.48	23.46	204.24	227.70	10.30	1.11	0.37	2.21	1.44	0	0	0	0	0	1	0
17 TOTAL	6256						6399.80	14153.40	20553.20						HI= 1 LOW=0				IS=1 IS NOT=0		

Table 5-4 COST/MARGIN ANALYSIS—SNACKS

	Item Name	No. Sold	Menu Price	Raw Food Cost	Sup. Food Cost	Total Food Cost	Item Cont. Mar.	Wgted. Food Cost	Wgted. Cont. Mar.	Wgted. Sales	% Item f.c.	% Total Sales	% Total f.c.	% Items Sold	% Wgted. CM	Sales Vol. Class	Food Cost Class	CM Class	Problem	Standard	Sleeper	Prime
0	mid point	185.68					2.73		724.23		36.15				2.40							
1	Snk Stk	165	4.95	1.30		1.30	3.65	214.50	602.25	816.75	26.26	2.11	1.56	1.91	2.40	0	0	0	0	0	1	0
2	Snk Clams	293	4.95	0.68		0.68	4.27	199.24	1251.11	1450.35	13.74	3.74	1.45	3.39	4.99	1	0	1	0	0	0	1
3	Snk Shrimp	129	7.95	3.04		3.04	4.91	392.16	633.39	1025.55	38.24	2.64	2.86	1.49	2.52	0	1	0	1	0	0	0
4	Snk Chk	370	4.95	1.57		1.57	3.38	580.90	1250.60	1831.50	31.72	4.72	4.24	4.28	4.99	1	0	1	0	0	0	1
5	Snk Combo	307	4.95	1.43		1.43	3.52	439.01	1080.64	1519.65	28.89	3.92	3.20	3.55	4.31	1	1	1	0	0	0	1
6	Shri mp Sal	246	5.95	3.05		3.05	2.90	750.30	713.40	1463.70	51.26	3.77	5.47	2.84	2.84	1	1	0	1	0	0	0
7	Chef	352	4.45	1.91		1.91	2.54	672.32	894.08	1566.40	42.92	4.04	4.90	4.07	3.56	1	1	0	1	1	0	0
8	Spin	280	4.45	1.88		1.88	2.57	526.40	719.60	1246.00	42.25	3.21	3.84	3.24	2.87	1	1	0	1	0	0	0
9	Chk Sal	551	4.25	1.94		1.94	2.31	1068.94	1272.81	2341.75	45.65	6.04	7.79	6.37	5.07	1	1	1	1	0	0	0
10	Taco Chk	206	4.25	1.66		1.66	2.59	341.96	533.54	875.50	39.06	2.26	2.49	2.38	2.13	1	1	0	0	0	0	0
11	Taco Chili	98	4.25	1.64		1.64	2.61	160.72	255.78	416.50	38.59	1.07	1.17	1.13	1.02	0	0	0	1	1	0	0
12	Changa	275	4.95	1.82		1.82	3.13	500.50	860.75	1361.25	36.77	3.51	3.65	3.18	3.43	1	0	1	1	0	0	1
13	Super	86	4.25	1.38		1.38	2.87	118.68	246.82	365.50	32.47	0.94	0.87	0.99	0.98	0	0	0	0	0	0	0
14	Beef-C	71	5.45	2.33		2.33	3.12	165.43	221.52	386.95	42.75	1.00	1.21	0.82	0.88	0	0	0	1	0	1	0
15	Turk-C	262	4.95	2.00		2.00	2.95	524.00	772.90	1296.90	40.40	3.34	3.82	3.03	3.08	1	0	1	1	0	0	1
16	Ham-C	139	4.85	1.83		1.83	3.02	254.37	419.78	674.15	37.73	1.74	1.85	1.61	1.67	0	0	0	1	0	0	0
17	Chk-C	81	4.45	1.86		1.86	2.59	150.66	209.79	360.45	41.80	0.93	1.10	0.94	0.84	0	1	0	1	0	0	1
18	Philly	912	4.75	1.60		1.60	3.15	1459.20	2872.80	4332.00	33.68	11.16	10.64	10.54	11.45	1	0	0	0	0	0	1
19	Club	264	4.75	1.50		1.50	3.25	396.00	858.00	1254.00	31.58	3.23	2.89	3.05	3.42	1	0	1	0	0	0	1
20	Chk Sal Sand	147	3.95	1.46		1.46	2.49	214.62	366.03	580.65	36.96	1.50	1.56	1.70	1.46	0	1	0	1	0	0	1
21	Reuben	257	4.95	1.52		1.52	3.43	390.64	881.51	1272.15	30.71	3.28	2.85	2.97	3.51	1	0	1	0	0	0	1
22	Dip	643	4.85	1.94		1.94	2.91	1247.42	1871.13	3118.55	40.00	8.04	9.10	7.43	7.46	1	1	1	0	1	0	0
23	Chk Sand	321	4.95	1.56		1.56	3.39	500.76	1088.19	1588.95	31.52	4.10	3.65	3.71	4.34	1	0	1	0	0	0	1
24	Q-Day	309	3.95	1.12		1.12	2.83	346.08	874.47	1220.55	28.35	3.15	2.52	3.57	3.49	1	0	0	0	0	0	0
25	Q-Ham	212	3.95	1.34		1.34	2.61	284.08	553.32	837.40	33.92	2.16	2.07	2.45	2.21	1	0	0	0	0	1	0
26	Q S/S	554	4.75	1.41		1.41	3.34	781.14	1850.36	2631.50	29.68	6.78	5.70	6.40	7.38	1	0	1	0	1	0	1
27	Q-Sea	196	4.65	1.68		1.68	2.97	329.28	582.12	911.40	36.13	2.35	2.40	2.27	2.32	1	0	0	1	0	1	0
28	Q-Sea S/S	238	5.35	1.86		1.86	3.49	442.68	830.62	1273.30	34.77	3.28	3.23	2.75	3.31	1	0	1	0	0	1	0
29	Soup/Sal	231	0.95	0.22		0.22	0.73	50.82	168.63	219.45	23.16	0.57	0.37	2.67	0.67	1	0	0	1	0	1	0
30	Muffin	341	0.85	0.27		0.27	0.58	92.07	197.78	289.85	31.76	0.75	0.67	3.94	0.79	1	1	0	1	0	1	0
31	Kid Chk	52	2.25	0.98		0.98	1.27	50.96	66.04	117.00	43.56	0.30	0.37	.60	0.26	0	1	1	0	0	0	0
32	Kid Stk	15	2.45	1.08		1.08	1.37	16.20	20.55	36.75	44.08	0.09	0.12	0.17	0.08	0	1	1	0	0	0	0
33	Kid Burger	40	2.25	1.01		1.01	1.24	40.40	49.60	90.00	44.89	0.23	0.29	0.46	0.20	0	1	1	0	1	0	0
34	KidShrimp	8	3.45	1.49		1.49	1.96	11.92	15.68	27.60	43.19	0.07	0.09	0.09	0.06	0	1	0	1	0	0	0
	TOTAL	8651				13714.36			25085.59	38799.95						HI=1 LOW=0			IS=1	IS NOT=0		

104

Table 5-5 COST/MARGIN ANALYSIS—ENTREES

	Item Name	No. Sold	Menu Price	Raw Food Cost	Sup. Food Cost	Total Food Cost	Item Cont. Mar.	Wgted. Food Cost	Wgted. Cont. Mar.	Wgted. Sales	% Item f.c.	% Total Sales	% Total f.c.	% Items Sold	% Wgted. CM	Sales Vol. Class	Food Cost Class	CM Class	Problem	Standard	Sleeper	Prime
0	mid point	185.68					2.73		724.23		36.15											
1	Cordon	148	6.45	1.90		1.90	4.55	281.20	673.40	954.60	29.46	4.64	4.39	2.37	4.76	0	0	0	0	0	1	0
2	BBQ Shrimp	240	7.45	3.18		3.18	4.27	763.20	1024.80	1788.00	42.68	8.70	11.93	3.84	7.24	1	1	1	0	1	0	0
3	8 oz	215	6.95	2.89		2.89	4.06	621.35	872.90	1494.25	41.58	7.27	9.71	3.44	6.17	1	1	1	0	1	0	0
4	10 oz	167	8.95	4.04		4.04	4.91	674.68	819.97	1494.65	45.14	7.27	10.54	2.67	5.79	0	1	1	0	1	0	0
5	Smo Stk	338	6.95	2.97		2.97	3.98	1003.86	1345.24	2349.10	42.73	11.43	15.69	5.40	9.50	1	1	1	0	1	0	0
6	Fr Shrimp	132	7.95	3.58		3.58	4.37	472.56	576.84	1049.40	45.03	5.11	7.38	2.11	4.08	0	1	0	1	0	0	1
7	S & S	161	8.75	2.81		2.81	5.94	452.41	956.34	1408.75	32.11	6.85	7.07	2.57	6.76	0	0	1	0	0	0	1
8	BBQ Chick	83	6.95	2.31		2.31	4.64	191.73	385.12	576.85	33.24	2.81	3.00	1.33	2.72	0	0	0	0	0	1	0
9	Smo Chick	203	6.75	2.01		2.01	4.74	408.03	962.22	1370.25	29.78	6.67	6.38	3.24	6.80	1	0	1	0	0	0	1
10	Fing Din	208	5.95	2.08		2.08	3.87	432.64	804.96	1237.60	34.96	6.02	6.76	3.32	5.69	1	1	1	0	0	0	1
11	Burger	330	3.95	2.16		2.16	1.79	712.80	590.70	1303.50	54.68	6.34	11.14	5.27	4.17	1	0	0	1	0	0	0
12	Burg Plat	729	4.65	2.28		2.28	2.37	1662.12	1727.73	3389.85	49.03	16.49	25.97	11.65	12.21	1	1	1	0	1	0	0
13	Eggs Benedict	401	4.25	1.75		1.75	2.50	701.75	1002.50	1704.25	41.18	8.29	10.97	6.41	7.08	1	1	1	0	1	0	0
14	Stk & Eggs	42	6.75	3.38		3.38	3.37	141.96	141.54	283.50	50.07	1.38	2.22	0.67	1.00	0	0	0	1	0	0	0
14	TOTAL	3397						8520.29	11884.26	20404.55						HI=1 LOW=0				IS=1 IS NOT=0		

Table 5-6 COST MARGIN ANALYSIS—DESSERTS

Item Name	No. Sold	Menu Price	Raw Food Cost	Sup. Food Cost	Total Food Cost	Item Cont. Mar.	Wgted. Food Cost	Wgted. Cont. Mar.	Wgted. Sales	% Item f.c.	% Total Sales	% Total f.c.	% Items Sold	% Wgted. CM	Sales Vol. Class	Food Cost Class	CM Class	Prob-blem	Stan-dard	Sleeper	Prime
0 mid point	185.68					2.73		724.23		36.15											
1 Royal	96	2.45	1.02		1.02	1.43	97.92	137.28	235.20	41.63	0.61	0.71	1.11	0.55	0	1	0	1	0	0	0
2 Cake	41	2.45	0.95		0.95	1.50	38.95	61.50	100.45	38.78	0.26	0.28	0.47	0.25	0	1	0	1	0	0	0
3 Delight	62	2.75	0.97		0.97	1.78	60.14	110.36	170.50	35.27	0.44	0.44	0.72	0.44	0	0	0	0	0	1	0
4 Kid Sundae	64	1.50	0.45		0.45	1.05	28.80	67.20	96.00	30.00	0.25	0.21	0.74	0.27	0	0	0	0	0	1	0
5 Rocky	226	2.45	0.97		0.97	1.48	219.22	334.48	553.70	39.59	1.43	1.60	2.61	1.33	1	1	0	1	0	0	0
6 Apple	195	2.45	0.97		0.97	1.48	189.15	288.60	477.75	39.59	1.23	1.38	2.25	1.15	1	1	0	1	0	0	0
7 B'day Cake	110	2.50	2.30		2.30	0.20	253.00	22.00	275.00	92.00	0.71	1.84	1.27	0.09	0	1	0	1	0	0	0
7 TOTAL	794						887.18	1021.42	1908.60												
															HI=1 LOW=0					IS=1 IS NOT=0	

106

Table 5-7 GRAND TOTALS

Total Menu Items	72
Number Sold	9098
Total Weighted Food Cost	$29,521.63
Total Weighted Contribution Margin	$52,144.67
Total Weighted Sales	$81,666.30

The *average weighted contribution margin (AWCM)* is the cutoff point for high versus low contribution margin items. The calculation is:

$$\frac{\text{Weighted Contribution Margin}}{\text{Total Number of Menu Items}} = \frac{\$52,144.67}{72} = \$724.23$$

Items that contribute an amount less than or equal to $724.23 are classified as low contribution margin items and those that contribute more are high margin items.

It is important to classify all menu items into one of the four menu categories for in-depth analysis and comparison to the popularity, PFC, and AWCM values. This breakdown will show the impact each menu category has on overall sales, costs, and contribution margin. (See Tables 5-3 to 5-6.)

The most valuable aspect of the cost/margin methodology comes when the spreadsheet data are graphically displayed, plotting each menu item by category by its food cost percentage and weighted contribution margin. A basic X-Y graph is used to plot individual menu items. The Y, or vertical, axis displays the food cost percentage and the X, or horizontal, axis the weighted contribution margin. Separate graphs should be prepared for each menu category calculating cutoff points *separately* for each one. It is important to compare items within their respective categories as it reveals a different perspective for assessing menu items. The different cutoff points for each menu category are shown in Table 5-8.

Although the graphs plot food cost percentage and weighted contribution margin, the figures really plot a third variable, popularity. Since cost/margin uses "weighted" contribution margin, popularity is reflected in the "weight" of the number sold of each menu item. Although not perfect, most of your popular menu items will be plotted to the right of the vertical AWCM line.

Note that each graph is divided into four quadrants by vertical and horizontal lines intersecting the plot of the potential food cost and average weighted contribution margin. (See Figure 5-4.) The interpretation of the graph is based on the location of each plotted point relative to the intersecting lines. In this example, the lines intersect at 36.15 percent and $724.23.

Items that fall below the horizontal PFC line are those considered low in food cost while those plotted above are considered high food cost items. Items plotted to the left of the vertical AWCM line are considered low in contribution margin while those plotted to the right are considered high.

Items that are both low in food cost and high in individual contribution margin satisfy both food cost and contribution margin standards and are referred to as *primes*. They are in the lower right quadrant. The more items in this

Table 5-8 MENU CATEGORY AVERAGES AND TOTALS

	Potential Food Cost	Average No. Sold	Average Item C.M.	Average Wgted. C.M.	% of Items Sold	% of Food Cost	% of Cont. Margin	% of Sales Dollars
Appetizers	31.41%	257.60	$2.26	$832.55	32.76	21.68	27.14	25.17
Snacks	35.35%	178.11	$2.90	$737.81	45.30	46.46	48.11	47.51
Entrees	41.76%	169.85	$3.50	$848.88	17.19	28.86	22.79	24.99
Desserts	46.48%	79.40	$1.29	$145.92	4.16	3.01	1.96	2.34
Totals	36.15%	185.68	$2.73	$724.23	100.00	100.00	100.00	100.00

COST/MARGIN ANALYSIS

Average Weighted
Contribution Margin $

PROBLEMS	STANDARDS
Low Contribution Margins High Food Cost Percentage	High Contribution Margins High Food Cost Percentage
	Potential Food Cost %
SLEEPERS	PRIMES
Low Contribution Margins Low Food Cost Percentage	High Contribution Margins Low Food Cost Percentage

(left axis) Food Cost Percentage

Weighted Contribution Margin $

FIGURE 5-4   Graph quadrants.

quadrant, the better the sales mix results in terms of lowering food cost and increasing contribution margin. It is not realistic to have all items in the primes quadrant and a menu will generally contain problems, standards, and sleepers.

Items located in the upper-right quadrant are high in food cost and high in contribution margin and are referred to as *standards*. They are the traditional items found on most table-service restaurant menus, (e.g., steaks, Prime rib, lobster, seafood). They are usually the highest priced items on the menu and have the highest food costs. All menus need to have standards to "balance" the menu with items that help raise the average check.

The items in the lower left are called *sleepers* because they are low in food cost and low in weighted contribution margin. The reason they are low in contribution margin is that they are not very popular menu items. They are often new dishes that are being tested. Every restaurant needs to test new menu items to keep its menu fresh, and often we seek to add low food cost items at low prices to create some demand. The inclusion of sleepers in the sales mix helps "soften" the negative higher-than-average food costs of problems and standards.

In the upper left are the *problems*, so called because they are high in food cost and low in weighted contribution margin. Often the items in this quadrant are children's menu items and desserts. Children's menu items may run 100 percent food cost in some restaurants where kids eat free with adults. As part of a marketing strategy to attract families, these items must be viewed differently than ordinary menu items.

It is important to point out that decisions on how to deal with problems is not made solely on quantitative data. If that were the case, the computer could replace management when it comes to adding and deleting items from the menu. Many nonquantifiable factors must be included in menu planning and pricing decisions. No simple quantitative rule of thumb is suggested here. Company policy, customer preferences, regional practices, competition, marketing policies, and company tradition are important factors that will over-ride purely quantitative factors and keep certain items on the menu regardless of cost or contribution margin. Hopefully, management can make changes in price, portioning, and menu positioning that moves sleepers into the primes quadrant and moves standards closer to the food cost cutoff line.

The menu items that fall closest to the intersecting lines are those easiest to improve or strengthen. Small changes in positioning or the menu to increase selection, adding and deleting accompaniments and portions to make an item either a better value to the customer or reducing the food cost and holding the price constant, or small incremental increases in price can improve item popu-larity and contribution margin.

The action taken on an individual menu item will also be influenced by how deeply it is positioned within a quadrant, its nearness to the intersecting lines, and whether it is above or below the PFC line or to the right of the AWCM. Generally, one would seek to move items downward and to the right on the graph toward the primes quadrant. Strategies for dealing with primes, problems, standards, and sleepers will be covered later in this chapter.

Appetizers

Upon examining the appetizers in Table 5-3 and Figure 5-5, one notes the con-centration of items in the sleeper quadrant. Items 2, 3, 6, and 7 appear the best menu items to improve. If the popularity of these items were improved, they

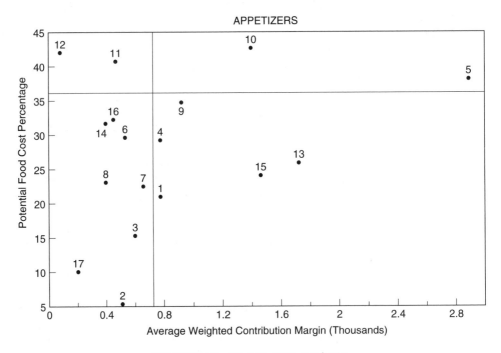

FIGURE 5-5   Cost/margin analysis.

could move into the prime quadrant. Any internal promotion that would call attention to the items and increase their chance of selection would be in order. The dispersion of appetizers on the graph represents a very good mix of items relative to food costs. However, contribution margin can be improved. Most items are below the PFC line and to the left of the AWCM line.

Snacks

In Table 5-4 and Figure 5-6, snack items 1, 3, 6, 8, 25, and 27 are the closest to the intersecting lines and therefore the best candidates for improvement. Closer examination of the items in the problems quadrant reveals the worst items are children's portions. These items are purposely priced low and, because they represent such a small portion of the total items sold, have minimal impact on the overall food cost percentage.

Entrees

Table 5-5 and Figure 5-7 shows the majority of entree items in the standards quadrant. If sales of entrees are increased, the PFC of the total sales mix will increase since most of the items carry a food cost higher than the 36.15 percent. The plotted points show menu items are fairly deep into the quadrant, indicating that movement downward to more favorable positions on the graph

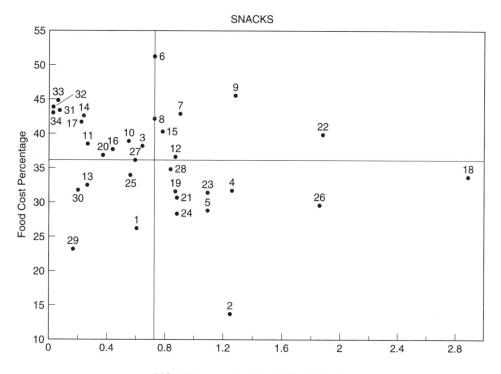

FIGURE 5-6 Cost/margin analysis.

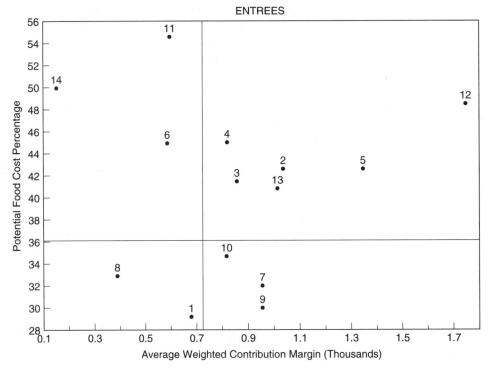

FIGURE 5-7   Cost/margin analysis.

will need several actions taken over an extended period of time. Drastic changes in price and portioning will be noticed by the customers.

Desserts

The desserts shown in Table 5-6 and Figure 5-8 are skewed severely to the left. Most items are borderline problems and may be moved into the sleepers quadrant if costs can be reduced or prices raised. These items might appear at first to have a negative effect on overall figures, but because they account for such an insignificant number of items sold, their impact on food cost and gross profit is negligible.

   The desserts present an example of why it is important to use a "desserts only" average for food cost percentage and average weighted contribution instead of the averages for the entire sales mix. If only desserts are averaged according to the formulas shown for cutoff points for food cost and average contribution margin, the food cost cutoff is 46.48 percent (compared to the 36.15 percent for the entire menu sales mix) and the weighted contribution margin cutoff is $145.92 (compared to $724.23). This would put dessert items 5 and 6 into the dessert primes category, whereas they show up as problems when compared to the overall sales mix. This is due to the fact that they have a lower markup, higher food cost percentage, and account for only 4.16 percent of all

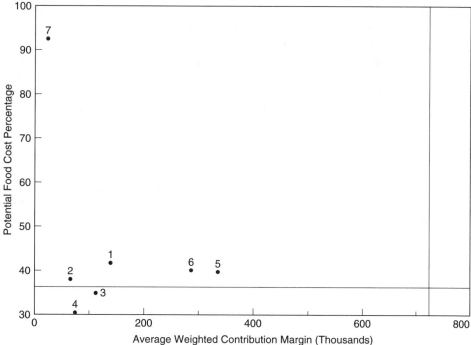

FIGURE 5-8   Cost/margin analysis.

items sold. A very low percentages of customers order desserts compared to snacks and appetizers.

The data in Table 5-8 on page 108 reveal that appetizers and snacks have a "lowering" effect on the PFC as both have average food cost percentages below 35.15 percent, the PFC for the entire menu sales mix. The highest volume items are in the appetizer category where the average number sold exceeds the menu average by 72 (257.60 minus 185.78). This is occurring at the expense of the entrees, which account for less than 18 percent of the total items sold. The data show that customers apparently order an appetizer or side order and do not consider entrees. This was partially due to the design of the menu, a multi-paged booklet where the entrees were located on the last two pages.

Snacks and appetizers made up 78 percent of the total items sold. These two categories have the greatest impact on overall cost, contribution margin, and sales revenue and deserve management's closet attention. They account for 68 percent of the food cost dollar, 75 percent of the contribution margin, and 72.5 percent of the sales revenue. (See Table 5-8.)

If this type of analysis is conducted on a quarterly basis, figures will reveal trends in popularity, costs, and contribution margin. An operator can quickly and easily see which items on the graph are the best candidates for improvement. If the graphs are printed on clear transparencies instead of paper, the movement of cutoff lines and menu item placement can be readily compared from one period to the next. If changes are made that lower the food cost line and move the average weighted contribution margin line to the right, the changes made are having positive effects on the sales mix.

Cost/margin analysis allows one to objectively view the effects of the menu design, pricing, and food cost changes through the plotting of the cutoff lines and menu items on a graph. Marketing and cost control efforts can be targeted to the menu categories and items where the greatest need exists. When changes are made, cost/margin analysis will indicate whether improvements to the sales mix have taken place.

The cost/margin analysis is applicable to fast-food operations. There is a separate column in the spreadsheet titled "Supplemental Food Cost," which can be used for including packaging materials like beverage cups and styrofoam containers. This can also be used to add a "direct labor cost value" for items requiring direct labor. In the case of alcoholic beverages, it can be used for the mix and garnish costs of the drink. The data can also be used by multi-unit operations to compare units.

THE SEVEN P'S OF MENU DESIGN

The marketing mix consists of the four P's of promotion, place, price, and product. We can apply a similar menu marketing mix of seven P's to examine the role of the menu in marketing items to the customers.

Through menu design, we can influence the sales mix of menu items by altering certain aspects within the following areas:

Purchase price: The purchase price of the ingredients can relate to the "quality" of the item. Higher quality costs more than lesser quality. You could "shop" for the best price of ingredients to lower your food cost without sacrificing quality.

Portioning: The portion size and the accompaniments that are included are treated in the same manner to project "value" to the customer. Larger portions and more accompaniments translate to increased value for the customer.

Positioning: Positioning has to do with the placement or prominence given to an item on the menu. Primacy and recency principles and gaze motion can be used to increase the likelihood of selection.

Promotion: Anything done to increase attention to certain items will increase its chance of selection; that is, table tents, suggestive selling, menu emphasis with graphics, bold typeface. When new items are added or old ones deleted, the number of portions sold of the items deleted will shift to other items. How much they affect the overall sales mix will depend on the promotion or attention given to the changes.

Product presentation: By doing something unique to the product and transforming it from a "commodity" to a "specialty" good allows you to create a monopoly of sorts, and with that designation come a group of distinctive advantages over the competition. The effective use of flatware and garnitures will certainly enhance the visual presentation and increase the value perception of the customer. We do not eat as much with our sense of taste as we do with our eyes. This also refers to the dining room amenities like tablecloths, candles, and fresh flowers.

Price (Menu): The price you charge can certainly influence selection. However, discounting or low price leaders are not the recommended way to build an image of quality and elegance that some restaurants seek to achieve. Pricing can also refer to whether the menu item is priced à la carte or table d'hôte. Further emphasis can be drawn to the item by price promotions such as discounting or by adding or deleting accompaniments or by giving larger portions.

Place: By altering the "place" aspects of marketing strategy, (i.e., home delivery, carryout service, picnic lunches, catering services) further competitive distinctiveness can be created.

These factors are used in any strategy to improve the position of items in your sales mix to enhance whatever it is you are trying to accomplish, whether it be lowering food cost, or increasing popularity (no. sold), the contribution margin, or the average check.

STRATEGIES FOR PRIMES, STANDARDS, SLEEPERS, AND PROBLEMS

Once the cost/margin menu analysis has classified the menu items into one of the four categories, a strategy for improving or optimizing their overall impact on the menu sales mix can be put into action. The characteristics of the menu items will point you in the direction of what specific strategy would be best.

Primes: Remember, primes are popular items that are low in food cost and high in weighted contribution margin. You want to sell the heck out of these items. Therefore you should utilize menu psychology design to make these items **STAND OUT** on the menu. Use techniques such as bold and oversized lettering, placing the menu item in its own outlined box, featuring it on a chalkboard or lit menu board, suggestive selling by servers, and so on.

Maintaining high visibility is recommended for primes. It is very important to keep quality high and portions adequate because these menu items are likely house specialties or signature items that are specifically sought by customers. Because they are popular, you might test for price elasticity and increase the price if you felt it was low relative to competing items on the menu and if an item was one of your moderate to lowest priced items in its respective menu category. Monitor quality and presentation standards to insure high standards on these items.

Standards: These are also popular items that have high food costs and high weighted contribution margins. You can test for price elasticity by raising the price to lower the food cost percentage. If the item were a signature item on your menu, this option is one you might consider. The proximity to the food cost line on the graph will tell you exactly how much you have to raise the price to move it on or below the food cost line. If it is only a matter of $.25 to $.95, it might be worth a try. If raising the price were not an option, if the portion were large, you could lower the food cost by reducing the portion without the customer noticing the change.

If you could do neither, you might move it to a less noticeable position on the menu to lower its selection odds. At the same time you may want to emphasize another item in its place that is lower in food cost and higher in contribution margin. Food cost can also be lowered by reducing accompaniments or perhaps finding a purveyor who has a lower price on some of the key ingredients. You may be able to develop a similar item that is combined with a low-cost ingredient (e.g., pasta or rice) and promote that item. Also, promote sleepers to soften the high cost aspects of the popular standards.

Sleepers: Since these items are slow-selling low food cost items, they also have a low weighted contribution margin. Therefore, anything you do to increase the likelihood that these items are selected by the guest is recommended. Prominently display them on the menu; feature them on menu boards; use table tents and suggestive selling by the servers. Since they are very low in food cost, you can lower the price via discounts or early bird specials to stimulate sales. Also, increase portions or accompaniments to create a better value at a low price to stimulate sales. Rename the item and promote it as a signature item.

Problems: These items are high in food cost and low in contribution margin. One of the first things you can do is raise the price and lower the product cost. If you cannot do either, hide it on the menu. Develop substitute items and promote. Combine with inexpensive ingredients to lower portion cost. If sales do not pick up, take it off the menu.

*Authors Note: For additional coverage of Cost/Margin Analysis see "Prime Numbers: Finding Your Menu's Strengths," Cornell Quarterly, Nov. 1985, Vol 26, No. 3, pp. 71-77.

"Cost/Margin Analysis: A third approach to menu pricing and design," International Journal of Hospitality Mgt. 1983, Vol 2, No. 3, pp 127–134.

Chapter Six

Menu Pricing Methodology and Theory

PRICING THEORIES

Regardless of the methodology used to mark up food and beverages, prices charged by commercial food services must not only cover costs but return a profit as well. Pricing is an important function that directly influences customer counts and sales revenues. The optimum price must not only include some contribution to profit but also be deemed fair and reasonable by the public.

One cannot remain in business very long if costs are not covered. However, costs are not the sole consideration in determining menu prices. Costs must be known in order to measure profit contribution on each sale. Some costs can be accurately determined and assigned to specific menu items while others must be subjectively allocated across the entire menu. At most, cost serves as a reference to begin developing a pricing strategy.

Many operators experience increasing competition for their customers and have to constantly deal with rising operating costs, labor shortages, and legislation impacting their business. Such factors will definitely impact their profits. Therefore, the pricing strategy they use is a major factor in developing an overall plan to deal with such obstacles.

Most businesspeople seek logical and objective criteria on which to base their pricing strategy. This is the main reason we start with determining the cost of a product or service. The costing process is objective and absolute. There is a tendency to rationalize price as a means of returning an amount that will reflect a fair profit for the risk incurred and the time, effort, and materials consumed.

Of all the business decisions a restaurateur has to make, one that causes much anxiety is pricing the menu. Whenever pricing decisions require raising prices, the operator mentally prepares for some adverse customer response. The usual feedback comes in the form of spoken comments and the dreaded dropping customer counts. Consequently, the task of menu pricing is beset with misgivings and uncertainty. Prices that are too high will drive customers away, and prices that are too low will sacrifice profit. The main reason for this anxiety may well be the highly subjective methodology used to price menus in the first place. Anxiety results over whether the approach to pricing is the best or the right one for the respective menu items, existing market conditions, and operational concept.

Prices partially influence which menu items will sell and therefore impact the overall profitability of the sales mix. The menu sales mix will, in turn, influence everything from equipment utilization to marketing efforts. Menu items will differ widely in cost, popularity, and profitability. In addition, the amount of labor required will differ from item to item. Thus, pricing is not a simple matter of markup over cost but an intricate combination of factors that involve both financial and competitive elements.

MARKET AND DEMAND DRIVEN PRICING

What it basically comes down to is that prices can be either *market driven* or *demand driven*, and depending on the uniqueness or monopolistic aspects of the menu item and operational concept, the approach to pricing will differ significantly. Prices that are *market driven* must be responsive to competitors' prices. Menu items that are relatively common (commodities in an economic goods sense) and found on most menus (e.g., hamburgers, barbecue ribs, Prime rib) and in markets where there are several restaurants for customers to get these items, must be priced competitively. This perspective on pricing is also used when introducing new menu items before any substantial demand has been established. Prices that are *market driven* tend to be on the moderate to low side of the pricing continuum.

In contrast are those prices that are *demand driven*, where the customers openly ask for the item and demand exceeds the supply of restaurants in the market able to offer it. The item becomes more of a "specialty good" in the economic sense, and a "monopoly" of sorts exists for the short term. Thus pricing an item that is demand driven is higher than on a market driven item until demand starts to wane or competitors add the item to their menus. When this occurs, prices will stabilize and become more market driven.

COST MARKUP

While costing out an entree and accompaniments is a relatively objective and logical process, establishing a selling price is more of an art. Whatever the pricing methodology, no *single* method can be used to mark up *every* item on any given restaurant menu. You must employ a combination of methodologies and theories. Therefore, when properly carried out, prices will reflect food cost percentages, individual and/or weighted contribution margins, price points, and desired check averages, as well as factors driven by intuition, competition, and demand.

If pricing were a purely quantitative exercise, a computer program that would incorporate operating costs, profit objectives, and raw food costs could be used to set menu prices. However, such an approach lacks important "qualitative" factors that enter into the pricing decision. It has been said of most retail products and services that the buyer determines the price, not the seller. Therefore, the seller must be able to offer a product or service and make a profit selling it at the price the customer is willing to pay. Value judgments are hard to program into a cost-markup pricing program.

Menu pricing philosophies are as diverse as political and theological beliefs and sometimes just as controversial. Initially it was the popular belief that only raw food costs should be marked up to obtain a targeted food cost percentage. More often than not, the targeted food cost percentage was arbitrarily determined by simply copying a successful competitor or trying to match some industry average. We have subsequently improved upon the method of determining a targeted food cost percentage and can analytically determine a realistic food cost standard based on each operation's financial and budgetary idiosyncrasies. However, a unit's financial limitations or profit demands may not be compatible or realistic with the existing economic or market conditions. If prices are too high relative to what competition is charging, quality too low, or portions so small as to negate the price-value relationship, sales and profit objectives may still not be realized.

DETERMINING THE PRICE TO CHARGE

A question often asked by restaurateurs is, "What price should I charge?" The response was, initially, "Charge the *highest* price you think the customer will pay." Finding that particular price point is not easy, and if you price at that point you can expect the customer to be more demanding and critical of the food and service.

A different perspective was offered by successful New York restaurateur Michael Weinstein during a past Multiple Unit Food Service Operators Conference, sponsored annually by Nation's Restaurant News. Rather than charging the highest price the customer will pay, his restaurants price at the lowest point at which they can still make a reasonable profit. His reasoning is that if you price at the high end, your operation must be on the "cutting edge" of excellence in food quality, preparation, service, and atmosphere. He achieves satisfaction from customers who praise the price-value offered on his menus. People almost always comment on the reasonableness of the prices, the large portion sizes, and the high quality of the ingredients. Therefore, the two perspectives on how much to charge are: Charge as much as you can or charge as little as you can. Keep in mind that the success of any pricing methodology is influenced by many factors including, among others, location, competition, clientele, and restaurant concept. What works on the Upper West Side of New York may flop in Atlanta, Georgia.

More often than not, prices are predominantly influenced by competition and/or customer demand. Whenever demand is greater than supply, pricing methodologies that favor higher gross profits and higher check averages can be effective in maximizing revenue. On the other hand, if customer counts are flat and strong competition exists for the products and services, such pricing could be disastrous.

The restaurant's menu prices must be in line with the price category in which the majority of its customers place the operation. If prices exceed that range, customers will not purchase many of those items. If your prices are too low, you run the danger of lowering your overall image and will find the check average falling.

The market ultimately determines the price one can charge. If you charge too much, your customers will go somewhere else. However, it is important to interject a warning at this point. Lower prices do not automatically translate into "value" and "bargain" in the minds of the customers. Having the lowest prices in your market may not bring customers or profit. Too often operators engage in price wars through discount promotions and find that profits fall and their image in the marketplace is lowered.

Once initial prices are determined, adjustments up and down will be made after examining the price spread between the lowest and the highest priced items. Every restaurant will be categorized by customers according to the prices it charges. Customers will place a restaurant into one of three categories: low-priced, moderate-priced, and high-priced. Specific numerical check averages are not given because customers, depending upon their incomes, will apply their own dollar ranges when rating restaurants in each category.

Some operators may temper markups on other factors besides food cost percentages. The desired check average, or price point, can strongly impact pricing philosophy, and it should be determined before the menu is initially priced. If you can forecast the number of customers you will serve at each meal period, a properly designed menu will help to influence your sales revenues by making it less likely for a customer to spend less than the predetermined amount needed to achieve your desired check average. This is a different definition of average check. Traditionally, it is calculated by dividing food and/or beverage sales by the number of covers.

For example, assume that sales were $2000 and you served 125 covers. The average check is therefore $16 ($2000/125). However, if you were seeking a $20 average check, you are $4 short of your objective. If a $20 check average is the goal or price point you want to achieve, this should be reflected in the prices charged. The majority of entrees (60 to 75 percent) should be priced within a range of $17.95 to $21.95 and predominantly positioned on the menu.

If the price range is as described and the check average is still below $20, the menu design may be encouraging customers to purchase lower-priced entrees. Menu design can influence customer selection. (See Chapter 5 on "Psychology of Menu Design.") Forcing a price point or check average will not be effective either. Price-value relationships must always be considered. Do not try to force up prices on common items offered by most competitors (e.g. steaks and Prime rib). Utilize house specialties and unique signature foods as your price point leaders. Because these items are unique to your operation, you enjoy the pricing advantages of having a monopoly—at least for the short run. This allows you to price closer to the high end of your price range.

As stated previously, menu prices must be in line with the price category in which the majority of its customers place the operation. If prices of some items exceed that range, customers will not purchase many of those items. If prices are too low, there is a danger of lowering the overall image and the check average may drop.

PRICING TO ACHIEVE A SPECIFIC FOOD COST PERCENTAGE

Exclusive reliance on a menu pricing philosophy that seeks to achieve an unrealistically determined food cost percentage can create problems. Assume that the food cost goal is the oft-quoted 40 percent. If *all* items are marked up 2 1/2 times their cost, one could theoretically achieve a 40 percent cost (allowances for employee meals and unavoidable waste factored in) and still not realize sales or profit objectives.

Clearly, food cost percentage cannot be the sole consideration in establishing the selling price. All items cannot be marked up the same amount. Pricing or markup is rarely exclusively cost driven. If it were, many items would be greatly underpriced relative to what the public is willing to pay, while others would be overpriced. In the case of the former, a simple cup of beef bouillon with a food cost of less than 2 cents per ounce would have a total cost of 10 cents for a 5-ounce portion. A 40 percent food cost would be achieved if it were sold for 25 cents. It could sell for $3.95 in a white tablecloth restaurant and not be considered overpriced by patrons.

In the same restaurant, pricing a 1 1/2-pound live lobster that costs $6.95 per pound would require a menu price of $26.00, without including the costs of accompaniments. Most patrons would consider this price excessive. In addition, marking up every item to achieve a single food cost percentage ignores price-value aspects of competitive pricing and does not allow for the fact that costs are not equally distributed among all items on the menu. Some items are purchased in convenience form and require little or no effort to prepare. An 8-ounce carton of milk, bottled or canned soft drinks, beer and wine, and coffee are examples. Such items do not require as high a markup as others requiring preparation and processing.

CUSTOMER PERCEPTIONS OF THE RESTAURANT AND THE PRICING DECISION

In addition to placing the restaurant into a price category, customers will evaluate a restaurant as a place to "eat out" or as a place to "dine out." If a restaurant is considered an eat-out operation during the week (a substitute for cooking at home), customers will be more price-conscious, because "mental accounting" has them allocating grocery budgeted funds to eating out. If a restaurant is considered a dine-out operation, the visit is regarded more as a social and entertainment occasion rather than merely a trip to satiate one's hunger. The "mental accounting" in this situation takes funds from an entertainment budget, which is more liberal than a grocery budget.

Rarely will a restaurant be rated as both an eat out and dine out category by the same patron. Frequency of visits to an eat-out operation will be greater than to the dine-out operation, but amounts spent will be considerably less than in the latter. Regular weekday customers may go elsewhere for special celebrations like anniversaries or birthdays. Weekend clientele may differ greatly from weeknight customers. For example, local residents may be the bulk of the traffic during the week, while weekends may bring visitors, tourists, or people traveling from outside the restaurant's normal market area. Such patrons categorize the operation as a dine-out or special occasion restaurant. "Diners" will travel farther than those patrons "eating out."

FOUR "COSTLESS" APPROACHES TO PRICING

One cannot arrive at a selling price without considering some highly subjective factors that have "refined" the interpretation of traditional economic theory on consumer buying behavior. Psychologists are teaming up with marketing analysts and economists to provide some new perspectives on pricing. The most common methods employed are logical in the accounting sense of the word. The methods offered here are largely subjective and, for the most part, ignore cost considerations. These "costless" approaches to pricing are (1) competitive pricing, (2) intuitive pricing, (3) psychological pricing, and (4) trial-and-error pricing (Schmidgall, 1990, pp 282–85). Regardless of what they are called, these approaches reflect two of the three critical factors in pricing: demand and competition; the third is cost.

Competitive Pricing

The "competitive" approach to pricing is very simple. The operator collects menus from competitors and then meets or beats their prices. This method is highly ineffective because it assumes that the customer makes the purchase decision based on price alone. It fails to take into account the many other factors that influence choice and preference such as product quality, ambience, service, and even location.

Intuitive Pricing

"Intuitive" pricing is practiced by operators who do not want to take the time to gather menu prices from competitors. They rely instead on what they can remember from past experiences and set prices based on what they feel the guests are willing to pay. This method relies on evaluating the competition and the demand for one's particular products or services.

Psychological Aspects of Pricing

In another pricing approach, "psychological" aspects, a number of interesting theories enter into the pricing decision and a few are offered here. Buyer "price consciousness" influences the way prices are perceived and the importance of price in the buyer's choice of products or services (Monroe and Kirshnan, 1984). Researchers have suggested that "price consciousness" is inversely correlated with social class, implying that price is more a factor to low-income customers frequenting lower-priced restaurants (Gabor and Granger, 1961).

When a buyer lacks specific qualitative information about a menu item and is unable to judge quality prior to purchase, higher prices are associated with higher quality. Price perceptions are sometimes based on the "last price paid" or reference price (Monroe and Petroshius, 1973). The reference price may be the price charged by a competitor, and if it was lower, value perceptions are lowered.

The order in which buyers are exposed to alternative prices affects their perceptions. Buyers exposed initially to high prices will perceive subsequent lower prices as bargains. However, dropping prices to meet a competitor's is not always effective (Della Bitta and Monroe, 1973). Low price does not always result in a dominant market position because people refrain from purchasing a product not only when the price is perceived as too high but also when it is perceived to be too low. When prices for two competing products are perceived to be similar, the price is unlikely to be a factor when a buyer chooses between similar products or services (Monroe and Petroshius, 1973).

Current evidence would suggest that it is the buyer's perception of the total relative value of the product or service that provides the willingness to pay a particular price for a given offering. The total relative value in the restaurant sense consists of such elements as atmosphere, convenience, quality, service, and location. The relative value is enhanced by either *value analysis* or *value engineering*. Value analysis concentrates on increasing perceived value through improving performance (service) relative to customer needs. Value engineering concentrates on increasing value by decreasing costs while maintaining performance standards (Monroe, 1986). The element of customer perception is an important determinant of buyer behavior. Buyers use such cues as product quality, corporate image, and name recognition, along with price, to differentiate among alternatives and to form impressions of product and service quality (Monroe and Kirshnan, 1984).

The driving force in psychological approaches to pricing addresses the important aspect of customer perceptions that will influence the purchase decision (Pavesic, 1989, pp. 43–49). Whether the customer will pay the price or balk is the question. Should one start off low and increase the price or start off on the high side and then discount? Answers to such questions depend upon one's market position, the demand for the product or service, and the stage in the market life cycle of the operation and/or product.

Another psychological theory on pricing looks at the impact of "mental accounting" (Thaler, 1985). This theory suggests that consumers mentally code purchases into categories (e.g., food, housing, entertainment) and that each category is controlled to some degree by a budget constraint. Consequently, the amount spent on a meal away from home will vary depending on whether the expenditure is debited to the food or to the entertainment expense.

In a football stadium, the price for a hot dog and Coke is higher than the price for the same at the neighborhood sandwich shop. However, there are no other choices so the customers accepts the price. This is analogous to the customer eating out while on vacation versus eating dinner on a weeknight in a neighborhood restaurant. Spending is more liberal in recreational or entertainment events.

Because restaurant expenditures can be assigned to the budget categories of either food, entertainment, or recreation, the objective is to get the expenditure classified into a higher budget category or to combine two categories together. The mental budget category may change depending upon the occasion and day of the week. Such considerations may prompt promotions such as early bird specials and discount coupons to entice weeknight diners using their food budget to eat out. Such strategy may not be necessary on weekends, when dining out is done primarily for entertainment or social purposes because spending constraints are more relaxed.

In any purchase decision there are elements of "pleasure" and "pain" to be derived from the transaction (Kahneman and Tversky, 1979). The pleasure comes from the enjoyment of or benefits derived from the purchase, and the pain comes from having to part with one's hard-earned cash. The pain–pleasure aspect of parting with one's money suggests two pricing perspectives: à la carte, and modified table d'hôte or combination pricing. In price-sensitive markets, operators in the low-price units usually price each menu component separately (à la carte) to keep prices down and leave it up to the customer to decide whether to purchase extra items. Up-selling strategy is employed by servers and order takers to increase check averages. The combination pricing, or table d'hôte, charges a higher price but includes accompaniments that otherwise must be purchased separately. The combination price is lower than the sum of the accompaniments purchased à la carte. These concepts are covered in greater detail later in the chapter.

In addition to these pricing perspectives, the practice of using certain combinations of numbers to stimulate sales has been studied (Kreul, 1982). The most popular terminal digits used for prices on restaurant menus are 5, 9, and 0. This "fine-tuning" of prices affects only the terminal digits and has little cost implication. Its greatest impact is on customer perception of the value when contemplating the purchase of two or more competing items. This has been referred to as "odd-cents" pricing. The assumption is that customers will perceive a price of $9.95 as a better buy than $10.00. The use of odd-cents pricing also makes price increases less noticeable to the customer, for example, $9.50 to $9.75.

Trial-and-Error Pricing

The last subjective method of menu pricing is simply "trial and error." This is another "non-cost" approach that claims to be responsive to customer perceptions of prices and is based on customer reactions and comments to pricing decisions. This can be employed on individual menu items to bring them closer to the price the customer is willing to pay. This "wait-and-see" perspective is not practical, especially when it comes to increasing prices.

The price differential between similar or competing items on the menu is another reason for adjusting prices upward or downward after initial pricing is completed. For example, consider the competitive similarity between baked chicken and roast duck. The cost of chicken will be much lower than the cost of duck, even if a larger portion of chicken is served. Duck can command a much higher price than chicken but has a higher food cost. If a menu offers both, the price differential between the two could be a determining factor in the customer selection process. By the same token, in the case of two similar veal dishes, with one requiring an inordinate amount of labor and ingredients and the other quickly and easily prepared, the former should be priced higher because of the preparation methods and ingredients. If the price spread is too close, the number sold of the more costly veal selection may increase. In both previous examples, two entrees had a lower food cost and lower price while the others had a higher food cost and higher price. The price spread can influence selection and therefore impact on check averages, food cost percentage, and gross profit.

Perhaps you have noticed on some restaurant menus that the price of a trip to the salad bar is within a dollar or two of the lowest priced entree that includes the salad bar. This is done partially to achieve a minimum expenditure from each guest and to encourage purchase of combination dinners rather than à la carte portions.

In addition, a steak house selling its steak trimmings as chopped sirloin at $7.95 may appear to be offering a bargain to price-conscious patrons when steaks range upward to $24.95. One must be cognizant of the desired check average and control the number of entrees priced above and below the average check target. The spread or difference between the highest and lowest priced entrees should be around 2-1/2 times the lowest priced entree. Therefore, if the lowest priced entree is $7.95, the highest should be around $19.95.

This is not a strict rule that forbids any entree from being priced above $19.95; however, if the menu has more than three or four items higher than this amount, adjustments should be made. Similarly, if there are more than three or four items at the extreme low end of the menu price range, one may find that the overall check average will be lowered if such items account for greater than 20 percent of items sold. The adjustments needed in order to bring pricing in line would mandate raising the prices at the low end, not lowering prices at the high end.

Operators also set menu price points to cover food costs and achieve a certain profit margin. This method is tempered according to what the competition is doing. Today operators must study customer demographics and market trends, and must give more thought to the wants and needs of their customers. In maturing and saturated markets, strategically set price points are critical to building and holding market share.

The challenge is to offer high value and low menu prices. This philosophy has spawned the introduction of lower-priced and lower-cost food items on many menus. Menus are showing upgraded à la carte offerings and increased variety. When prices are lowered, check averages decline, but the hope is that traffic will increase and build unit volumes. Portions on high-cost items are being reduced or combined with inexpensive accompaniments because patrons are balking at paying higher prices and seem less inclined to eat so much food at one sitting. The strategy with à la carte pricing is to build check averages through add-on sales of lower-cost side dishes and desserts. However, price-value perception does not evolve solely from low price; it is a feeling that the customers have about receiving their money's worth when they pay their check. It is a combination of price, quality, portion size, ambience, service, and psychological aspects.

INDIRECT COST FACTORS IN MENU PRICING

Up to this point the discussion has been primarily on rational pricing methodologies that have traditionally employed quantitative factors to mark up food cost, beverage cost, or food and labor costs. These costs can be allocated to specific menu items. There are, however, a number of indirect costs that can influence the price charged because they provide "added value" to the customer or are affected by supply/demand factors. They are (1) market standing, (2) service commitment, (3) ambience, (4) customer profile, (5) location, (6) amenities, (7) product presentation, (8) desired check average, and (9) price elasticity (Pavesic, 1988).

Market Standing

Market standing relates to the operation's position in a particular market segment; that is, whether it is a "leader" or a "follower." Is it considered the "number one" operation in its concept category or one that is just marginally competitive? Usually, the first one into the marketplace has an advantage over others that follow. Eventually, "copycat" operations go head-to-head in the same market. The one that was there first can usually be more aggressive in its pricing strategy than the "clones;" however, competition will eventually moderate aggressive pricing strategy. This holds true for both fast-food operations and the higher check average, table-service restaurants. The number one operation in a particular food service segment usually finds that the competition tries to outdo it. To do so, copycats must go at least one step further than the leader in menu selection, service, ambience, and value in order to gain ground. The leader can never become complacent and let standards decline or market share may begin to erode.

Service Commitment

The service element can be just as important as the actual food being served in the customer's decision on which restaurant to patronize. This is especially true when the differences in product quality, quantity, and price are seen as negligible by the customer. In addition, the costs of providing table service versus self-service must be reflected in pricing structure. When the customer performs many of the duties of service personnel, prices must be lowered to compensate for the inconveniences. But even self-service restaurants have opportunities to provide service that will distinguish them from their competition. The "invisible product"—the service component—is becoming an important measure of competitive distinctiveness.

Truly personalized service, driven by the needs of the customer, becomes an intangible that is recognized as an added value by the customer and can be reflected in the prices charged. Increased competition leads to increased demand for services, and service can become the basis for improving one's market position.

Ambience

The atmosphere and decor of a restaurant can add much to the enjoyment of a meal. It can turn the experience of eating out into a pleasant social occasion. People want quality food products regardless of whether they pay a little or a lot. However, the perception of value is certainly enhanced for the customer eating in a beautifully decorated, carpeted, appointed, and lighted dining room. Some operators spare no expense in trying to create atmosphere in their restaurants. The atmosphere can be informal or formal, casual or elegant. The more luxurious the atmosphere, the higher prices are likely to be. The customer does not usually object to paying a little more to dine in such surroundings.

Customer Profile

Although the type of clientele that regularly frequents a restaurant is influenced to a great degree by all of the factors listed, the pricing structure can dictate the status or economic class of clientele it will attract. The higher the average check or price range, the more selective and limited your customer base will be. Whether you are attempting to attract professional businessmen and women on their lunch hour, teenagers, baby boomer adults, or families with small children, the target customer will dictate to a great degree the prices you can charge.

Location

Where the restaurant is located significantly influences the prices the customer will be willing to pay and whether the operator should price at "what the market will bear" or at relatively competitive levels. Usually, restaurants with lower check averages and prices must be located in areas of dense population and high traffic. They require many transactions to achieve sales goals. On the other hand, white tablecloth restaurants serving French and continental fare will need fewer covers per meal period and make up for it with high average checks.

Location also refers to geographic area of the country (i.e., Northeast, South, Midwest) and even to certain parts of a city. These conditions may predispose a restaurant operator to a menu pricing structure; for example, Lower Manhattan versus the Upper West Side of New York City, Chicago's South Side versus the Rush Street area, a small rural town versus a large metropolitan city, and a residential neighborhood versus a commercial district. If a location is accessible to tourists more than to local residents, higher prices are more likely than if only local customers are sought.

Amenities

Amenities cover a number of factors that can raise the value-added perceptions of the customer. Most definitely, with all other things being equal between two competing restaurants, one with live entertainment could have a competitive edge over one without it, in terms of customer perceptions of value. Other examples may be free valet parking, complimentary hors d'oeuvres in the lounge, taking reservations, fresh flowers on the table, and house charge accounts. Such extras must eventually be reflected in prices charged.

Product Presentation

This marketing concept proclaims, "Sell the sizzle, not the steak." The product presentation is very important in the patron's value perception. It is often said that "we eat with our eyes." If it looks good the guests are likely to enjoy it. The same concept works for alcoholic beverages. Restaurants spend considerable time and money selecting appropriate china and glassware to "display" food and drink. They do many things to make the product stand out and be noticed by the customer ordering it. Some even turn the presentation into a production that causes other diners in the restaurant to take notice.

The presentation can be enhanced by visual or audio accents. The hot sizzle platter (audio) used by some steak houses can get the patron's attention when the waiter places the steak in front of the guest. A seafood assortment served on a fish-shaped platter is not common and will elicit favorable comments from customers. One restaurant serving "London broil for two" created attention by serving from a cart that was rolled through the dining room. When it reached the table, the maitre d' would hone the carving knife before slicing the London broil. The slices were placed on a super-heated steak liner that sizzled and steamed when a ladle of au jus was added. Since this was the most expensive dinner on the menu, its presentation was deserved.

This type of presentation costs very little in relation to the additional price that can be charged. Another example pertains to alcoholic beverage service. If you have ever been to Pat O'Brien's in the French Quarter of New Orleans or at a luau at the Polynesian Village at Disney World, you probably ordered or saw many unique drinks being served in hollowed out pineapples, melons, and coconuts as well as glasses and mugs of unique shapes and sizes. They were colorfully garnished with fruit, flowers, and bamboo parasols. You probably paid in excess of $4.00 for what amounted to less than $.50 worth of liquor and fruit juice. Nobody complained about the prices because the presentation was unique and not available anywhere but in New Orleans or at Disney World.

Desired Check Average

One cannot rely on what is referred to as the "secondary sales effect" to reach a desired check average if entrees are priced too low (secondary sales effect: sell appetizers, side dishes, and desserts at à la carte prices to build check averages). The reason for this is that although every customer will buy one entree, less than 50 percent will likely order an appetizer, side dish, or dessert. The addition of such add-ons cannot be relied upon to upgrade a $6.95 entree to achieve a $10 average check. Pricing structure should be designed to make it impossible for a customer to spend less than a specified amount.

Price Elasticity

Although related to the aspect of market standing, price elasticity for a product or service is a key element in the pricing decisions. Whenever demand is high (if the restaurant has waiting lines every night), the approach to pricing can be more aggressive than if the operation were one of four similar operations all within a mile of one another. In the latter situation, supply is greater than demand. In such a market, sales volume may be very sensitive to a change in price. (See the discussion on discount pricing later in this chapter.)

However, certain items on the menu can be priced higher because of their uniqueness. Signature items or house specialties can be priced at the higher end of your price range because they are only available at your operation. You create a "monopolistic" pricing situation where you can charge the "highest price the customer is willing to pay." This type of aggressive pricing cannot be employed on highly competitive or common items like Prime rib or sirloin steak. It will be limited to unique appetizers, entrees, and desserts prepared from scratch with the owner's, manager's, or chef's "secret" recipe.

À la Carte and Table d'hôte Pricing

Two approaches to pricing menu items are used in concert with one another. They are à la carte, where each course is priced separately, and table d'hôte or combination pricing, where several courses or accompaniments are included at one price. The price of the items purchased à la carte should always be higher than the combination price for the same entree accompaniments.

Combination pricing is a modified table d'hôte that includes everything from appetizer to dessert and beverage at one price. The more accompaniments or courses, the higher the price that must be charged. It is a pricing strategy that "packages" menu items to make it easier for the customer to order. Most club breakfasts are typical examples of combination pricing. A club breakfast that includes two eggs, bacon, toast, juice, hash browns, and coffee may be offered at $4.95 whereas the same items ordered à la carte may come to $5.25.

Combination pricing also helps to increase the check average. Even fast-food operations that have exclusively priced items on an à la carte basis are promoting "value meals" which combine a hamburger, french fries, and soft drink at a reduced price. À la carte pricing allows the customers to select accompaniments with greater freedom and control the amount they spend.

The classical table d'hôte pricing, appetizer to dessert at one price, is being modified to include fewer courses in order to keep prices down and give customers greater choice. Most patrons do not want a seven-course meal. Most menus will be a mix of à la carte and combination pricing where appetizers, side dishes, and desserts are priced à la carte and the entree, bread, and vegetable or salad are included at one price.

When pricing combinations that provide choices among two or more accompaniments—for example, baked, french fried, or mashed potatoes; French, thousand island, or blue cheese salad dressing—it is much better to price the

Table 6-1 MENU LISTINGS FOR PRICING

OLD WAY		BETTER WAY	
Spaghetti with Meatballs	$3.60	Spaghetti Marinara	$3.50
Spaghetti with Sausage	$3.95		
Spaghetti with Mushrooms	$3.70	Spaghetti with meatballs, sausage,	
Spaghetti with Meat Sauce	$3.80	mushrooms, or meat sauce	$3.95
Spaghetti Marinara	$3.50		
Small Pizza with cheese	$6.95	Small Pizza with cheese	$6.95
Pepperoni	$7.50	One Topping	$7.50
Sausage	$7.75	Two Toppings	$7.75
Peppers and Onions	$7.25		
Anchovies	$7.80		

combination slightly higher and not make additional charges for sour cream or blue cheese dressing. Many times the customer is not informed of the extra charge and is annoyed when the check arrives. In addition, the server may fail to charge for these extras.

The practice of offering several choices at one price is even more practical when pricing such items as pizza toppings and sauces for spaghetti or lasagna. Instead of having five different prices differing by less than $.50 for meatballs, sausage, mushrooms, ground beef, and clam sauce, have one premium price for the choice of any one of them.

Most pizza restaurants list prices according to the number of toppings and allow the customer to select any combination from the full offerings. There is rarely a need for price differentiation to be less than $.25 to $.50 between certain combinations of accompaniments. This is especially true when servers must price each item manually and memorize prices (see Table 6-1).

The food cost range may vary 1 to 7 percent, depending on the topping at the single price, but the sales mix will result in a food cost reflecting a weighted average of all items. The item with the highest cost will likely set the upper limit on the price to charge, but if that particular item is ordered only 2 to 3 percent of the time and the lowest cost item is the most popular, the average single price charged can be lower than the upper limit item would be on an à la carte basis.

CHANGING MENU PRICES

When cost of ingredients or other expenses increase, the operator must adjust menu prices upward. However, a price increase can often result in an immediate drop in the demand for an item and generally, as average check moves up, the number of meals served begins to level off and sometimes begins to decline. The operator cannot always pass on cost increases to the customer in the form of higher prices. This is especially true in fast-food and moderate-priced food-service operations. The higher average check white tablecloth restaurants seem to show less sensitivity to price increases because their clientele are in higher income brackets.

Changes in restaurant prices should always be done with merchandising skill and finesse. The less attention called to price increases the better, and the less chance of adverse customer responses. The following suggestions are offered as ways to disguise the fact that prices have been raised (Pavesic, 1988).

1. Use increments of .25, .50, .75, and .95 for the digits to the right of the decimal point. An item raised in $.25 increments from $4.25 to $4.50 is less likely to stand out and be noticed by the customers.

2. Never raise prices when you change the design of the menu. Raise prices on the last reprint of the old menu. Patrons will be more price conscious with a new menu because they expect prices to increase and will therefore be more sensitive to changes.

3. Never cross out old prices and write over them with a pen. However, this would be effective if prices were lowered, as a bargain is implied when a higher price is crossed out.

4. Hold off as long as possible on price increases that change the dollars digit (e.g., $9.95 to $10.25), as these changes are most likely to be noticed.

5. If a price increase cannot be avoided, consider increasing portions or accompaniments to create a "new" and "improved" item and give it a new name. In this way, one provides "added value" that becomes a trade-off for the price increase.

6. Reposition items that have been noticeably increased to less visible parts of the menu and emphasize lower priced substitutes in their place.

7. Consider reducing portions or accompaniments in lieu of raising prices. This may be appropriate strategy in highly competitive markets that are price sensitive. Many operators have dropped either the vegetable or salad accompaniments in lieu of raising prices.

8. Never raise prices across the board. It is better to raise only a few items with each reprinting of the menu. It is also better to increase popular items by a small amount than to try to recover costs by sizable increases in marginally popular items.

9. Items with volatile and unpredictable costs should be listed as "market priced" so prices can be verbally quoted. Remember that prices of à la carte accompaniments must be adjusted to remain in line with combination prices. The à la carte prices should always be higher than the same items priced together.

10. Do not align prices in a continuous pattern and never list menu items in price sequence. Doing either makes price dominate and biases the purchase decision. The most commonly used menu format aligns prices in a straight line down the right side of a column or page (see Figure 6-1). The price range can be quickly determined and price comparisons easily made. Descriptive menu copy that has been written to "sell" the customer on each respective item may be overlooked. If this occurs, the price becomes the major determinant in the purchase decision. To overcome such shortcomings, do not align prices. Instead, place the price immediately after the last word in the menu description. The price will not be placed in any set location and the focus is transferred to the "sell" copy (see Figure 6-2).

SPECIALTIES

Veal Francese   **20.95**
A Trotters tradition with lemon-butter sauce

Veal and Mushrooms   **19.95**
Tender milk-fed veal sauteed in fresh cream with mushrooms and herbs and served with fettuccine

Sauteed Medallions of Veal   **19.95**
With tomato and basil cream sauce

Calves Liver   **13.95**
Thinly cut and sauteed with bacon and raspberry-vinegar sauce

Long Island Duckling   **15.95**
Roasted and grilled with thin pancakes; served with a black currant sauce

Rack of Spring Lamb   **20.95**
Roasted with an herb breading and served with a rich brown sauce

FIGURE 6-1   Traditional alignment of prices.

POISSONS ET CRUSTACÉS

NORWEGIAN SALMON STEAK BARBECUED ORIENTAL STYLE
With Sesame Seeds, Ginger, and Garlic   17.75

DOVER SOLE FILLETS POACHED IN SAUVIGNON BLANC
With Shrimp, Mussels, and Mushrooms   20.00

GULF SNAPPER FILLET
In Romaine Lettuce with Beaujolais Sauce and Mediterranean Eggplant   18.00

DOVER SOLE FILLETS SAUTEED GOLDEN BROWN
"Noisette Butter" and Lemon   20.00

SWORDFISH PICCATA
With Linguini, Spinach, and Tomato Concasse   17.75

SEA SCALLOPS WITH LEEK SAUCE
In Phylio Crust   18.00

FIGURE 6-2   Recommended placement of prices.

Although the concept of primacy and recency says to list the higher-priced and higher-profit items first or last in a list to improve the likelihood of their being ordered, it is not recommended to list them in perfect price order. Customers may never read past a certain price point and usually the lower-priced entrees will dominate, dropping the check average. When prices are listed in a mixed (not random) order, there is a greater likelihood that the customer will read through the entire list of selections before making a decision. Some operators of formal dining establishments, particularly private clubs and hotel dining rooms, will omit the price completely on all but the host or hostess menu, and where price is shown it is written out in words rather than arabic numerals (e.g. twenty-one dollars rather than $21.00). These practices are only appropriate in high average check operations, and arabic numerals will be used in the majority of restaurants.

DISCOUNT PRICING

In an attempt to increase volume, many operators have employed some form of discount pricing strategy. The National Restaurant Association reported that 56 percent of its members polled were using price or coupon discounts (Haugh, 1983). Discounts are being renewed so often that regular menu prices have almost become meaningless. The increasing use of discount promotions would seem to endorse its effectiveness, but many operators remain unconvinced that discounting is cost-effective. Many fear that repeated use of discounting erodes pricing policy, detracts from one's image, and attracts fickle bargain hunters by "buying" their loyalty.

There are two considerations with discounting: its appropriateness or effectiveness as a strategy for increasing traffic, attracting new clientele, and introducing new products; and the consequences discounting has on overall financial results. Profit margins are lowered with discounting and may be too low to cover costs.

The use of discounting assumes that demand is elastic or price sensitive. The philosophy of discounting states that reduced prices will increase demand. Failure to realize sufficient increases in sales volume to offset the lower margins of each discounted transaction can have detrimental effects on financial outcomes.

The increased redemption rates necessary for high value discounts (e.g. two-for-one) may not be realized. The higher the discount and the greater the percentage of discounted transactions, the more sales volume must rise to achieve the same return realized prior to the discount (Pavesic, 1985, pp 67–73).

Sales volume must improve if the costs of discounting are to be recovered. The break-even point is increased, because discounting increases the food cost percentage. This variable cost increase can be offset only by a decrease in the percentage of fixed costs, which in turn can occur only if sales volume increases.

The operator needs to examine the impact of any given discount on profit margins and check averages. Each discount has a "trigger point" of increased volume that must be reached to offset the reduced margins of each discounted sale. A simple calculation, using a variation of the traditional break-even formula, can be used to estimate the approximate increase in sales required to reach the "trigger point."

The operator first needs to estimate an increase in sales and set a discount rate that is appropriate to existing competitive conditions, historical sales trends, and realistic redemption rates. Before discounting can be successful in a financial sense, overall sales must increase so that the percentage of fixed costs declines more than variable cost percentage increases.

The chances of realizing an increase in overall profit from a discount promotion is greatly improved if the business is already operating at or above break-even. Because the gross margin per sale is reduced by discounting, an operation that is below break-even will take longer (more sales) to reach break-even.

For example, assume that "buy-one-get-a-second-at-half-price" is contemplated. Start with an estimate of the number of discounted entrees you expect to serve. If you assume that 10 percent of the entrees served will be discounted, the equivalent of a 5 percent reduction in sales revenue will result.

> 10% of entrees @ 50% discount
> 90% of entrees @ 100% (no discount)
> $0.10 (.50) + 0.90 (1.00) = 0.95$ or 95%
> $100\% - 95\% = 5\%$ reduction

Table 6-2 shows the break-even point without the discount. Theoretically, the 5 percent reduction in sales would cause the food cost to increase by 2 percent. Instead of $1000 in sales, only $950 would be received, and if the same

Table 6-2 BREAK-EVEN WITHOUT DISCOUNT

	Amount	Percent
Sales	$1,000*	100
Less Variable Costs:		
Food Cost	(380)	(38)
Operating Expenses	(160)	(16)
	(540)	(54)
Contribution Margin	$460	46
Less Fixed Costs		
Labor Cost	(280)	(28)
Occupational Expenses	(180)	(18)
	(460)	(46)
Net Profit (Loss)	$0	0

*Break-Even Sales = $460/0.46 = $1000

Formula: $\dfrac{\text{Fixed Cost \$}}{\text{Contribution Margin (100\% − Variable Cost 54\%)}}$

number of dinners are served, the total food cost would still be $380. The new food cost percentage would therefore be 40 percent, not 38 percent.

Table 6-3 shows how break-even is affected by the discount. Assume that although customer traffic may increase slightly, total sales do not increase. If all other costs remain constant, a loss of 2 percent will be incurred. Realistically, promotion costs would likely increase expenses and result in a greater loss than 2 percent.

Total variable costs have increased from 54 to 56 percent. Because sales did not increase, the percentage of fixed costs remained the same. However, you can estimate the approximate increase in sales necessary to be no worse off than before the discount. Table 6-4 presents the figures in statement format.

The calculation for the "trigger point" is simply,

$$\frac{1}{1 - \text{Var. Cost \% with Discount}} \times (\text{Change in Variable Cost \%})$$

Table 6-3 LOSS AFTER DISCOUNT WITHOUT SALES INCREASE

	Amount	Percent
Sales	$1,000	100
Less Variable Costs:		
Food Cost	(400)	(40)
Operating Expenses	(160)	(16)
	(560)	(56)
Contribution Margin	$440	44
Less Fixed Costs		
Labor Cost	(280)	(28)
Occupational Expenses	(180)	(18)
	(460)	(46)
Net Profit (Loss)	$(20)	(2)

Table 6-4 BREAK-EVEN WITH DISCOUNT

	Amount	Percent
Sales	$1,045	100
Less Variable Costs:		
Food Cost	(418)	(40)
Operating Expenses	(167)	(16)
	(585)	(56)
Contribution Margin	$460	44
Less Fixed Costs		
Labor Cost	(280)	(27)
Occupational Expenses	(180)	(17)
TOTAL	(460)	(44)
Net Profit (Loss)	$0	0

The variable costs before and after the discount are 54 and 56 percent, respectively. Substituting into the equation:

$$\frac{1}{1-.56}(.56-.54) = \frac{1}{.44}(.02) = 2.273\,(.02) = 0.04546 \text{ or } 4.546\%$$

$$0.04546\,(\$1000) = \$45.46 \text{ increase in sales to } \$1045.46$$

Therefore, the 2 percent increase in variable costs can be offset if sales increase by 4.546 percent, because fixed cost percentage will be reduced from 46 to 44 percent. The sales increase can be expressed in customer counts by simply dividing sales by the average check.

The check average before the discount was $10 ($1000/100 covers). If 10 percent of the entrees were discounted by 50 percent, the new check average would be approximately $9.50 ($950/100 covers). Therefore, an additional 10 covers must be served in order to break even when the discount is running ($1045/$9.50 = 110 covers).

The operation would need to serve more than 110 covers before any incremental profit would be realized. If the promotion increased customer traffic and sales improved by 20 percent, the financial results would resemble that shown in Table 6-5, assuming that only 10 percent of the entrees were discounted.

Although the contribution margin remained at 44 percent, a sales increase of 20 percent reduces the percentage of fixed costs by 5.7 percent, to 38.3 percent. It is important to understand that the greater the value of the discount and the higher the percentage of discounted transactions, the greater the resulting increase in the variable food cost percentage and the higher the break-even point will go.

Table 6-5 PROFIT AFTER DISCOUNT WITH 20 PERCENT INCREASE IN SALES

	Amount	Percent
Sales	$1,200	100.0
Less Variable Costs:		
Food Cost	(480)	(40.0)
Operating Expenses	(192)	(16.0)
	(672)	(56)
Contribution Margin	$528	44.0
Less Fixed Costs		
Labor Cost	(280)	(23.3)
Occupational Expenses	(180)	(15.0)
TOTAL	(460)	(38.3)
Net Profit (Loss)	$68	5.7

In the example given, only 10 percent of the meals were discounted and food cost increased by 2 percent. If 15 percent of the meals were discounted, the food cost would increase to 41 percent.

$$15\% \text{ @ } 50\% \text{ discount}$$
$$85\% \text{ @ } 100\% \text{ (no discount)}$$
$$0.15 \, (.50) + .85 \, (1.00) = 0.925 \text{ or } 92.5\%$$

This is theoretically equivalent to a reduction in sales of 7.5 percent. Sales would therefore be $925 with a food cost of $380 or 41 percent. Food cost will continue to increase as the percentage of discounted meals rises. Having a dining room full of customers redeeming coupons could be financially disastrous. There needs to be a substantial number of customers paying full price along with the bargain seekers to "soften" the effects of the discount.

Further, if a "buy one, get one free" discount were employed, the consequences would be as follows: Assuming that 20 percent of the meals are discounted and 100 covers are served, food cost would increase from the original 38 percent to 47.5 percent. This would require that sales increase by 26 percent just to break even. This requires an additional $260 in sales and 58 more covers to reach the "trigger point."

$$20\% \text{ @ } \text{Free} = 0$$
$$80\% \text{ @ } 100\% = .80$$
$$100\% - 80\% = 20\% \text{ reduction in sales}$$
$$\$1000 - \$200 = \$800/100 \text{ covers} = \$8.00 \text{ average check}$$
$$\text{Food Cost } \% = \$380/\$800 = 47.5\%$$

$$\frac{1}{1 - .635} \, (9.5\%) = \frac{1}{.365} \, (0.095) = 2.74 \, (0.095) = 0.26 \text{ or } 26\%$$

$$\$1260/\$8.00 = 158 \text{ covers}$$

Using this information, the operator can examine actual cover counts to see if the promotion is drawing enough additional business. If the promotion does not draw more than 58 additional covers, it should be adjusted or discontinued because the operation will be in worse financial condition than it was before the discount.

The trigger point is not an absolute number and will vary up or down depending on the percentage of discounted meals served and the sales mix of accompanying items sold. Studies have revealed that too large or too small a discount does not pay off relative to additional sales, customer counts, and profits. Overdiscounting can cause profits to be reduced, even with increased traffic and sales. The amount of the discount is important to optimizing sales increases and profit return. Small price reductions do not stimulate traffic, and overdiscounting does not bring in significantly more traffic than slightly smaller discounts would have captured ("Restaurant Technology," 1984).

It is therefore logical to conclude that every promotion offering some discount has a "relevant" range such that the optimum increase in sales allows the operator to offset the increased costs and improve on the return that would have been realized had the discount promotion not been used. Using the simple calculation, one can estimate the increases in traffic needed to make the discount pay off in the financial sense. If the increases are unrealistic, given competitive and historical redemption rates, the discount can be altered to improve the likelihood of financial success.

Discounting prices is therefore a somewhat risky pricing strategy. Additional sales cannot be guaranteed, especially in markets experiencing flat or declining customer counts. The additional cost incurred in offering a discount raises the break-even point. Therefore, the amount of the discount must be adjusted to achieve financial benefits that can be seen in the form of bottom line profit return.

PRICING IN PRIVATE CLUBS

Pricing menu items in private clubs is largely influenced by the markup limits mandated by the club's board of directors. Prices charged by clubs may be somewhat lower than prices for comparable items offered by commercial restaurants, and food cost percentages in clubs may sometimes exceed 50 percent.

In those clubs that desire just to break even on their food and beverage operations, price markup will cover only raw food cost and labor. Some may include an additional 3 to 5 percent markup as a "safety factor" to cover cost overrides. To avoid having to assess members if costs are not covered, clubs charge members monthly food and beverage minimums to cover fixed overhead expenses. Therefore, the budget and policies of each club's board of directors will determine the markup on food and beverage items.

PRICING IN NONPROFIT OPERATIONS

Many industrial or institutional food services set prices on the basis of a minimum markup to cover costs. The rationale is that there is an average cost incurred in serving every patron and if this average cost is recovered on every sale, break-even is assured. The allocation of cost is based on dividing total costs by the number of customers. However, if customer counts are less than projected, costs will not be covered unless prices are increased. This pricing method is used in state and federally subsidized convalescent homes, where residents are charged a daily rate for meals regardless of their individual dietary requirements. In commercial operations, a minimum cover charge would be required.

Nonprofit operations do not utilize cost percentages for control and pricing the way commercial operations use them. Most often, institutional food services operate on budgeted cash allowances per meal, per person, per bed, or per day. For example, a nursing home may have a yearly allowance of $2400 per person to feed and care for the patient. This allowance may be allocated as follows: food, 50 percent, labor, 30 percent, supplies and overhead, 20 percent. This breaks down to $6.58 per day, with a food portion of $3.28 for meals and snacks.

Determining prices in nonprofit or subsidized operations primarily involves recovering costs or staying within a budgeted amount per day, per person, or per meal. This approach is taken by public schools and state-run institutions such as prisons and nursing homes, and in some cases by employee food services operated by business and industry.

Cost markup varies because the cost may be covered all or in part by federal or state funds or by company subsidy. The patrons pay only a portion of cost, as with school lunch programs and employee cafeterias. Generally, pricing in nonprofit operations involves selling at cost and there is no need to include margin for profit in the price. At most, they are required to stay within a budget and perhaps add a small allowance above cost as a safety factor to make up for fluctuations in costs and volume.

Covering costs becomes critical to keeping within budgets. Accurate cost information must be assembled and updated to be sure that costs remain in line. Monitoring of standardized purchase specifications, recipes, and portions are critical elements in nonprofit operations.

In some institutions, a cost allowance is established based on specific quantities of foods from different food groups allocated per day or per meal. The allowance is based on providing a balanced diet from the four food groups. The cost allowance per person is determined after combining the items from each food group making up the entire meal. Our armed forces operate on a system referred to as a "ration allowance." In many state tax-supported institutions, such as hospitals and prisons, ration systems are used.

Ration allowances are determined by standards developed by the United States Department of Agriculture based on current prices of commodities. There are three levels for these allowances—low, moderate, and liberal—based on the quantities needed by elementary school children, elderly patients, or military personnel. When a ration system is used, only the cost of food is used to establish allowances per person. Other costs must be kept separate (e.g., labor, overhead).

EMPLOYEE MEALS

Policy regarding employee meal allowances is determined by each operation. There is no requirement to provide free meals to employees in the wage and hour law. Employers may charge employees full price, discount meals, or give them away without charge. The wage and hour laws do allow operators who provide free meals to take a credit against the minimum wage in an amount equal to the reasonable cost of the food and beverage provided.

Employee meals are often considered a fringe benefit, and the cost is included as a payroll related expense. Employee meals must be monitored because the food used can account for over 2 percent of the cost of food consumed. Employees are often limited as to what they can eat for free, and additional charges are made if they choose to order from the regular menu. Regardless, some type of employee meal policy needs to be made, for it is generally expected that meals will be part of the overall compensation.

PRICING CATERING

Since caterers often provide more than just the food and beverage, price is determined more by the perceived value for the management of an entire event and is not a simple markup of food cost. In fact, pricing one's services too low may result in lost sales.

The right price matches the customer's perceived value. Cost is merely a minimum that helps you determine whether you can afford to sell the function for the value the client assigns to it. Never forget that catering is a personal service; too often one reduces the services to a list of groceries. You must understand your clients' needs. Ask them to describe the party they have in mind; that is, buffet or sit-down dinner, self-service or servers, silver chafing dishes or ceramic bowls. Once you get an idea of their budget, you can offer a price range. Their reaction to your price range will be an indication of their interest.

Your objective is to get past negotiating over price. Once they feel that you are going to provide an affair that will satisfy their guests, price will not be as much a factor. In pricing catering, determine what value the clients place on your services and give them their money's worth. The minimum price can be assumed to be 100 percent markup, or double your total costs. But remember, this is a minimum price. Sell the party for what it is worth to the customer—what the market will bear. Other caterers may sell it cheaper, but they may not provide a better catered event. If the customers are satisfied, they will feel that any price was worth it (Mossman, 1987).

Once a menu has been initially priced, there will come a time when prices must be raised. It is not an easy task for management because of the likelihood of adverse customer reactions. In setting price strategies, pay attention to consumer price sensitivity and changing customer demands and expectations. Current food service wisdom says that caterers must offer strong price-value to capture consumers.

In past years, caterers set menu price points to cover food costs and achieve a certain profit margin. This decision was tempered according to what the competition was doing. However, today caterers must study customer demographics and market trends, and must give more thought to the wants and needs of their clients. In maturing and saturated markets, strategically set price points are critical to building and holding market shares.

For every caterer who prices the menu by marking up cost, there is one who says prices are market driven. Realistically, it is a combination of the two, but more and more market pressures and not cost pressures are driving menu prices. To achieve the right mix of prices, caterers must be willing to adjust prices up and down as needed.

THE TEXAS RESTAURANT ASSOCIATION (TRA) PRICING METHOD

Most menu pricing methodologies covered in books and articles on the subject are cost driven or are intuitive, subjective, and arbitrary. Pricing must be carried out with the ultimate objective of planning for a profit, and costs must be covered; that is a must. The question is, however, how much over cost should one charge? Charging too much drives down demand and sales while charging too little sacrifices marginal income.

The first step in pricing out a menu is to get a firm grasp of the cost structure. Food cost and profit standards for any given type of restaurant cannot be based solely on such factors as industry averages or established by simply copying a competitor's prices. In the early 1960s, a group of restaurateurs in Texas developed a method that remains an efficient way to assess cost structure implications prior to pricing decisions. No two restaurants are exactly alike in all costs, even if they are chain affiliated. Therefore, if the food cost objectives of two operations were set at the same percentage, and even if this food cost were achieved, there is still no guarantee that bottom line profit and return on investment would be the same.

The reason for this is that every restaurant operation has distinctly different and unique costs, investment, and financial idiosyncracies that will cause cost standards and profit goals to vary. This is the reason why copying the budget of another operator will not achieve the same results. In addition, due to different menu sales mixes, food cost objectives cannot be the same. Yet multiple unit operators continue to apply a single food cost standard to all units under their supervision.

The Texas Restaurant Association (TRA) method answers the question, "What does the food cost need to be in order to achieve the desired profit?" The TRA methodology works equally well with proforma financial information of proposed properties and with existing operations.

The TRA methodology follows the identical procedures explained in Chapter 3 on the discussion of *maximum allowable food cost*. Start with a realistic estimate of costs and revenues if working with a proforma. Actual costs should be expressed in dollar values rather than percentages. Do not heavily rely on industry averages; instead, call insurance agents, utility departments, and the telephone company, and get cost figures based on actual billings in the market of the proposed building and property. Labor costs can be determined by preparing a manpower schedule based on staffing requirements and the going wage rates. Most operating costs have a large "fixed" portion and are therefore better expressed in dollars than in percentages. Be liberal when estimating expenses; you are better off overstating costs. After all costs have been estimated, impute a minimum profit expectation. Be reasonable; don't set it unrealistically high, as it will impact the food cost figure. Food cost is the only expense that is not estimated. It is calculated after other costs and profit have been projected.

The next step is estimating sales revenues for a comparable accounting period that relates to the cost projections. Be conservative in the sales forecasts; in fact, show three different sales levels—the best or highest volume expected, the worst, and a realistic level somewhere between the high and the low. However, for purposes of the proforma, use the lowest sales projections to determine the food cost percentage.

Sales are projected based on estimating check averages and customer counts by meal periods and days of the week. If there are three meal periods per day using different menus, project sales of each separately. Once sales are projected, convert expenses to percentages of sales, add the profit percentage based on the minimum sales projections, and subtract this total from 100 percent. The difference is the food cost percentage objective used in pricing decisions. To achieve the profit objective, food and operating cost percentages must stay within the expense projections. Compare these figures to industry averages to see if they are in line. In reality, actual revenues should be higher and expenses lower than the projections, not the other way around.

As an example, assume that the following figures have been derived from an existing operation. Start with an unbiased accounting period, one that is neither too high nor too low in sales. A six-month or year-to-date average can be used. Separate costs into two categories: labor, and all other operating expenses including controllable and fixed expenses but *excluding* food cost. Profit must also be expressed and is a critical element in determining the food cost goal. All expenses must be expressed as dollars initially and then converted to percentages of the sales for the same accounting period. Assume that the following totals were calculated for the accounting period used:

Sales Revenue	$30,000	
Labor Cost	$ 6,900	23%
Overhead	$ 7,500	25%
Profit	$ 3,000	10%
Total Cost and Profit w/o food cost =	$17,400	58%

$$100\% - 58\% = 42\%$$
$$42\% \times \$30,000 = \$12,600$$
Proof: $12,600 + $17,400 = $30,000

This tells us that we must achieve a food cost objective of 42 percent or less to realize a 10 percent profit. Because these expenses are unique to this particular operation, the food cost goal is equally unique and demonstrates why this exercise must be performed on an individual unit basis. The computed food cost percentage becomes the basis for pricing the menu. Every item cannot be marked up the same amount. The TRA uses subjective markups based on such factors as menu category (i.e., appetizers, entrees, and desserts), the popularity of the item, its perishability, and preparation requirements. This is where objectivity ends and the "art" enters into the menu pricing decision.

The TRA menu pricing methodology is demonstrated in the following example. Assume that we are concerned with two menu items, one a half of broiled chicken and the other an 8-ounce top sirloin steak. The food costs, including salad, potato, and bread, are $1.75 for the chicken and $4.50 for the steak.

The TRA arrives at the initial price by dividing raw food cost by a desired food cost percentage. We previously calculated the TRA desired food cost percentage to be 42 percent (100% − 58%); therefore, the starting point for pricing the chicken would be $4.16 ($1.75 divided by .42) and $10.71 for the steak ($4.50 divided by .42). Remember, these are just starting points for the menu price, as the pricing decision cannot be exclusively cost driven.

Pricing to achieve a 42 percent food cost should return a profit of 10 percent. If you can charge more and achieve a lower food cost percentage, profit will increase. If the chicken is plain broiled or barbecued, a minimum price must be charged. However, if it is "honey basted" or "mesquite broiled," it may get a premium price. You may further adjust the price upward to close the spread between the highest and lowest priced entrees. The competitive position in the marketplace may allow you to charge the highest the customer is willing to pay, or it may require a price below the competition. The price must be tempered with subjective, competitive, and economic considerations.

The steak, initially priced at $10.71, may not be acceptable in the marketplace. If the operation is not noted for its steaks and has them on the menu to accommodate a small percentage of the customers, it should not price them at the high end of the market. In such a case, market position and competition may require lowering the price to $8.95. This would increase the food cost to over 50 percent, eight points higher than our 42 percent target. However, we may not be competitive at $10.71 and need to set the price on something other than the food cost percentage; for example, the gross profit or contribution margin. It represents the difference between the menu price and the raw food cost. In this case it is $4.45 for the steak ($8.95 − $4.50) and $2.75 for the chicken ($4.50 − $1.75). Although the food cost is higher on the steak, it brings in $1.70 more in gross profit. We are reminded that we bank dollars, not percentages, and are likely to sell more steaks at $8.95 than at $10.71.

The TRA methodology recognizes that the menu price is determined primarily by the market. However, a higher markup is taken when the risk of a loss or spoilage increases. Regardless of this logic, the customer will determine the correct price. The pricing methodology cannot force a food cost percentage or gross profit by charging a price that the customer does not deem fair and acceptable. You may employ low markups on high-cost items to stimulate sales, and although the food cost percentage may be higher, as with the steak, hopefully the gross profit will make up for it. Fast-selling items can have only moderate markups, as the volume allows for sizable gross profit return. High markups can be taken on specialty items that are unique to the operation, as there is little competition and one enjoys a monopolistic position.

In summary, the procedures for using the TRA menu pricing methodology are as follows.

1. Select an unbiased accounting period and divide expenses into the following categories:
   Labor and related expenses
   Overhead (which will include controllable as well as fixed expenses, but without food cost)
   Profit (minimum profit expectations)
2. Express all costs and profit as dollar values (e.g., labor $6900, overhead $7500, profit $3000, sales $30,000).
3. Convert dollar values to percentages by dividing by sales (e.g., labor 23%, overhead 25%, profit 10%, total 58%).
4. Total the percentages to arrive at total operating costs and profit without food costs. Subtract from 100% to determine the TRA food cost percentage (100% − 58% = 42%).
5. Divide the raw food cost of each menu item by the TRA food cost percentage to arrive at the initial price (e.g., chicken: $1.75/0.42 = $4.16; steak: $4.50/0.42 = $10.71).
6. Adjust the price upward or downward depending on such factors as perishability, popularity, uniqueness, and demand.

The most important aspect of the TRA methodology is that it forces the operators to study their true operating costs. The figures used in the calculation must be realistic, accurate, and reflect the operation's unique financial and competitive position. Covering costs is a basic tenet of any business; however, in addition to the raw food cost, prices must reflect the risks of doing business and the nature of the product itself. For example, more must be charged if the product is delicate or highly perishable and the risk of loss or spoilage is great.

The old saying, "Volume hides a multitude of ills," refers to spoilage, waste, and operating inefficiencies and their effects on bottom line profits. The higher the total sales volume, the lower the markup has to be because such "ills" are absorbed in the marginal profits realized. The other side of the coin is that low volume requires higher markups because the bottom line cannot absorb much loss. Each item in the menu must be assessed and priced according to uniqueness, popularity, and whether you want to price at the high or low end of the market. No simple quantitative formula can be used in menu pricing. A proper and effective pricing policy results from management's understanding of costs, sales, volume, profit, competition, and customer demand.

PRIME COST PRICING METHODOLOGY

Another major cost-driven menu pricing philosophy states that the cost of preparation labor must be added to the raw food cost of all menu items made from scratch. In some instances the cost of direct preparation labor can exceed the cost of the ingredients. St. Louis restaurateur Harry Pope is credited with introducing this pricing theory. He noted that certain items on his menu had considerable labor involved in their preparation. The conventional method of marking up only raw food cost often omitted a significant part of the cost incurred in making an item ready for service to the customer.

The theory of including direct labor with raw food cost is referred to as the *prime food cost pricing methodology*. Direct labor is precisely defined as that labor incurred as a result of making an item from scratch on the premises. Direct labor is labor specifically involved in the "preparation" of menu items (e.g., butchering meats, vegetable cutting, and in-house baking). The operation must pay the meat cutter, salad maker, and baker because the restaurant manufactures its own products in-house. If the operation were to purchase precut steaks, premade salads and dressing, and baked goods from a commercial bakery, it would not employ or schedule labor to prepare such items from scratch (see Figure 6-3).

However, the price of convenience foods (items that are purchased partially processed) will cost the operator more per pound or unit of purchase, because the price paid reflects both raw food and labor for processing. Therefore,

---

PRIME COST = RAW FOOD COST + DIRECT LABOR
Direct Labor: Any labor incurred as a result of making an item from scratch on premises

Direct Labor	Indirect Labor
Prepreparation	Bus Staff
Meat Cutting	Dishwashers
Baking	Wait Staff
Vegetable/Salad Preparation	Hostess
	Cashiers
	Line Servers

FIGURE 6-3   Prime cost.

both cost aspects of items prepared on premises should be considered when determining markups. Examples of items that incur more labor costs than food costs are homemade soups, pastries, decorative garnishes, canapes, and hors d'oeuvres. Main entrees requiring cleaning, peeling, cutting, breading, partial cooking, or other time-consuming processing add a labor element that needs to be reflected in the total cost of the item.

Prime cost methodology, when used, raises the markup on items with high food costs and little direct labor and lowers the markup on items that have low food costs and considerable direct labor. Convenience foods, with built-in labor costs, will not be marked up as high as they would with the more conventional Texas Restaurant Association method because the cost of the labor is already reflected in the higher purchase price.

In order to assign labor costs to the specific menu items causing the labor to be incurred in the first place, you must first divide your menu items into two categories, those items needing direct preparation labor and those that have little or no direct labor. Labor that cannot be directly charged to specific menu items is designated "indirect" labor cost and is allocated evenly across all menu items, just like overhead expenses. Wait staff, line servers, and cooks used to "finish cook" items are not direct labor. Remember, direct labor is essentially initial production labor or preprep labor.

The cost of this direct labor can be determined by having employees note the amount of time they are involved in direct preparation activities each day. Not all of a kitchen worker's time will be classified as direct labor. For example, the head cook may cut steaks only 20 percent of the time; the rest of the time he or she may be working on the serving line plating food or finishing cooking entrees. Only the time used to cut the steaks is considered in prime food cost.

By noting the amount of time an employee spends in the preparation of a recipe, the labor cost per unit produced can be determined. Include the time it takes to assemble ingredients, utensils, and equipment. This is referred to as the "get-ready" stage. Washing, peeling, cutting, trimming, weighing, mixing, breading, and preliminary cooking such as parboiling and blanching must be considered direct labor. Do not forget to include the cleanup process that concludes the task. Once the time has been determined, the labor cost can be quickly calculated by multiplying the hours by the hourly wage. This labor cost is then divided by the number of pies, salads, or steaks produced to determine the labor cost per unit. When this is added to the raw food cost, prime food cost will be determined.

If a restaurant elects not to recognize the direct labor aspect in menu pricing, then the cost of steak cutting, baking, or salad preparation will be charged to menu items that do not benefit from the labor. Spaghetti, baked chicken, Prime rib, and other items with little or no direct labor must carry an unfair burden of recovering the expense of the meat cutter. Prime cost allocates the direct labor incurred to the item that caused it to be incurred in the first place.

Those that argue against prime cost may assume that direct labor will be covered by spreading the cost throughout the entire menu sales mix. However, smart operators quickly realize that they are not assured of selling one spaghetti for every steak sold. They recognize the benefit of a method that equitably costs out and prices each item to obtain the necessary return.

Pricing the steak with the prime cost method requires the inclusion of the direct labor element with the raw food cost. The operating budget is the same as that given in the TRA example. The first step is to calculate the portion of the total labor expense that is direct labor.

Assume that the total labor hours worked per week are 100, and of that 25 hours are required to trim and cut steaks. Assume that the total payroll is $500 and the average hourly wage is $5 per hour ($500/100 hours). The direct labor cost would then be $125 ($5 × 25 hours). If 500 steaks were produced during this time period, the direct labor cost per steak would be $.25 ($125/500 steaks). If the steaks were purchased precut, we would not have to schedule the meat cutter for the 25 hours. In the TRA example, we considered only raw food cost and made no distinction between direct and indirect labor.

The prime cost of the steak is $4.50 + $.25, or $4.75. The chicken is not priced with the prime food cost methodology because it does not require any direct labor to prepare and serve. The amount of direct labor, $125, represents one fourth of the total labor, or 25 percent ($125/500). Since a portion of the total labor cost is added to the raw food cost, do not use the formula, Raw Food Cost divided by Desired Food Cost Percentage, to arrive at a starting point for pricing.

If one divides the prime cost by the TRA calculated food cost, the markup double-charges for the direct labor. If one fourth of total labor is direct labor, represented by the $.25 per steak, the total labor cost percentage needs to be reduced to reflect this fact. The remaining three fourths, or 75 percent of the total labor, is indirect labor that is allocated across all menu items. The direct labor will be added only to steaks cut on the premises. Figure 6-4 shows all the costs in a pie chart format.

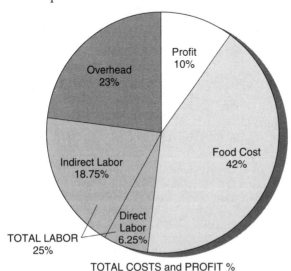

FIGURE 6-4   Prime food cost.

The total labor percentage must be reduced by the direct labor portion of one fourth of 25 percent, or 6.25 percent. Therefore, the indirect labor portion is 18.75 percent (25% − 6.25%). The prime food cost percentage can be determined by adding the indirect labor percentage to overhead and profit and subtracting this total from 100 percent (18.75% + 23% + 10% = 51.75%). The prime food cost percentage is therefore 48.25 percent (100% − 51.75%).

The prime cost price, $9.84, is calculated by dividing prime food cost by the prime food cost percentage ($4.75/48.25% = $9.84). When you examine the difference between the TRA and prime cost methodology in pricing the steak, the prime cost method needs to generate only $2.07 in sales for every dollar of prime cost ($1.00/48.25%), compared to $2.38 for every dollar of raw food cost with the TRA or conventional markup theory ($1.00/42%).

In summary, the steps in determining the prime cost markup are:

1. Determine the percentage of total labor that is direct labor. ($125/500 = 25%)
2. Multiply the total labor percentage by the percentage of direct labor. (0.25 × 0.25 = 6.25%)
3. Subtract the percentage of direct labor from total labor to determine indirect labor. (25% − 6.25% = 18.75%)
4. Add the indirect labor to overhead and profit and subtract the sum from 100 percent to get the prime food cost percent. (18.75% + 23% + 10% = 51.75%; 100% − 51.75% = 48.25%)
5. Divide the prime food cost by the prime food cost percentage to arrive at a starting point for price evaluation of the item. ($4.75/48.25% = $9.84)
6. Adjust the price upward or downward depending on competitive and economic factors.

Since the chicken does not require direct labor, it is priced using the TRA or conventional markup with appropriate adjustments up or down based on product uniqueness and the relevant indirect cost factors that may apply.

BY-THE-OUNCE PRICING FOR SALAD AND FOOD BARS

A new pricing strategy is being tried in operations offering self-service salad and food bars. Restaurants are experimenting with pricing *by the ounce* as an alternative to the traditional per-person price for all you can eat. One of the ideas they are testing is whether pricing by the ounce will increase the marketing value of all-you-can-eat promotions to nutrition- and diet-conscious patrons. In addition, all-you-can-eat operations that do not permit carryouts or doggy bags for leftovers can do so with pricing by the ounce. With the increasing demand for takeout service, by-the-ounce pricing would allow operations to offer the same price value to both carryout and dine-in customers. Restaurants can basically charge customers for only what they take.

Arriving at a by-the-ounce price is complex because items offered range from inexpensive croutons and bean sprouts to the more costly chicken and salmon salad. A random check of operations pricing by the ounce revealed prices ranging from $.15 to $.28 per ounce. The per-person prices for all you can eat ranged from a low of $1.99 for a basic salad bar to double digits for elaborate buffets with meat and seafood entrees. How does one arrive at a price that is acceptable to the customer's price-value perceptions and the operator's profit and food cost goals?

The most widespread method used today for pricing all-you-can-eat food bars is the set per-person price. Operations offering smorgasbords, buffets, and the traditional Sunday brunch typically charge one price for all you can eat. Other operations serve family-style at-the-table for a set price per-person. In each case, the portion size and food cost varies with each man, woman, and child that partakes. These two key cost factors make it difficult to arrive at a single price point that is acceptable to all customers because of the individual differences in *perceptions* of what constitutes *value*. Unlike the controlled plating of food served from a kitchen, there is no such thing as a controlled *standardized portion*. The variance in individual portions complicates the task of determining a single food cost that will serve as the basis for a single price for all adult customers.

The National Restaurant Association's study on price-value relationships at restaurants reported that value is not absolute and cannot be determined without considering price and cost. Consumers determine the value of a restaurant meal based on the combination of goods and services they receive for the price paid. Customers see themselves as more *quality* and *value* conscious as opposed to *price* conscious (February 1992, pp. 30).

Pricing by-the-ounce provides the operator with an opportunity to establish perhaps what is the most *equitable* menu pricing methodology for all customers regardless of sex, age, or income level. The operator seeks to set a price that will cover costs and return the desired profit margin. Arriving at a set price per-person requires an estimate of the average food cost per customer. The question is, how does one determine the average cost of food per customer when on any given day the mix of customers may range from senior citizens to growing adolescents? When a single price is used, it must reflect the wide range of portion sizes that are consumed by the total mix of customers.

The set price per-person pricing decision begins by determining the food cost for all the items needed to set up the bar plus the backup inventory used to replenish the bar during the meal period. Assume that $794 represents the beginning inventory of food and $258 represents the food remaining at the end of the meal period. The cost of food consumed is the difference between the opening inventory and the ending inventory, which in this case is $536. If the number of customers going through the buffet that day was 223, the average cost per customer served can be determined by dividing the number of customers into the cost of food consumed ($594/223). In this case, $2.40 is the average food cost per customer. This procedure is repeated for each meal period for two to three weeks. The average food cost per customer will vary slightly from day to day because the mix of customers, the meal period, and day of the week all impact business. A weighted average can be calculated to approximate a *standard portion cost* for a set price per person. Although this is a satisfactory way to estimate average food cost prior to setting the price, certain customers, especially women, dieters, and older patrons, are likely to question the price-value.

With per-person pricing, the light eaters subsidize the heavy eaters because they pay just as much as the customer who goes back for seconds and thirds. Nutrition-conscious customers are not as motivated to purchase by all-you-can-eat promotions. In fact, all you can eat may be viewed negatively by those who want only salads and vegetables and feel that they should pay less than those eating meats and desserts. Operators that use multiple price categories for children, adults, and seniors are often challenged by the customer, and in all likelihood, charges are not consistently applied by the servers who must classify the customer into a price category.

Pricing by-the-ounce addresses two other difficulties sometimes associated with per-person pricing of all-you-can-eat food and salad bars. They are (1) the customer who shares food with another member of his or her party who did not order and (2) the issue of taking home leftovers in doggy bags. Carry-out meals could also be sold by the ounce, thereby allowing customers to pay only for what they take and so creating additional marketing opportunities.

The process of arriving at a price per ounce is not difficult. However, there are items whose weight and density are at different ends of the weight continuum. For example, three ounces of bean sprouts will fill a medium salad bowl while three ounces of potato salad would amount to only three or four tablespoons. Items usually measured in *liquid* ounces must now measured by *avoirdupois* ounces. It cannot be assumed that two liquid ounces will weigh two avoirdupois ounces. When pricing by-the-ounce, all items must be weighed. Divide the weight, expressed in ounces, into the total recipe cost to arrive at the cost per ounce for each item on the salad or food bar. Calculations will reveal costs ranging in cost from $0.02 to $0.30 per ounce. Table 6-6 shows the cost per ounce of common salad bar items.

A cost markup based on highest cost item will result in grossly overpricing the salad bar. When pricing by the ounce, consider the customer's perspective on the quality, quantity, and value. Keep in mind the price range the market for the concept will permit. For example, students and faculty patronizing a college cafeteria have expectations of lower prices there than at a nearby commercial cafeteria serving identical food. There are definite price points for each concept, menu, and service delivery system that must be considered before setting the price.

Setting a price per ounce that will achieve a specific average check is important. First estimate the weight of an average portion in ounces and divide the number of ounces into the desired average food check. If the average check target is $3.95 and the average portion size is 16 ounces, a price of $.25 per ounce is needed in order to achieve the desired average check. However, *forcing* a price to achieve a desired average check without providing value to the customer would be a mistake.

Table 6-6 STANDARD SALAD BAR ITEMS

Item	Price per Ounce
Canned Pickled Beets	$.02
3 Bean Salad	$.04
Shredded Carrots	$.03
Yellow Onions	$.01
Green Peppers	$.06
Garbanzo Beans	$.02
Sliced Cucumbers	$.02
Iceberg Lettuce	$.02
Broccoli	$.03
Yellow Squash	$.03
Croutons	$.06
Imitation Bacon Bits	$.05
Mixed Citrus Fruit Sections	$.05
Pineapple Chunks	$.03
Peach Halves	$.04
Cottage Cheese	$.05
Kidney Beans	$.02
Ranch Dressing	$.05
Italian Dressing	$.04
French Dressing	$.05
Bleu Cheese Dressing	$.06
Thousand Island	$.03

In a survey of costs of *premium* salad bar items is shown in Table 6-7. The cost per ounce of *premium* items like pasta salads with tuna or shrimp, chicken salad, and ham salad can reach $.30 per ounce, especially if premade products are used. Technically, a customer could fill the plate with high-cost items such as anchovies and smoked salmon and exceed the average portion cost target. One should not be overly concerned when this happens because it will generally average out over the month. The rounded straight average for all items found on *typical* salad bars is approximately $.05 per ounce. With a price to the customer of $.20 per ounce, the food cost is a respectable 25 percent.

A bar with both cold salads and hot entrees will be perceived as a better value than one with only cold items. A national supermarket chain with in-store food bars prices both by per person and by-the-ounce. Its dine-in-store all-you-can-eat price is $4.29 per person, and the take-home price is $2.99 per pound or $.187 per ounce. Hot selections include fried chicken and pot roast and desserts like banana pudding and cherry cobbler. The food bars found in many budget steak houses offer similar low-cost hot food items, that is, meat loaf, fish sticks, and spaghetti and meatballs. The cost of most items will still be under $.10 per ounce. *One quarter of adult customers purchase meals from a supermarket, convenience store, or deli one to three times per month according to the NRA study on pricing (1992).*

Table 6-7 PREMIUM SALAD BAR ITEMS

Item	Price per Ounce
Fresh Mushrooms	$.15
Sliced Tomatoes	$.12
Shredded Cheddar	$.11
Parmesan Cheese	$.19
Real Bacon Bits	$.19
Chicken Salad	$.25
Tortellini Salad	$.26
Provolone Cheese	$.24
Broccoli Salad	$.22
Hot Chicken Wings	$.22
Ham Salad	$.22
Sliced Pepperoni	$.30
Potato Salad	$.07
Cole Slaw	$.04
Jello w/fruit	$.08

Premium cold items like pasta, chicken, and tuna salad provide value and command higher prices. Even the quality of the salad dressing can impact price-value perceptions of the customer. Does the blue cheese dressing contain chunks of real blue cheese? Specialty items like anchovy fillets, stuffed manzanilla olives, and pickled corn are premium items too.

Cost markup of salad bars and buffets is typically lower than plated items in full-service operations. The overall food cost percentage with a food bar or buffet will usually run four to six percentage points higher than with table service. This translates to a better value on the plate. The added costs are recovered from the lower labor cost associated with self-service. In high-volume operations, once the sales exceed the break-even, every percentage point that fixed costs are lowered goes directly to bottom line profit.

Eleven food service operations in a large southeastern city offering all-you-can-eat salad or food bars were surveyed to ascertain offerings and prices. Only one commercial operation priced its salad bar by the ounce; it charged $0.25 per ounce. Four of the restaurants offered only cold items with prices that ranged from $2.50 to $5.45 per person. The higher price was indicative of more extensive offerings, the higher quality of their selections, and intangibles such as location, ambiance, and service. Six operations offered hot entrees along with salad items with prices ranging from $3.99 to $6.49 per person. Carryout was permitted in all but one of the operations, and the price was the same as the dine-in price.

Pricing by-the-ounce does have some weaknesses that need to be considered before switching over. For example, the *daily* average check may fluctuate and run lower than with a set price per-person. However, this does not necessarily mean lower overall revenue if daily customer counts increase to offset lower check averages. In addition, digital portion scales must be purchased, and the logistics of having to weigh each plate before the customer is seated may be disruptive to the service delivery system already in place. Many customers like to return to the bar for seconds, and pricing by the ounce precludes return trips, which could lower the value perceptions of the customer who expects to return for seconds.

Pricing of all-you-can-eat salad and food bars in commercial food services by a per-person charge is the most widely used pricing strategy largely for reasons of marketing, logistics, and customer price-value perceptions. Institutional food service operations and retail grocery stores may find that pricing their food and salad bars by the ounce is an acceptable alternative pricing strategy. Hotels and private clubs offering elaborate buffets containing boiled shrimp, Prime rib, and other premium items may find a per-ounce pricing structure impractical. Changing over from a per-person price would likely lower the price-value perceptions of regular customers. For the present time, commercial operations featuring food and salad bars are likely to remain with the per-person price for all-you-can-eat and leave the institutional food services to experiment with pricing by-the-ounce.

DETERMINING THE AVERAGE COST PER OUNCE

1. Make a list of all items offered.

2. Determine the recipe cost for each item. Calculating the cost per servable pound/ounce on items with shrinkage or waste in preparation (e.g., beef roasts and fresh fish) or items that increase in volume and weight (e.g., rice and pasta) are more difficult to compute than on products that basically combine ingredients that neither shrink or expand. Carefully weigh raw products and ingredients before and after cooking or preparation. Keep in mind that your total food cost is the same before and after cooking or preparation. However, depending on the yield, the cost per servable pound will likely increase considerably. Assume you start with 25 pounds of raw headless shrimp (as-purchased price of $124.75, or $4.99/lb) that weigh only 13 pounds when peeled, deveined, and cooked. Exclusive of the cost of added spices and other ingredients, the cost of the shrimp is now $9.60/lb ($124.75/13). In addition, direct labor costs are added to items requiring extensive amounts of preparation labor and when added will increase the cost per servable pound/ounce even more.

3. Record the weight of each batch of product prepared.

4. Divide the weight of the item into the raw food cost of the item.

5. List the cost per pound of each item and then convert to the cost per ounce.

6. Rank order the items by cost per ounce from most to least.

7. Estimate the popularity of each item and the quantities you will likely consume each day. These key items will shape your price per ounce.

8. Compute a weighted average price per ounce of the entire list of ingredients. Method: pounds consumed per meal × the cost per pound. Do this for each item on the salad and food bar. Divide the total weight into the total food cost. This is your weighted average cost per pound. Estimates are adjusted after an actual sales analysis can be taken and estimates of consumption are replaced with actual figures. Daily inventories and monitoring of high-cost items should be done. The determination of the quantities consumed of each item on the food bar will allow you to recalculate the weighted cost of the food consumed. This will impact your overall food cost and the price you must charge to recover cost and return a fair profit.

9. Determine your desired average food check for the meal period. This is an imputed amount based on realistic customer counts and minimum sales needed to cover costs and produce a profit.

10. Estimate the "average" portion size of an "average" customer.

11. Divide the weight of the average portion into your desired check average. This is what you need to charge *(price)* per ounce in order to achieve your desired average check based on the average portion. You want to compare this figure to the *cost* per ounce calculated in step 8.

12. Subjectively adjust your price per ounce. You are the only person who can effectively do this; there is no magic formula for marking up your food cost and establishing a menu price. The two ends of the pricing continuum are (a) charging the highest price the market will bear and (b) charging the lowest price that will still produce a profit.

Regardless of the menu pricing philosophy, in the long run it is the customer who ultimately determines what price is acceptable. Therefore, only after knowing the acceptable price does cost come into play. The operator must be able to make a profit selling at the price the market says he or she must charge.

What is the proper price? From the customers' point of view, it is the one that makes them buy. From the seller's perspective, the successful price is one that moves the product and produces a profit. If a menu item is common or ordinary and offered by many competitors, the price will likely be at the low end. However, if the item is special or unique and not easily duplicated by the competition, it can be priced at the high end. It behooves management to have several "specialty" items on the menu to create some competitive distinctiveness. Competitive distinctiveness can be enhanced by other factors such as location, atmosphere, service, entertainment, and unique product presentation (Pavesic, 1994).

For an in-depth discussion of pricing, see <u>Menu Pricing and Strategy</u>, 4th ed., by J. Miller and D. Pavesic (Van Nostrand Reinhold Publishers, 1996).

REFERENCES

"Computer Applications in Marketing." *Nation's Restaurant News,* July 1984.

"Coupon Promotions." *Independent Restaurants,* February 1985, pp. 68–71.

Degen, James M. "How Price Promotions Affect Profits." *Restaurant Business,* April 1, 1983, pp. 169–170.

Della Bitta, A. J., and Kent B. Monroe. "The Influence of Adaptation Levels on Subjective Price Perceptions." In *Advances in Consumer Research,* Vol. 1., eds. Scott Ward and Peter Wright. Ann Arbor, MI: Association for Consumer Research, 1973, pp. 353–369.

Ferguson, Dennis H. "Hidden Agendas in Consumer Purchase Decisions." *Cornell Quarterly,* 28, no. 1 (May 1987), 31–39.

Gabor, André, and Clive Granger. "On the Price Consciousness of Consumers." *Applied Statistics,* 10 (November 1961), 170–188.

Haugh, Louis J. "The Pitfalls of Over-discounting." *Nation's Restaurant News,* 17, no. 5 (February 18, 1983), 77.

Haugh, Louis J. "MVP Contest Shows Advertising Support For Promotions Down." *Nation's Restaurant News,* 17, no. 14 (July 4, 1983), 58.

Jeffrey, Don. "The Battle for the Spotlight." *Nation's Restaurant News,* 17, no. 17 (March 28, 1983), 31, 33–34.

Kahneman, Daniel, and Amos Tversky. "Prospect Theory: An Analysis of Decision under Risk." *Econometrica,* March 1979, pp. 263–291.

Keister, Douglas C. *Food and Beverage Control.* Englewood Cliffs, NJ: Prentice Hall, 1977.

Kotschevar, Lendal H. *Management by Menu.* Wm. C. Brown Publishers, National Institute for the Foodservice Industry, 1987.

Kreul, Lee M. "Magic Numbers: Psychological Aspects of Menu Pricing." *Cornell Quarterly,* August 1982, pp. 70–75.

Levinson, Charles. *Food and Beverage Operation: Cost Control and Systems Management.* Englewood Cliffs, NJ: Prentice Hall, 1976.

Miller, Jack and Pavesic, David. *Menu Pricing and Strategy,* 4th ed. New York: Van Nostrand Reinhold Co., 1996.

Monroe, Kent B. "Techniques for Pricing New Products and Services." Virginia Polytechnic Institute, 1986.

Monroe, Kent B., and Kirshnan. "The Effect of Price on Subjective Product Evaluations." Pp. 209–231 in *Perceived Quality,* eds. Jacob Jacoby and Jerry C. Olson. Lexington Books, 1984.

Monroe Kent B., and Susan M. Petroshius. "Buyer's Perceptions of Price: An Update of the Evidence." *Journal of Marketing Research,* 10 (February 1973), 70–80. Published by American Marketing Association.

Mossman, John. "How to Set Prices." *Restaurant Management,* June 1987, pp. 76, 85.

Pavesic, David V., "Indirect Cost Factors in Menu Pricing," *FIU Review,* Vol. 6, No. 2, Fall 1988, pp. 13–22.

Pavesic, David V., "Psychological Aspects of Menu Pricing," *International Journal of Hospitality Management,* Vol. 8, No. 2, 1989, pp. 43–49.

Pavesic, David V., "Taking the Anxiety Out of Menu Price Increases," *Restaurant Management,* February 1988, pp. 56–57.

Pavesic, David V. "The Myth of Discount Promotions," *International Journal of Hospitality Management,* Vol. 4, No. 2, 1985, pp. 67–73.

Pavesic, David V. "By-The-Ounce Pricing for Salad Bars," *Journal of College and University Foodservice,* Vol. 1(4), 1994, pp. 3–11.

"Price-value relationships at restaurants," National Restaurant Association Research and Information Service Department, Feb. 1992, p. 30.

"Restaurant Technology, Computer Applications in Marketing." *Nation's Restaurant News,* July 2, 1984, Sec. 2, p. 33.

Schmidgall, Raymond S., *Hospitality Industry Managerial Accounting,* 2nd ed., East Lansing, MI: Educational Institute of the American Hotel and Motel Association, 1990.

Thaler, Richard. "Mental Accounting and Consumer Choice." *Marketing Service,* Summer 1985, pp. 199–214.

Chapter Seven

Financial Analysis

THE NEED FOR FINANCIAL MANAGEMENT

When you hear and read about successful restaurants, whether independent, franchise, or chain operated, you must realize that their success didn't happen all by good luck and timing but as a result of some very careful and detailed planning. In order to make a profit, one must plan for a profit. All aspects of an operation must be designed to achieve the profit plan. Richard Melman, chairman of Lettuce Entertain You Enterprises, perhaps the most successful restaurant concept developer, addressed the attendees at a past National Restaurant Show in Chicago. His company has launched over 30 different restaurant concepts, most of which have been great successes. His words to the audience were that 85 percent of a concept's success is determined before a restaurant opens its doors to the public. This speaks directly to the importance of due diligence in all areas of site selection, menu, equipment selection, layout, staffing, and the like. The unsuccessful entrepreneur did not plan to fail; he likely *failed to plan*.

Many food service operations offering well-prepared and served food, in attractive surroundings, in good locations, and having adequate customer counts still go out of business. The reason that many businesses fail is the inability of the owner-manager to manage the financial aspects of the business. Now while it is true that volume will make up for minor flaws in your managerial style, poor cost control management will eventually be fatal.

While operators cannot avoid many of the consequences brought about by factors affecting the economy as a whole, those who are prepared in advance can often "weather the storm" while the less prepared close their doors. The critical function of financial management goes hand in hand with cost control. Financial management has three perspectives for assessing the profitability of an enterprise. First, in the beginning and growth stages of the business, decisions surrounding long-term assets and capital expenditures for physical facilities and equipment must be made. The decisions management makes today are a future commitment and long-term financial obligation that must be well planned.

The way these assets are financed is the second perspective from which management must assess its financial commitments. The ratio of borrowed funds to owner's investment should not put a strain on the cash flow. Ideally, it should provide an adequate rate of return to the investors while not taxing the operation's ability to retire the debt. Third, current assets and operating capital must be monitored on a day-to-day basis to detect variances from operating standards and serve as the basis for management planning and control in both the short- and long-term decision-making process.

Financial management stresses the *interpretation* rather than the preparation of financial statements and internal reports. Preparation of the forms is an accounting function, but to interpret the data, one must have an understanding of what each figure or ration represents. This requires an insight into the relationships between revenues and expenditures.

FINANCIAL SEMANTICS

Let us distinguish the sometimes subtle differences in meaning of several terms used in the area of financial management. There are many kinds of financial records, and their preparation depends upon who ultimately has to interpret them. *Financial accounting* is primarily intended to provide *external user groups* with information concerning the current status of the firm and the results of its operations. It is historical in nature and must be reported precisely and without bias. Reports for the Internal Revenue and Securities and Exchange Commission demand this kind of reporting. Accounting information is the basis for cost standards, budgets, and departmental controls. The information provided by the accounting function is essentially financial in nature and is used by management to compare actual to projected results, direct daily operations, and assist in controlling costs.

Distinctively different is the concept of *managerial accounting*. Where financial accounting provides information concerning the financial status of the firm and the results of its operations, managerial accounting attempts to provide *internal users* with data and information that will serve as a basis for day-to-day operational decision making. Because its use is internal, report preparation is more specific and emphasizes departmental operations; uses nonfinancial data like customer counts, menu sales mix, and labor hours; draws from other disciplines (e.g., marketing, human resources, and production); and supplements financial accounting information.

Cost accounting is a concept that utilizes techniques designed to standardize and systematize the accumulation and analysis of cost data for use in financial management decisions. This is a two-step process. First, management must set the control standards that will be compared to the actual costs incurred. Second, through the use of a cost accounting system, the actual unit costs must be accumulated. Variances between standard and actual costs identify areas for management emphasis either to maximize returns or minimize losses. Knowledge of current and past cost trends allows management to better forecast the future. Pricing policy is also dependent upon cost accounting analysis.

With *managerial accounting,* internal reports break down revenues and expenses by department, day, and meal period to make them easier to interpret and to locate the areas that need attention. The aggregate figures on the standard income statement do not allow management to pinpoint the causes of variances. Each revenue producing department must be analyzed separately and compare expenses incurred to the revenue produced.

This is why financial statements must be designed as *management tools.* They should *not* be just IRS forms for income tax purposes. The most important financial statement from an operational perspective is the Statement of Income and Retained Earnings, also known as the Statement of Profit and Loss, which summarizes the historical results of operations for a previous period, usually one month. Management needs the information it contains much more frequently than once a month; daily and weekly reports must be prepared to see emerging trends.

The monitoring of current assets—for example, food and beverage inventory in particular—and operating capital is accomplished through the interpretation of the daily and weekly operating reports prepared for internal control purposes. *Working capital,* defined as the excess of current assets over current liabilities, is the liquid cash the business has to work with. Working capital turnover is a measure of short-term cash position. Because the majority of transactions are for cash rather than extended credit terms, a restaurant per se does not need as much working capital as a retail operation. Lending institutions and creditors sometimes use working capital to assess the financial position of the borrower. Adequate working capital gives the business protection against financial stress and is a strong indicator of being able to meet current debt.

The restaurant industry has a considerably smaller percentage of its total assets in current assets as compared to retail or industrial firms. This is due to the small inventories of perishable commodities that are turned over frequently and the fact that restaurants deal primarily in cash transactions. Credit card charges are debited daily to bank accounts and are treated as cash.

Effective internal reports contain departmental data that can be directly measured and controlled by unit management. Prompt remedial action can be taken when unacceptable variances are detected. Major costs or recurring costs are monitored closely. An effective internal reporting systems organizes operations by revenue centers and assigns cost and income to each. The monitoring of cash receipts and accounts payable is a daily function of management. Cash flow management is perhaps the most critical task for the owner/manager. Funds must be allocated to pay the outstanding bills in a timely manner.

TURNING THE COMMON INCOME STATEMENT INTO A COST CONTROL TOOL

The standard income statement format shown in Figure 7-1 can be improved even further to be a useful tool to management in financial analysis. It is the recommended system format for restaurants according to the seventh edition of the *Uniform System of Accounts for Restaurants*, published by the National Restaurant Association.

The major weakness of this format is that it provides only *summary* information that totals income and expense during a particular period of time. In order for management to be on top of day-to-day operations, the financial data must be supplemented with *managerial accounting* information, much of which is nonfinancial data.

The income statement needs to include information that will provide specific facts about the operation that put detail into the financial information it reports. Most financial statements are prepared only once a month. The supporting information is compiled weekly and even daily.

The daily and weekly internal operating reports emphasize departmental breakdowns of both financial and nonfinancial statistics; for example, customer counts, labor hours, and menu sales mix. This information is needed to pinpoint variances and check compliance to cost standards. The traditional income statement merely *summarizes* accounting data where departmental reports emphasize specific detailed operating statistics.

The assumption is made that in the absence of departmental reports, the income statement will be the primary tool for assessing operational efficiency. This makes it imperative that financial data is presented in a manner that provides management with a clear picture of revenues and costs.

The general organization of the income statement shown in Table 7-1 indicates a *detailed* breakdown of sales and expenses. The IRS does not require this kind of detail. Management, on the other hand, needs to have separate sales figures for food, beverage, and banquets broken down separately. This detail is missing from most monthly income statements; your accountant should provide you with the information you want, not just what a computer is programmed to prepare for some generic accounting software program.

Expenses should be similarly separated to correspond to the same sales breakdowns. The section of the statement, *Direct Departmental Expenses*, groups all expenses that can be directly attributed to the revenues they produce.

NAME OF RESTAURANT
PERIOD COVERED BY STATEMENT

	$ Amounts	% Percent
Sales		
Food		
Beverages		
Total Sales		
Cost of Sales		
Food		
Beverage		
Total Cost of Sales		
Gross Profit		
Food		
Beverage		
Total Gross Profit		
Other Income		
Total Income		
Operating Expenses		
Salaries and Wages		
Employee Benefits		
Direct Operating Expenses		
Music and Entertainment		
Marketing		
Energy and Utility Services		
Administrative and General Expenses		
Repairs and Maintenance		
Total Operating Expenses		
Income before Occupancy Costs, Interest, Depreciation, Corporate Overhead, and Income Taxes		
Rent		
Property Taxes		
Property Insurance		
Total Occupancy Costs		
Income before Interest, Depreciation, Corporate Overhead, and Income Taxes		
Interest		
Depreciation		
Corporate Overhead Charges		
Income before Income Taxes		
Income Taxes		
Net Income		
Retained Earnings, Beginning of Period		
Less Dividends		
Retained Earnings, End of Period		

FIGURE 7-1 Statement of income and retained earnings. (*Source:* Uniform System of Accounts for Restaurants, 7th Ed, National Restaurant Association, 1996.)

Table 7-1 MONTHLY INCOME STATEMENT\INTERNAL MANAGEMENT
TOOL FORMAT

	$ Amount	% of Sales	Cost per Cover
Sales			
Food	34,499	70.5	$6.63
Beer/Wine	5,919	12.1	$1.14
Liquor	8,107	16.6	$1.56
Vending	23	.0	$.0
Promotional Sales	368	.8	$.07
Cash Over/Under	35	.1	$.0
Total Sales	**48,951**	**100.0**	**$9.41**
Direct Departmental Expenses			
Cost of Food Consumed	14,696	42.6	$2.83
Less Employee Meals	(690)	(2.0)	($.13)
Cost of Food Sold	14,006	40.6	$2.69
Beer/Wine	1,378	23.3	$.26
Liquor	1,443	17.8	$.28
Cost of Beverage Sold	2,821	21.1	$.54
Promotional Items	294	79.9	$.06
Food Wages	7,850	22.7	$1.51
Beverage Wages	1,000	7.1	$.19
Total Wages	8,850	18.2	$1.70
Employee Meals	690	2.0	$.13
Payroll Taxes/Insurance	760	1.5	$.14
Total Departmental Expenses	**27,421**	**56.0**	**$5.27**
Gross Margin	**21,530**	**44.0**	**$4.14**
Operating Expenses			
Laundry and Uniforms	950	1.9	$.18
Bar Supplies	250	.5	$.05
Kitchen Supplies	275	.6	$.05
Cleaning Supplies	459	.9	$.09
Utilities	1,350	2.8	$.26
Telephone	50	.1	$.01
Repairs and Maintenance	250	.5	$.05
Equipment Leases	475	.9	$.09
Printing and Menus	168	.3	$.03
Credit Card Expense	125	.25	$.02
Advertising	900	1.8	$.17
Total Operating Expenses	**5,252**	**10.7**	**$1.00**
Profit before Admin. and Gen. Expense	**16,278**	**33.3**	**$3.13**
Administrative and General Expenses			
Management Salaries	4,000	8.3	$.77
Management Benefits and Taxes	810	1.7	$.16
Office Expense	525	1.0	$.10
Travel and Entertainment	195	.4	$.03
Automobile	275	.6	$.05
Accounting and Legal Fees	325	.7	$.06
Licenses and Fees	25	0	$.0
Total	**6,155**	**12.6**	**$1.18**

(*continued*)

Table 7-1 *(continued)*

	$ Amount	% of Sales	Cost per Cover
Profit before Occupational Expenses	**10,123**	**20.7**	**$1.95**
Occupational Expense			
Rent	2,500	5.1	$.48
Interest	400	.8	$.08
Property Taxes	325	.7	$.06
Insurance	475	.9	$.09
Total	3,700	7.5	$.71
Profit before Depreciation	6,423	13.2	$1.24
Depreciation	200	.4	$.04
Pretax Profit	6,223	12.8	$1.20

NONFINANCIAL DATA

Food Labor Hours	2,160
Beverage Labor Hours	200
Total Labor Hours	2,360
Wage per Food LH	$3.63
Wage per Beverage LH	$5.00
Average Wage per LH	$3.75
Sales per Food LH	$15.97
Sales per Beverage LH	$70.13
Average Sales per LH	$20.56
Customer Count	5,200
Average Sales per Cover	$9.33
Labor Cost per Cover	$1.70
Covers per LH	2.2

Operating Expenses are those costs that can be at least partially controlled by management and follow in the format. Expenses such as laundry and uniforms, utilities, and supplies are examples.

They are followed by *Administrative and General Expenses,* commonly grouped under the category with fixed and noncontrollable expenses. They are typically not a responsibility of the operational management team in an absentee owner operation. Included here are management salaries, fringe benefits, licenses, and fees.

Another category of expenses are identified as *Occupational Expenses,* also referred to as fixed expenses, that includes rent, interest, property taxes, and depreciation. Note that regardless of the classification, every revenue and expense is expressed as a dollar value, a percentage of *total* sales and as a cost per cover.

Ratios and percentages are not effective in localizing trouble spots or measuring performance of individual departments unless they can be calculated by figures taken exclusively from their respective departments. For example, the *total* cost of beverage sold is 21.1 percent, but there is a 5.5 percent differential between beer/wine and liquor cost that would not have been readily noticed were they not broken down and reported separately.

Operators like to compare their percentages with industry averages published in trade journals as a reference point for their cost standards. The fact that a difference is found or that they have identical numbers does not necessarily mean that cost optimization has or has not been achieved. The reasons that can be causing the differences or similarities can be due to prices, costs, and menu sales mix.

One of the likely reasons for differences in payroll, food cost, or beverage cost percentages comes from the way revenues and expenses are separated. For example, if beer, wine, and spirits are all grouped into the categories "beverage sales" and "beverage costs," the percentages that result will be significantly different from another operator who separates the three. Restaurants typically sell more beer and wine than mixed drinks, thereby driving up the overall beverage cost percentage. See Chapter 12 for more beverage cost information.

Unless identical records are kept, it is not likely that two independent operators can use each other's cost standards interchangeably. The same caution holds true for food and labor cost comparisons. If salaried personnel are included with hourly workers, the percentage will be greater than if they were separated. The message here is simply to be aware when comparing operational data with industry averages or other operations.

When the standard accounting information is combined with certain nonfinancial data on the income statement, it becomes much more valuable as a management tool. Most of the nonfinancial data is already assembled on daily cash reports and payroll records so it is easy and inexpensive to incorporate it into your income statement format.

Daily sales reports will give you sales by meal periods and corresponding customer counts. Labor hours are tallied for every hourly paid employee and are recorded every time a payroll is processed. By simply separating time cards by job categories—that is, busboys, cooks, servers, and so on—labor hour distribution among employees can be seen.

Sales can then be shown on a per labor hour basis and supplement the traditional labor cost percentage used by all operators. Evaluating the number of customers served for every labor hour worked will indicate the true productivity of the employee. Calculation of average wage per labor hour worked and customer served can indicate far more specific causes of payroll problems than an aggregate ratio of total labor to total sales can. Refer to Chapter 11 for detailed report formats.

While food, beverage, and labor costs get the majority of management's attention, and rightly so, what remains cannot be ignored. With the nickels and dimes that are made or lost on each dollar of sales, even the smallest expense must be kept in line. By calculating the *cost per cover* for all the controllable expenses over a period of time, comparisons to past periods can reveal much in the search for causes of profit declines.

In the example statement provided, Table 7-1, total wages were $8850, or 18.2 percent of total sales. But further breakdown indicates that food related payroll of $7850, was 22.7 percent of *food* sales and that beverage payroll of $1000 was 7.1 percent of *beverage* sales. This is an example of why it is important to separate revenues and costs by department. Food related payroll makes up 88.7 percent of the total payroll, indicating that improvements made there are likely to be reflected in a lower overall payroll percentage.

Payroll records show that 2360 labor hours were worked (2160 in food and 200 in beverage). The average cost per labor hour was $3.75 ($8850/2360). By separating food and beverage labor, the cost per labor hour proves to be $3.63 in the food area ($7850/2160) and $5.00 in the beverage area ($1000/200). This information can be broken down further by individual job categories so the average cost per labor hour can be shown for servers, cooks, busboys, cocktail waitresses, bartenders, and so forth.

Sales per labor hour can be similarly calculated and compared. The average sales per labor hour worked was $20.56 ($48,525/2360). When broken down by food and beverage, it is $15.97 ($34499/2160) and $70.13 ($14,026/200), respectively. The figures can be broken down further by meal periods to see the times of day when sales per labor hour are highest.

Although this type of information can increase the management value of the income statement and help establish standards for forecasting and costs, it is subject to distortion and therefore inaccurate interpretation. Inflation and wage and menu price increases will require some type of adjustment over time to keep comparison of present figures to past figures relevant. The inclusion of customer counts is very important because it is perhaps the one true inflation-proof figure.

During the statement period, 5200 covers were served. This information was obtained from guest checks and server counts. Utilizing this with the previous revenues and cost breakdowns, the value of the income statement as a management tool increases.

The labor cost per cover served is $1.70 ($8850/5200), and the average number of covers served per labor hour was 2.2 (5200/2360). The initial calculation of this type of information becomes more useful over time as comparisons of one period to another are made. You can begin to see trends that are developing and the highs and lows in sales and costs.

Every item on the income statement can be expressed as a cost per cover served. The data can be presented to show current period, year to date, and the previous year's results (not shown). Computer software makes such detailed financial statement reporting easy and inexpensive to produce. The majority of management's time no longer is spent on the preparation of the cost control documents, but in the interpretation of the data.

BREAK-EVEN ANALYSIS FOR RESTAURANT OPERATIONS

A helpful technique that provides additional information in making financial and operation decisions is *break-even point analysis* (BEP). Break-even is a cost accounting tool commonly defined as the volume point at which an operation becomes profitable. You need to understand the general effects of what is referred to as the *volume-cost-profit relationship*. When a change occurs in either sales volume or cost, the profit will be affected. Therefore, there is no single or absolute BEP for a restaurant. It is constantly changing and may actually be several hundred dollars more or less than the theoretical calculated BEP.

The reason for this is that costs are *not perfectly fixed or variable*. Many expenses on the income statement possess, at different levels of volume, both fixed and variable cost components. *Semi-fixed* is used on those fixed costs with some variable cost tendencies, and a *semi-variable* is used to describe variable costs with some fixed properties. If purely fixed and variable costs were shown on a graph, like those in Figures 7-2 and 7-3, they would make the break-even analysis much more precise. Some expenses behave like those shown in Figure 7-4, with both fixed and variable properties at different sales volumes.

All restaurants have fixed costs, and these fixed costs continue to be incurred, even if a restaurant is closed. When it opens for business, it will incur additional variable costs. However, consider the fact that fixed costs can be either *discretionary*, as with an advertising budget, or *committed*, as with rent or principal loan payments.

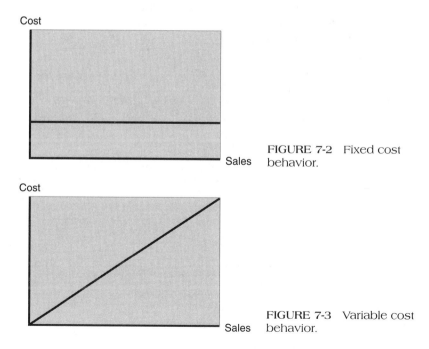

FIGURE 7-2   Fixed cost behavior.

FIGURE 7-3   Variable cost behavior.

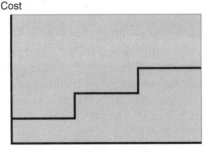

Cost

Sales

FIGURE 7-4 Semi-variable/fixed cost behavior.

Another term for *discretionary* is *managed,* in that fixed costs are *totally controlled* by management. They may be planned or budgeted, or they may be deleted if management sees that the restaurant is not deriving any additional business from the advertising. Expenses like depreciation and rent cannot be easily changed with just a management decision, as they require other parties to approve and negotiations must take place. While they are not *absolutely* fixed, they are fixed for purposes of the accounting definition. Fixed cost behavior is not tied to or influenced by the level of business volume.

In contrast, variable costs increase and decrease at a predictable percentage amount when volume increases or decreases. The two most exemplary variable costs are food and beverage cost. As long as the sales mix of food and beverage remains consistent to past sales mixes and prices, portioning, and recipe costs are held constant, the food and beverage percentage will be the same regardless of whether sales are $1000 or $10,000.

However, some conditions cause these variable percentages to vary, and they have to do with the elements previously mentioned. If a discount promotion is run, it will change the sales mix, food costs, and sales volume. See Chapter 6 for coverage of discount pricing. Happy hours in the lounge or discount coupons in the paper will cause the cost of sales to increase.

Semi-fixed costs have characteristics of both fixed and variable costs. They are fixed to a point but after volume reached a certain level, they will increase. Utilities are an example: When the volume of business increases, more gas and electricity will be needed for cooking, washing dishes, and cooling or heating the premises. These expenses may increase 4 to 5 percent in response to a 10 percent increase in volume.

Labor is another example of a semi-fixed expense. Labor cost is fixed at the "skeleton crew" level of staffing. Regardless of the slowness of business, management must schedule this minimum staff to open the doors. The skeleton crew can handle a pretty good number of customers, but after a certain number, additional employees must be scheduled in certain job categories to meet the quantitative and qualitative service standards. Typically, a restaurant will schedule additional service employees as the number of cooks, bartenders, and hostesses remains the same.

Since BEP analysis must assume that costs are purely fixed or variable, something must be done with these *semi*-costs so they fit into one of the two classifications of cost. What you can do is separate them into their fixed and variable components through statistical methods or what I call an "educated estimate."

The terms *marginal income, contribution margin, profit-volume ratio, gross profit,* and *gross margin* have been used to describe basically the same thing; the amount that remains after variable costs have been deducted from sales. However, always check the meaning of the term used by an author when these terms are used because they may mean something other than what has been defined here.

In this book, the preferred term is *contribution margin*. It is expressed as a percentage calculated with the formula: 100% − Variable Cost Percent. If total variable cost were 63.5 percent, the contribution margin would be 36.5 percent, which is the amount left to pay the remaining fixed-occupancy costs. Accounting and finance tell us that this represents the actual cost behavior and that every dollar brought in above the break-even point will produce added profit equal to the contribution margin ratio. The truth is that the ratio fluctuates because of the changes in costs or volume.

The traditional break-even formula seems so simple and easy to follow. It is the numbers and percentages you use in the formula that are difficult to compute accurately. The following assumptions are made for BEP in this chapter:

1. Food and beverage costs are 100% variable.
2. Hourly payroll is semi-fixed and management salaries and benefits are discretionary fixed costs.
3. Advertising and promotion are discretionary fixed costs because they can be increased, decreased, or totally eliminated by management.
4. Rent and occupancy expenses are committed fixed expenses. However, if you really want to split hairs, an expense like insurance has two elements, fixed for personal property coverage and variable for products and customer liability. Liability insurance premiums are sometimes determined by the sales volume much like workers' compensation insurance is computed as a percentage of your total payroll.

To take the BEP out of the realm of theory and put it to practical use, you must first recognize its limitations. The factors of cost and volume affect it in the following ways:

1. Changes in fixed costs will change the BEP but not the contribution margin percentage.
2. Variable cost changes will alter both the BEP and the contribution margin percentage.
3. Changes in menu prices will alter both the BEP and the contribution margin.

In order for BEP to work perfectly, the following must occur:

1. Prices will not change.
2. The sales mix will remain constant.

3. Variable costs will vary in direct proportion to sales.

4. Fixed costs will remain constant at all sales levels.

If all these conditions are met, the calculated BEP will remain the same for all levels of volume. This is rarely the case in the hospitality industry. Understand that a calculated BEP is *not* an absolute value calculated down to the exact dollar. It has value to management for use as a "what if . . ." in financial decision making.

Managers can consult BEP as they consider alternatives to a variety of operational problems and conditions. Some applications for BEP are:

1. The effects on BEP when sales rise or drop
2. The effects on BEP when variable costs rise
3. The effects on BEP when menu prices are increased/decreased
4. The effects on BEP of labor-saving devices or training
5. The effects on BEP from long-term capital expenditures
6. The sales levels needed to achieve a specific profit amount
7. The profit growth from expansion of the business
8. What increase in sales is necessary to offset a price reduction?
9. Should the restaurant stay open or close for given day/meal period?

Examples of BEP Analysis

Assume that management is considering putting additional seats in the restaurant's lounge and dining room. The plan calls for 10 additional seats in the bar and 30 more seats in the dining room. Further assume that the restaurant's sales volume has leveled off at $80,000 per month. The profit structure resembles that shown in Table 7-2.

Table 7-2 FINANCIAL SUMMARY FOR CAL-MAR RESTAURANT

	$ Amounts	% Percent
Sales	80,000	100
Cost of Sales (all variable costs)	30,400	38
Gross Margin	49,600	62
Operating and All Other Costs		
Variable Costs	20,800	26
Fixed Costs	17,600	22
Totals	38,400	48
Operating Profit before Taxes	11,200	14
Taxes	5,800	7.3
Net Profit	5,400	7.7

The following monthly increases in fixed costs are anticipated from the expansion:

Utilities	$150
Rent	$250
Depreciation	$300
Administrative	$300
Total	$1000

The new fixed costs are $17,600 + $1000 = $18,600. The total variable costs are 38% + 26% = 64%. Therefore, the contribution margin is 100% – 64% = 36%. Substituting into the break-even formula, Fixed Cost $/Contribution Margin, or $18,600/0.36 = $51,667. The break-even without the expansion is $17,600/0.36 = $48,339. Therefore, it has increased $2778 per month. That works out to about $650 a week in additional business, or $92 per day based on a seven-day week. This does not seem to be an unreasonable volume to achieve.

What sales level must be attained to make a $11,200 profit? Using the same formula, we treat profit as a fixed expense and add it to the fixed cost in the numerator of the equation: ($18,600 + $11,200)/0.36 = $82,778. The previous sales level to achieve the same profit was $80,000 so an increase of only $2778 per month is needed.

Since the expansion requires a cash investment, management expects an additional $1000 in profit per month. The BEP to achieve a $12,600 profit is $85,555 ([$18,600 + $12,200]/.36). Is an additional $5555 per month a realistic amount given the competition and customer traffic in the restaurant's trading area? If volume has plateaued at $80,000 due to supply and demand, expansion may not increase customer counts. Perhaps money should be spent on marketing to increase business.

What is the profit before taxes at a sales level of $85,000 without expansion costs? The formula is Profit = Sales × Contribution Margin – Fixed Costs. In this case, $85,000 × .36 = $30,600 – $17,600 = $13,000.

What sales volume is needed to earn a $15,000 profit? Again, profit is treated in the formula as if it were a fixed expense. So instead of fixed costs of $17,600, we have $32,600 in the numerator of the formula: $32,600/0.36 = $90,555.

What sales volume is needed to maintain the present profit if a discount promotion is run that, in effect, will decrease overall prices by 5 percent? Assume that $11,200 profit is acceptable. We already know that at regular prices sales of $80,000 are needed to earn $11,200 in profit. The formula is:

$$\frac{\text{Desired Profit} + \text{Fixed Costs}}{1 - \dfrac{\text{Present Variable Cost \%}}{100\% - 5\%}}$$

$$\frac{\$11,200 + \$17,600}{1 - \dfrac{0.64}{1.00 - .05}}$$

$$\frac{28,800}{1 - \dfrac{0.64}{0.95}}$$

$$\frac{\$28,000}{1 - 0.6736} = \frac{\$28,000}{0.3264} = \$88,235$$

The discount promotion would need to bring in an additional $8235 to equal the profit the restaurant is earning without the discount. An increase in sales volume of over 10 percent is needed. That should be translated into the number of additional customers needed on the nights the discount is offered.

Food cost will increase as a result of the discount reducing the contribution margin and increasing the BEP. Remember, BEP assumes that costs remain constant or vary in the same proportion to sales. It is doubtful that this could be the case with a 10 percent increase in volume. Labor would most definitely have to increase. The actual BEP is probably much higher than this figure. It makes you wonder about the financial impact of discount promotions. See Chapter 6 for a full explanation of discount pricing.

What is the effect on profit if fixed and variable costs are changed? Assume that we lease $3000 worth of new equipment that will enable us to reduce variable costs by 20 percent. A new contribution margin ratio needs to be computed. Present variable costs are 64% so a 20% reduction would be $0.20 \times 0.64 + 12.8\%$. 64% = 12.8% = 51.2%; 1.00 − 0.512 = .488, the *new* contribution margin. Fixed costs will increase from $17,600 to $20,600 because of the equipment lease: $20,600/0.488 = $42,213. The new BEP is lowered from $51,667 to $42,213. Go out and lease that equipment!

If sales were $85,000, how much profit would we earn with the leased equipment installed? The formula is Sales × Contribution Margin − Fixed Costs, or $85,000 × 0.488 − $20,600 = $17,480. This is almost $4500 more than the profit we calculated earlier on this sales volume without the expansion in seats. *Remember, every time there is a change in fixed or variable costs, the break-even point must be recalculated.*

THE CONCEPT OF CLOSING POINT

Is a restaurant better off financially to close its doors earlier on certain days or cease to operate during a particular season of the year? Is it possible for an operation to make more money by closing one day a week or by operating one meal period instead of two? Should a restaurant expand its hours of operation to early in the morning? Whether you are trying to determine the most profitable hours or days of the week to open, the *closing point analysis* can help you make an informed decision.

Every operation has a break-even point and a closing point. Closing point is that point where sales revenues do not cover the costs of opening; for example, payroll, extra utilities, supplies, linens, and the like. If the operation remained closed, such "opening" expenses would not be incurred.

The closing point of any operation is based on the relationship of minimum opening costs to total sales. For example, as sales volume and customer counts drop, the cost-minded manager or owner will purchase and prepare less food, schedule fewer employees, and cut costs wherever possible. Yet, eventually he will reach a point where costs are fixed and cannot be further reduced if the business is to remain open and standards of food, beverage, and service are to be reasonably maintained.

In table-service operations, regardless of customer counts, when the doors are opened, food will be purchased and prepared and a minimum skeleton crew will need to be scheduled and paid. These minimum costs are fixed and the restaurant cannot open without incurring these opening costs. Consequently, sales revenue must be sufficient to recover these minimum opening costs. If sales fall below the closing point, not only will you have to pay the "sunk" fixed costs like rent, insurance, interest, and utilities, you will incur the additional expenses of opening. Simply stated, if it costs $100 to open the doors and you take in only $90, it will cost you $10 more than it would to remain closed in the first place.

To illustrate, if you decided to close your restaurant for any one day or perhaps at an earlier closing hour each day, you would save the expense of labor, food, and beverage, reduce your utility bill, not use up supplies, consume hot water, or turn on cooking equipment.

When you open the doors, you will incur these expenses and your sales must cover these operating costs. Of course, the alternative to closing is to try to increase sales volume and make it profitable to remain open. If your sales were $110 instead of $100, your would not only cover the costs of opening but an additional $10 of your sunk fixed costs. In that case, you are $10 better off by opening than staying closed.

Many operations have hours of the day and days of the week when they operate below their break-even point. But as long as they are above the closing point, they are better off remaining open than closing.

To determine your operation's closing point, classify your costs into two categories: fixed and variable. Fixed costs are those that continue when you are closed. The remaining costs are not absolutely variable as the opening costs have a "programmed" fixed portion. For the sake of example and simplification, the only purely variable costs are food and beverage. These costs are expressed as percentages. Fixed costs are expressed in dollars.

The most logical expense of opening to express in dollar value would be your labor cost. Based on hourly wages and management salaries of those scheduled for the day, meal period, or hour, you can arrive at a definite dollar cost of labor for opening. Add any additional costs in dollars that you will incur by opening (e.g., laundry and linen, utilities, supplies, etc.). Compute a contribution margin by adding the food and beverage variable cost percentages, and subtract it from 100 percent. Divide the contribution margin into the fixed costs of opening to arrive at the closing point or sales level that will cover the costs of opening the doors to the public.

Assume the following costs of opening are:

Labor $150
Variable Costs   46%
Contribution Margin = 100% − 46% = 54%
Closing Point = $150/0.54 = $278

Sales would need to exceed $278 to cover the costs of opening for the period of time the expenses represent.

Break-even and closing point analysis is best used for short-term periods like meal periods, days, and weeks. When break-even is calculated, try to express your costs from monthly or weekly figures. If you have annual figures and simply divide by 12 to get a monthly BEP and then by 4.3 to get a weekly figure, the figure you get is not exact to what BEP may be. BEP analysis is a helpful tool if costs used in its calculation are representative of the actual costs incurred. Most costs of operating a restaurant are not purely fixed or variable; they are a combination of each. This complicates the calculation of BEP and explains why it is just an estimated sales point and not an exact number.

REFERENCES

Pavesic, David V., "Financial Management for Hospitality Enterprises," in *Introduction to Hotel and Restaurant Management*, Robert A. Brymer, Editor, 4th Ed., Kendall-Hunt Publishers, 1979, pp. 212–216.

Chapter Eight

Internal Controls

REASONS FOR INTERNAL CONTROLS

Restaurant owners and security experts estimate that about five cents on every dollar spent in U.S. restaurants is lost to theft. To discourage theft, management establish clear controls and must be sure they are in fact followed and practiced. The most fundamental aspects of internal control are the separation of duties and the recording of each transaction. Most of us are guided by a high degree of personal integrity and moral standards that keep us honest. The total humiliation of being accused, let alone being arrested, is also a huge deterrent to honest people.

The procedural checks and balances discussed in this chapter and the perseverance of management toward fraud will strongly limit the opportunity to steal and increase the likelihood of being detected. However, one's personal circumstances can reach such a desperate point that previously honest and law-abiding employees are driven to steal, often as a result of severe debt or catastrophic financial loss. Tax-free money becomes very tempting to an individual experiencing such stress.

Internal controls are a critical component to any cost control program. They identify the authority and responsibilities of all members of the organization at each and every level. They also define the ways by which cost objectives will be achieved. Many operations install a management information system (MIS) for data accumulation, preparation, analyzing, and reporting.

MANAGEMENT INFORMATION SYSTEMS (MIS)

Management information systems help establish clear and proper rules for consistent and prompt reporting. MIS sets up efficient paperwork flow and data collection that reduces errors and omissions so not to compromise their interpretation and decision making. The accumulation and preparation of reports must be done economically to keep duplication and overreporting to a minimum.

A MIS seeks to prevent fraudulent conversions at all levels. Although no system will prevent all fraud because the cost could far exceed the losses from it, a soundly designed system that is followed and maintained will reveal areas of loss if fraudulent conversions do occur. A system will not identify specifically what caused the loss or variance from standard, but it will alert management that investigation is warranted. For example, when the sales records show fewer items were sold than were used, the food cost will certainly be affected. However, at this stage one cannot determine whether the kitchen or dining room is the cause and who in particular is as fault. The system alerted management to a potential problem and now they must investigate.

The Association of Independent Certified Public Accountants (AICPA) defines internal controls as follows: *Internal control comprises the plan of organization . . . adopted to safeguard the assets of a business, check the accuracy and reliability of its accounting data, promote operational efficiency, and encourage adherence to prescribed managerial policies.*

The definition goes beyond simple checks and balances in paperwork flow, using cash registers, prenumbered guest checks, time cards, and inventory records. It includes such techniques and control devices as:

1. Budgets
2. Standards of performance
3. Personnel policies
4. Statistical analysis
5. Physical safeguards
6. Sales and production planning and forecasting
7. Continuous follow-up and appraisal to compliance and accuracy of reports and activities.

A well-designed system of control is so important to the efficient conduct of the business that it is incumbent upon management to continually review and evaluate their control system. From time to time, controls might break down from the lack of supervision and continuous review. This may happen when an employee fails to perform a particular procedure one time and, because no one challenged the lack of procedure, the employee continues to omit the procedure periodically; for example, putting guest checks in numerical order and matching kitchen copies with hard copies to detect walkouts and missing checks.

The key to internal control is *entering the transaction into the system*. That may be accomplished electronically as with a computer driven sales system or when a handwritten, serially numbered guest check is given to the cook or bartender to fill an order. If food or beverage can be obtained by servers or customers without being entered into the system, the system is flawed and control can be compromised.

The basis for all control is comparison. Menu sales mix analysis is useful only when the totals can be compared against the amounts on hand, issued, and remaining in inventory. The figures are compared to either a preestablished or concurrently established standard or goal.

Most activities performed in a restaurant are cyclical and begin with preparation, proceed to action, and then the cycle starts over again. By inserting a comparison stage in the cycle you create a control sub-system that becomes the basis for your system of internal control. The sub-systems interlock and feed into a reporting cycle since the final stage in a control system is a written report of the results. It is used to assess the persons responsible for the reported activity as well as the activity itself.

In addition to establishing a control point against which results can be compared, five other general cost control concepts are integral to control systems. They are:

1. Documentation: A description of the task, activity, or transaction including a physical record of the result. Written procedures and report forms are essential.
2. Supervision and review by someone familiar with performance standards.
3. Segregation of duties so no one person is responsible for or involved in all parts of the task cycle.
4. Timeliness: All tasks must be performed within the appropriate time. Comparisons must be made at established control points and reports made available at scheduled times in order to solve problems that are detected.
5. The cost-benefit relationship of procedures used and benefits derived must exceed the cost of implementing the controls.

The basic control procedure is an independent verification at a control points during and after the completion of a task. Although normally done visually or manually, verification is now being accomplished through written reports and the use of electronic devices and generated reports. The verification, however accomplished, is for the purpose of determining one or more of the following:

1. Proper authority to perform the task
2. Quantity available must be verified
3. Quality must meet preset standards
4. Performance results must be in accordance with proper guidelines

Techniques used include observation, inspection, and physical counts. The cycles of control must be examined from the perspectives of control objectives, control sub-systems, control points, and special procedures and techniques. The aspects of control include operational control, accounting control, and administrative control.

DAILY SALES REPORT

An MIS is a network for the generation and communication of pertinent and timely quantitative and qualitative information to all levels of management to be used for planning, directing, and controlling the operations of an organization. Internal managerial accounting records are necessary for the control of day-to-day operational activity.

The primary record is perhaps the daily sales report. If a restaurant has more than one cash register, it will require reports for each register. A sample of a restaurant's daily report is shown in Figure 8-1.

The information contained on a sales report can include any of the following information:

1. Register readings, beginning and ending
2. Sales breakdowns, by meal periods, types of sale (e.g., food, beverage, merchandise, cigars, candy, etc.)
3. Type of payment (i.e., cash, charge, check, employee, discount, or complimentary)
4. Over-rings, under-rings, voids, paid-outs
5. Comments on activity, weather, special parties, events affecting business
6. Sales tax
7. Amount of deposit
8. Name of person preparing report
9. Customer counts

GUEST CHECK REGISTER

Forms that monitor guest checks, if check books are issued to servers, are an important control when the guest check is used to requisition food and beverage from the kitchen and bar. A guest check register should record the beginning numbers of all check books. See Figure 8-2. Checks should not be left out in the open but kept under lock and key with unused checks turned in at the end of the shift and the ending number written on the check register. Servers should write their name on all their checks when issued a new book to discourage others from using their checks when they are not working.

Checks should be sorted by server and put in numerical order to check for missing checks. If a soft duplicate copy (dupe) is used to requisition food from

DATE ___/___/___   **RESTAURANT DAILY REPORT**

DAY OF WEEK _____ WEATHER _____

NAME _____

ADD BEGINNING REGISTER CASH _____
ADD CREDIT CARDS NOT DEPOSITED TO DATE _____
ADD NSF CHECKS ON HAND _____

(MEMO ONLY) SALES		(MEMO ONLY) NON TAX SALES OR CONTROL INFO.	SALES CATEGORIES	CLOSING READINGS		LESS: OVERRINGS & UNDERRINGS	TOTALS
FORWARD	MONTH-TO-DATE						
			FOOD				
			LIQUOR				
			BEER				
			WINE				
			PROMOTIONAL SALES				
			VENDING				
		(B)	TOTALS (F)			ADD TOTAL SALES → (A)	

COMMENTS _____
_____
_____
_____
_____
_____
_____
_____

ADD SALES TAX COLLECTED: USE ONLY FOR THE AMOUNT OF SALES TAX NOT ALREADY INCLUDED IN (A) ABOVE:

1. AMOUNT COLLECTED PER SEPARATE REGISTER KEY
   ———— OR ————
2. TAXABLE SALES: (POSSIBLY JUST TAXABLE FOOD) TIMES ____%

(SEE A/R PAGE) ADD COLLECTIONS ON CHARGE SALES

◄——————(EXPLANATION) ADD OTHER INCOME OR RECEIPTS

EQUALS TOTAL TO ACCOUNT FOR (C)

PAID OUT OF REGISTER CASH

PAYEE AND DESCRIPTION	FOOD	LIQUOR	BEER	WINE	PROMO SALES			
TOTALS								

ADD TOTAL PAID OUTS ——————►

PERPETUAL REGISTER READING RECONCILIATION	
PERPETUAL READING TODAY	
LESS: PERPETUAL READING YESTERDAY	
= AUDIT TOTAL	
LESS: TODAY'S READINGS ((F) ABOVE)	
= DIFFERENCE TO ACCOUNT FOR	

(MEMO ONLY) DISCOUNT	**DEPOSITS**	
	CASH	
	MASTERCHARGE	
	VISA	

ADD TOTAL DEPOSITS ——————►

SEE A/R PAGE FOR CREDIT CARD RECEIVABLE CONTROL SECTIONS	**OTHER CREDIT CARDS**	
	AMERICAN EXPRESS	

CONTROL & ANALYSIS SECTION				
		LOCATION	LOCATION	LOCATION
TICKET CONTROL	TOTAL			
CLOSING TICKET # +				
OPENING TICKET # −				
TICKETS ISSUED =				
TICKETS VOIDED −				
TICKETS USED = (G)				
CUSTOMER ANALYSIS				
AVG. CHECK (A) ÷ (G)				
CUSTOMER COUNT				
AVG. PER CUSTOMER				

ADD TOTAL CREDIT SLIPS SUBMITTED FOR COLLECTION ——————►

(SEE A/R PAGE) ADD CHARGE SALES _____

ADD OWNER CASH WITHDRAWALS _____

ADD ENDING REGISTER CASH _____

ADD CREDIT CARDS NOT DEPOSITED TO DATE _____

ADD NSF CHECKS ON HAND _____

EQUALS TOTAL ACCOUNTED FOR (D)

CASH OVER/(SHORT) TODAY (D) MINUS (C) _____

CASH OVER/(SHORT) MONTH TO DATE _____

FIGURE 8.1   Daily sales report. Permission granted by Edwin K. Williams & Company, Waco, TX 76707.

Date: *7-22-98*		Shift: *Lunch*		Prepared By: *DVP*			
Checks Issued		Server Initials	No.	Checks Returned		Server Initials	No.
Beginning Number	Ending Number			Beginning Number	Ending Number		
001	*025*	*RRF*	*25*	*016*	*025*	*RRF*	*15*
026	*050*	*DDR*	*25*	*036*	*050*	*DDR*	*10*
051	*075*	*PRC*	*25*	*069*	*075*	*PRC*	*18*

Missing or Voided Check Record				
Check Number	Server	Comments		Mgt. Authorization
065-067	*PRC*	*Checks voided due to beverage spill. New checks prepared. Voids attached.*		*DVP*

FIGURE 8-2 Guest check register.

the kitchen, kitchen copies should be collated with the customer copy to detect missing checks or omitted food items. Checks should be audited for register verification of payment and the amounts verified. Price extensions and additions should also be audited.

If food and beverage can be obtained without submitting a guest check (i.e., oral orders), the system has a flaw. Once an item is written on a check or entered electronically, it can be tracked. That is why so many operations have eliminated oral transmission of food and beverage orders. All cross-outs of food and beverage items should be initialed by management. If they cannot present it orally, it must be written. Checks that have been filled should be marked or perforated to keep them from being resubmitted. If checks are monitored, controls will be effective.

The data assembled on the reports may be pertinent enough to be presented in raw data form for decision-making purposes. More often data are included with other information for comparative and ancillary purposes. For example, the sales mix information taken from guest orders or checks is useful to the kitchen manager to forecast preparation quantities. This same information is used by the buyer to determine what and how much to purchase. All they need is summary information of what was recorded on the guest checks, not the checks themselves.

The actual guest check in passed from server to guest to cashier. Sometimes the server also acts as the cashier and keeps a personal bank. If a separate cashier is used, the guest check is collected when paid for future auditing. The sales data needed by the kitchen and buyer may be extracted electronically with a point-of-sale system. In the absence of such technology, the sales mix information will be collected manually. The checks are also audited for errors in addition, price extensions, and verification stamps that checks have been paid. Most cash registers will print PAID on the check and the amount tendered.

A detailed sales report of the daily sales for food and beverage is also garnered from the guest check. Sales reports are prepared and management uses this information to compare to forecasts, standards, and budgets. It also provides information helpful to management in scheduling workers and forecasting business activity. Finally, the information on sales is compiled and entered into sales journals for financial reports where further decisions will be made after interpreting the information.

BASIC PRINCIPLES FOR CASH CONTROL

No matter which method of cash collection is used by an operator, basic principles apply.

1. With all systems, any handwritten check should be added up with an adding machine. The tape should be stapled to the check so the customer can see that the bill has been added correctly. This also speeds up the auditing of prices and extensions.

2. The guest check should be rung into a cash register that cancels the check by printing a paid total on the check so it cannot be resubmitted for payment. In coffee shop operations where the same check is used to requisition food from the kitchen and given to the guest at the end of the meal, some marking or perforation should be done when the order is filled to prevent the check from being reused on another table. In the case of alcoholic beverages, the simple grease pencil line drawn under the order indicates it has been filled.

3. Require that the guest check be submitted *before* food or beverage will be prepared. Do not under any circumstances fill requests from oral orders. Remember, it must be written on the guest check or entered electronically for it to be tracked by the cost control system.

4. All checks should be rung up individually and the cash drawer should be closed after each check is rung up. The checks should be audited to see that the verified amount paid is the same as the written total on the check. A newly hired cashier under-rang checks totaling $1200, which we did not discover until after she had left town. The system was there but management failed to check for compliance.

5. Use a pre-check or dual system of ordering. Checks not only are to be written out but also rung into a pre-check register under the food or beverage key. The check must be verified by the register stamp or receipt before an order is filled. At the end of the night, the totals from the pre-check register are compared to those at the cashier station.

6. Require management initials on all altered checks, especially once the food order has been issued from the kitchen.

7. Limit the access to the cash register to as few individuals as possible. Verify the contents of the drawer whenever there is a shift change. Conduct random drawer changes in the middle of a meal period to check for under-rings.

8. Do not allow the register to be "Z'ed out." Remove the ability to set the register reading back to zero. Make sure register tapes are included with the drawer contents at the end of the shift. The ending reading should be verified by the tape.

9. Guest checks should be custom printed and serially numbered. Issue checks to specific servers and have them turn in unused checks at the end of the shift. Keep unused guest checks in a secure location. Sort used guest checks by number order and compare ending number of unused book to verify that all checks have been accounted for.

10. Have management initial any checks that are over-rung or under-rung and attach an over/under-ring slip. See Figure 8-3. Do not make up over-rings by under-ringing checks. If a check is under-rung, put it in sideways and ring the shorted amount.

11. Develop a uniform set of menu abbreviations for handwritten guest checks, and develop a format that divides the check into sections for food and beverage.

12. Have management approve all voided checks and do not discard voided checks no matter how soiled or torn they may be.

13. Do not deviate from your procedures for cash and check control.

14. Print notices on the checks, menu, and at the cashier's station that inform the customer as to how and whom to pay.

15. If you have a cashier, do not allow servers to collect cash. Direct customer traffic in such a manner that those who pass the cashier's stand without paying can be detected.

16. Use a duplicate check or pre-check system for main dish items and all food items issued from the kitchen. Inventory pies and other desserts so you can check the sales records against the usage at the end of a meal period.

17. Inventory all bottled beers and wines before and after each meal period and compare to guest checks.

```
+-----------------------------------------------------------+
|                                                           |
|              Regan's Restaurants, Inc.                    |
|                                                           |
|   Unit Location:                                          |
|                                                           |
|          CASH PAID-OUT VOUCHER                            |
|                                                           |
|   +---------------------------------------------------+   |
|   | Date:                        Amount $:            |   |
|   |                                                   |   |
|   | Paid To:                                          |   |
|   |                                                   |   |
|   | Justification:                                    |   |
|   |                                                   |   |
|   |                                                   |   |
|   | Expense Category:                                 |   |
|   |                                                   |   |
|   | Paid Out By:                                      |   |
|   |                                                   |   |
|   | Received By:                                      |   |
|   +---------------------------------------------------+   |
|                                                           |
|      RECEIPT MUST ACCOMPANY THIS VOUCHER                  |
|                                                           |
+-----------------------------------------------------------+
```

FIGURE 8-3   Cast paid-out voucher.

18. Audit checks regularly for correct prices, price extensions, and addition.

19. Use secret shopper services to see that correct procedures are being followed.

20. When coupon promotions are used, require that coupons be stapled to the guest check prior to payment at the cashier to reduce coupon fraud by the cashier or server.

21. If management makes bank deposits, set strict procedures on how often deposits are made. This is especially important for out-of-town locations. Have deposit slips turned in weekly or even better, obtain electronic verification of deposit amounts from bank. This is a particularly vulnerable area where large losses can occur. Management typically prepares and completes sales and deposit reports. If they also count or prepare the daily deposit, ownership must be especially vigilant in monitoring these activities.

22. Paid-out and correction vouchers (Figure 8-4) should be reviewed and approved. Authority to approve these vouchers should not be given to persons involved in the cash or check register duties.

Sometimes management can directly contribute to putting employees in a position that the temptation to steal and go undetected is too much. Ironically, the

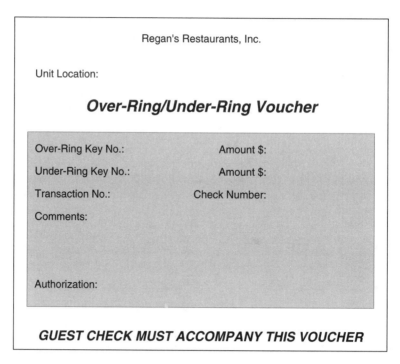

FIGURE 8-4 Over-ring/under-ring voucher.

techniques used by employees to steal are not sophisticated or complicated. A large percentage of the theft goes undetected simply because management does not consistently follow up on the very procedures they have in place. I recall a situation I faced at one restaurant that we were just not happy with the amount of profit given the volume of business the restaurant was doing. We suspected that food cost was too high and concentrated our efforts in the back of the house on waste, portioning, and purchase price. We inventoried items that were not rung into the register to tally against the guest checks. Nothing could be detected.

It was not until a friend and regular customer, who stopped in for breakfast before his weekly golf game, related that his waitress never gave him a check and made change from her apron. When confronted the waitress admitted to taking an average of $12 a day for the previous 6 years. We estimate that she took over $30,000. This was made possible because we wanted to save money on a cashier and did not schedule one until 8:00 A.M. when the restaurant opened at 6:00 A.M.

TELLTALE SIGNS OF POSSIBLE THEFT

A number of "danger signs" can point toward the possibility of theft. Sometimes the thief is the person you least expect. It may be a loyal, long-term employee, a close friend, or even a relative.

1. Are you at a loss to explain why your restaurant is not making the profit it should, given the volume of business you are doing?
2. Is any employee or manager overextended to creditors?
3. Has any employee incurred extensive personal or family medical bills without a way to pay them?
4. Has any employee displayed spending habits that surprise you given his or her pay rate (e.g., new car, furniture, clothes, recreational equipment)?
5. Does any employee appear to have a drug or drinking problem and a habit of "partying"?
6. Is any employee openly showing dissatisfaction with his or her rate of pay?
7. Is any employee unusually friendly with one of your supplier's sales or delivery personnel, or your regular customers?
8. Have you been receiving more than the normal number of calls from creditors to verify employment of one employee in particular? Have collection agency personnel or creditors called your company because of one of your employees?
9. Is any employee openly lobbying you to give him or her more responsibility in one or more of the following tasks: receiving cash, recording to accounts, preparing bank deposits, auditing guest checks, or checking deliveries?
10. Is there any employee who constantly asks for advances on his or her pay? (Source: Thomas L. LaJeunesse, "Is Your Company Safe from Embezzlement?" *The Bottomline*, August–September, 1987, pp. 7-7, 11).

POINT-OF-SALE SYSTEMS FOR CONTROL

One effective way to reduce and control the loss of cash receipts is through tight inventory control and point-of-sale procedures. If servers are unable to obtain food or beverage without a hard-copy check or entering the sale electronically, you have eliminated 99 percent of the opportunity for theft. Once a check has been written or entered into the system, an audit trail is established.

Several great products are available to the industry to speed up data accumulation, sorting, and report preparation. Total systems require extensive training of the entire staff as well as management. At first, employees will be intimidated by the new hardware and software. It may take longer for the older employees to feel comfortable and accept the registers and dispensers than the younger ones.

Once installed, operators report a significant reduction in pilferage and theft. Food cost and liquor cost savings often pay for the system in a very short time period. This is referred to as the "Big Brother Syndrome." Employees are uncertain of the system's capabilities and are therefore inclined to watch their step. Some operators will report that long-time employees will quit or retire.

One restaurant manager who asked my advice about which system to purchase, related the true story of two long-time employees who left soon after he purchased a system. One was his head bartender and the other his cashier. His head bartender never took a vacation, and his cashier always came out exactly to the penny when she reconciled her register drawer. We surmise that both were stealing heavily from the business.

With a press of a key, a manager can discover which items sell the best at different times of the day. The manager can then order more efficiently and keep inventory to a minimum, eliminating overstocking and running out. The option on the point-of-sale system is referred to as "menu explosion." It has the ability to subtract out of inventory all the ingredients used in the preparation of the item sold.

Example: When a cheese enchilada is sold, the prescribed amounts of cheese, lettuce, and tomato, spices, and corn enchilada are used. You compare the amount the standardized recipe says you should use to the actual amount left in inventory at the end of the month. What in essence the system does is compare cost of food sold to cost of food consumed. If there is a significant variance in one or more of the ingredients, it "flags" that item on the printout. While it does not tell what was causing the over-usage of a particular ingredient, it alerts the operator to a potential problem area for management to investigate. In this case the variance could be caused by the service person not putting the item on the check, a cook's over-portioning, the ticket not being rung, and so on.

The data such a system provides can be used to track server productivity, initiate promotions and contests for servers, and keep the servers with their customers and not in the kitchen. These systems can also give you sales on a monthly, weekly, daily, meal, or hourly basis. Peak periods can be discovered to assist in scheduling workers more efficiently.

The majority of what is stolen in restaurants comes out of the bar. In a tightly run operation, cash is more likely to be taken by management-level employees than by hourly workers. They know the system better, have a much greater access to cash and inventory, and have considerable autonomy. Hourly employees are more likely to take things. If there is any food or beverage near an open back door, you increase the opportunity for theft.

One of the deterrents management uses to slow down thieves is simply making them aware that they suspect someone to be stealing and letting them know that they are investigating to determine who the person or persons are. In addition, the announcement that management will prosecute to the full extent of the law is also a significant deterrent to petty theft. The habitual thief or person who has a drug problem will not be as motivated not to steal, but it will slow them down for a while.

The internal control process is built from all the rules, regulations, policies, and procedures in place for ordering, receiving, storage, preparation, portioning, and the like. Every activity occurring within the restaurant is linked to your internal controls.

The transmission of information for such controls includes visual inspections or observations. However, it also means checking to see that schedules are manned properly and taking the necessary action when they are not (e.g., calling in another employee and disciplining the absentee). Information flows horizontally and vertically in the organization as well and through the formal and informal communication channels.

PAY BY CHECK, NOT CASH

In the restaurant industry, the central collection point for data is the accounting department or, in the case of an independent operation, the accounts payable function. A systematic record-keeping system must be established to record daily sales and organize invoices for payment. It is recommended that all your bills be paid by check and that you open two checking accounts for the business. One is your *general account* into which you deposit your daily sales and from which you write checks to pay your bills. The second checking account is used exclusively for *payroll*. You move funds from your general account to the payroll account as payrolls are processed. Basically, the payroll account "zeros out" each pay period when employees cash their checks.

By using checks to pay 99.9 percent of you bills, only small cash paid-outs are allowed. The check register, along with your invoices, inventory, and deposit slips, is all your accountant needs to prepare your financial statements for the month.

MANAGEMENT REPORTS

As the level of management for which the reports are intended moves higher, the nature of the information contained in the reports changes. At the departmental or unit manager level, the information is rather detailed and frequently is expressed in such terms as cover per labor hour or labor cost per cover served. These reports provide information that allows the department heads to immediately isolate deficiencies in the operation under their direct control.

At higher levels of management, the information tends to become broader and more summarial in nature. At the level of chief executive, the information is presented in the form of financial statements, operating statistics, departmental performance, budgets, or special reports. Since upper management is responsible for the performance of the total operation, it must be able to take the appropriate action, preventive or corrective, in the event of unsatisfactory performance.

An efficient method of keeping management informed, but not buried in data, is through what is referred to as *exception reporting*. Here management can be kept informed about the current deficiencies and favorable information that exceeds standards. Standards are set that provide for an acceptable range of performance. Only data that deviates to an unacceptable level from the standard are flagged for upper management's attention.

The frequency of reports should be closely related to management's ability to influence or control items included within particular reports. Food and beverage reports must be frequently prepared, but schedules showing insurance and or depreciation schedules are not readily controllable and thus compiled less frequently.

Some reports will contain only objective quantitative information while others may have more subjective qualitative information, as with secret shopper reports on quality of food and service. Examples of both types of reports are given throughout this book and include both financial and statistical information. Financial information requires reporting of absolute dollar values as with the monthly financial statements. Statistical information includes percentages, ratios, and averages; other statistics include units of activity, number sold, customer counts, and productivity indices.

The period of time a report covers is related to the length of the reported activity covered. For example, dining room sales could be reported over the time period of the whole day, meal period, or hour while the report is transmitted to management every day.

The length of time between the end of the reporting period and the delivery of the report must be kept to a minimum. It is related to the time it takes to prepare the report and deliver it. Daily reports, for example, are prepared early the following day to maintain their value for prompt corrective action. The problem with the traditional accounting reports was the time lapse between their preparation and delivery to appropriate management. The fifteenth of the following month was not timely enough. With electronic data processing, reports can be compiled in one third the time it previously took to prepare monthly financial statements.

Internal control covers a broad field and involves far more than cash and check control. Prevention is the key to internal control as it is impossible to completely eliminate fraud when an employee, customer, or purveyor is motivated to steal. Such internal controls are needed most in operations with absentee ownership. Actual visual observation is not sufficient to insure adequate control. Written reports and adherence to standards are critical to minimizing the occurrence of internal theft.

Chapter Nine

Food Purchasing and Ordering

We start with distinguishing the difference between *purchasing* and *ordering.* The distinction is more than semantics; they are two different functions. Independent operators and corporate executives set purchasing policy; chain general managers and franchisees only order quantities of specified brands and grades. Purchasing involves setting policy as to which purveyors, brands, grades, and varieties of foodstuffs will be ordered. These are referred to as *standardized purchase specifications.* Prices, credit terms, delivery schedules, discounts and returns, and allowances are all part of the purchasing policy that is negotiated between the distributor and the owner or corporation. Therefore, the decision of what and from whom to buy is a *purchasing* decision.

PARAMETERS OF EFFECTIVE ORDERING

Managers of corporate or franchise restaurants are not given "purchasing" authority. They do have authority to *order* necessary quantities of the specified merchandise from approved purveyors. Therefore, *ordering* determines the *quantities* that will be purchased and kept in inventory. Ordering can be delegated; purchasing authority is not. A purchasing agent for a hotel chain makes both ordering and purchasing decisions as do some corporate chefs and club chefs.

Efficient ordering brings together the right items, in the right quantity, in the right place, at the right price, at the right time. Once menus have been written offering items that will result in optimum customer satisfaction and will return the desired food cost percentage and gross profit, a purchasing program designed to assure profit margins can be developed.

To order efficiently and effectively, the buyer will need the following information:

1. Product descriptions and specifications
2. Unit size per case or individual package
3. Unit price
4. Purveyors who carry items
5. How much to order and keep on hand

Any efficient purchasing program must also incorporate the following:

1. Standard purchase specifications based on,
2. Standardized recipes that result in,
3. Standardized yields that with portion control allow for,
4. Accurate costs based on portions actually served

Standards assure consistency in each area, and if standards change, costs must be recalculated. Once you have determined the specific varieties, grades, and brands, you must adhere to these specifications. Although a bid process is usually undertaken to determine possible suppliers, rarely is the decision on which purveyor to use based on price considerations alone. Other factors that enter the decision process will be covered in detail later in this chapter. The exceptions are state and municipal governments that are bound by statute to go with the lowest bidder. As those who have to follow such regulations have told me, there are also disadvantages, and low initial price does not always translate to low cost over the long run. Given the choice, another vendor might be selected even if the price were a little higher. The missing element in making a buying decision on the basis of price alone is *service after the sale.*

One thing that both chains and independents strive for with their menus is consistency in taste, appearance, and cost. If different brands of product are purchased without regard for standardized recipes, consistency will fluctuate wildly. As any kitchen manager, chef, or cook knows, mayonnaise quality is not the same with all brands. The same holds true for salad dressings and most other foods. Consider the color, taste, and consistency of the brands of French dressing available on the market today. An order placed with three different purveyors for French dressing will produce three different-tasting products ranging from sweet to a definite vinegar tartness. In addition, the color may range from a deep orange color to a pale orange or yellow.

There is an old saying in the pizza business: "You don't have to make the best pizza sauce, just be consistent." After a while, your customers will become accustomed to your sauce. If it changes in taste and texture on subsequent visits, customers will complain. They do not want to be surprised when they get their salad with French dressing and find it different from the last time they ate in the restaurant.

Ordering for a restaurant operation is complicated by the fact that a restaurant is essentially a manufacturing operation producing a large number of highly perishable products. Some restaurants serving breakfast, lunch, and dinner have three different menus to order for each, containing dozens of different items at different times of the day.

In order to effectively carry out the ordering function and control costs, the operator must be able to do four things: accurately predict how much will be needed, maintain purchase specifications, follow standardized recipes, and enforce portioning standards. Only when these four things are under control can the person doing the ordering determine the optimum quantities to keep on hand.

It is important to understand that written standards are not a guarantee that they will be effective. There can be compliance in the absence of written standards. It is not what is *written* that makes it formal, but what is actually *practiced*. Standards are followed to the extent that management demands. It is management and employees who make standards work, not the mere fact that they are codified in some policy manual. There must be continual follow-up and appraisal because employees will deviate from prescribed standards only as far as management allows.

If the ordering function is not done properly and shortages occur, food cost will fluctuate and standardized recipes may be altered. Ingredients may be left out of a recipe or substitutions made that not only affect the taste but the cost as well. Quantities can be accurately predicted if standards of purchasing, preparation and portioning are followed.

THE BUYER'S CREDENTIALS

Purchasing is an administrative function requiring technical knowledge about the products being purchased and the market dynamics that affect prices and supply. To fill the position of purchasing agent, the buyer should be experienced in food production procedures. The buyer must understand the workings of a kitchen and be familiar with equipment and the skill levels of employees in the kitchen. It is also critically important to be familiar with market trends and sources of supply and to keep up with new products coming on the market. The buyer needs to know how the primary markets impact prices paid in local markets and how quickly the prices in local markets will change relative to the major market indicators.

The purchasing agent should be able to judge if a fair price is being quoted by a distributor based on current market reports. Foodstuffs and supplies ordered must be matched to the purchase specifications for each outlet. For example, the specifications for a fast-food versus a full-service restaurant will find that more prepared or convenience products are used in the former. Also impacted will be the grade, variety, size, or count of food items ordered. The lack of space, equipment, and skilled employees may require pre-portioned or processed ingredients be purchased.

If ordering is to meet the needs of the system it serves, the buyer must be familiar with the use to be made of each food item as this will impact the various types, grades, and forms in which they will be purchased. The buyer must also know the grading criteria, labeling terminology, and the standards of quality used in grading.

Buyers need to follow market conditions closely as supply and price follow predictable seasonal variations. The United States Department of Agriculture (USDA) provides free reports indicating the percentage of total crop that is marketed during each of the twelve months of the year. The greater the probability of price and supply changes, the greater the need to follow the market closely, especially on items purchased in significant quantities. Some of the USDA reports are available for seafood, fruits and vegetables, and beef, pork, veal, and lamb.

A very few buyers may physically go to the market to select their own merchandise. Exclusive restaurants sometimes purchase directly from farmers, fishermen, and growers who sell organically raised products. They are willing to pay a premium for these products as are their customers.

TYPES OF BUYING

Different types of buying are employed in the food-service industry. *Open* or *informal buying* is where the contact between the buyer and seller is made through a sales representative in face-to-face meetings or over the phone. Negotiations are largely oral, and conditions of purchase and product specifications are given orally. This is not unlike a unit manager calling a produce supplier checking supply and prices of items needed.

Formal buying means that the terms are put in writing and procedures for payment of invoices and terms are stated as conditions for quoting prices and service commitments. This is what corporate administrators will arrange for multi-unit purchasing programs. However, individual operators also enter into formal buying agreements with suppliers.

The traditional purveyor representative will usually make weekly stops at the company's top accounts to get the order directly from the manager or purchasing agent. Some may also collect payment for last week's delivery. Occasionally, they will bring in new product samples; they are sales representatives first and foremost. The role of the sales rep cannot be overstated as companies realize that anyone can sell a particular product and that the determination of who gets the order is not simply based on the purveyor with the lowest price. If the price advantage is neutralized, the customer will make the purchasing decision on other services and benefits received from dealing with a particular purveyor and their sales rep.

SALES REPRESENTATIVES

The most important aspect of purveyor selection is perhaps customer service. It is here where the purveyor representative has to be much more than an *order taker*. Representatives not only must be knowledgeable about product lines but also must have an understanding of the needs and problems of the operator and be able to offer suggestions. The major food-service distributors are offering a package of what is being called "value-added services," or buyer benefits. These include such things as recipes for products, point-of-sale information, training sessions for kitchen and service personnel, special reports detailing the use levels of all items purchased, and special presentations on new products.

Professional sales representatives will not take up a lot of an operator's or manager's valuable time and interrupt his or her daily routine just to get an order. However, they want to sell to you every week and would very much like you to expand what you purchase from them. They gain your confidence by offering solutions to your food related problems.

Some of the old-time sales reps will take as long as you let them to get an order. They will stand around chatting with the kitchen personnel and dining room staff and keep them from being productive. These types give sales reps a bad reputation; but they will stay only as long as management allows them to stay. Many managers will only see sales reps with appointments or at a set time each week.

With certain items like dairy products, fountain syrups, coffee, crackers, and bread, the delivery person and the sales rep are one and the same. Orders are prepared at the time of delivery after counting what is currently on hand. A par level of stock is usually kept with the approval of the operator. In cases of product sold on guaranteed sales, day-old bread and outdated dairy products are replaced for credit unless they were specifically ordered by the operator. This kind of conditional sale is a self-regulating inventory process. There is little benefit in overstocking when the product has to be returned for credit and returns are subtracted from the commission of the sales representative.

However, I recall one restaurant where the bread delivery person had his product stocked in the freezer of the restaurant. The manager did not realize that he was paying for this unused inventory when it should have been credited to his account. In addition, I have observed occasions where nonperishable items were overstocked by ambitious commissioned sales reps. Paper suppliers and dish detergent sales reps should always be required to obtain management approval on all reorders. If you are not careful, you will be tying up your cash in excess inventory.

Some managers, myself included, prefer to give their order over the phone to eliminate the time spent dealing with sales representatives. This is the practice with most chain restaurant operations. It is unnecessary for the sales representative to make personal visits because the prices and products supplied have been agreed upon by corporate executives and payment is not made from the individual unit. The manager has no authority to change product specifications and cannot authorize purchase of items not preapproved by corporate. The weekly visits to restaurants still occur within the independently owned and operated units that account for roughly 60 percent of the 595,000 commercial food-service units.

Most commercial restaurants purchase from distributors and orders are placed over the phone, given to sales representatives, or submitted in writing. The amount of formality varies, but there is negotiation and agreement over the terms of sale that specify quantities, prices, deliveries, payment of invoices, and notification of price increases.

PURCHASING CHANNELS

The path that food products take to ultimately end up in the storerooms of the food service operation is quite complex. As products move from the grower or producer to the end user, costs increase with each successive transfer. The route begins with the producer and grower, who in turn sell their products to a processor. Often, an intermediary, called a *concentrator*, is necessary to gather the output of many small producers and growers into transportable quantities. Examples of concentrators are grain elevators, receiving plants, and cooperative marketing organizations. They primarily aid the small farmers in getting their goods to the larger markets.

A *broker* represents a packer or processor who in turn sells the processed products, canned tomato products, for example, to distributors and wholesalers who may put their private label on the can. They in turn will sell direct to the end users, the restaurants, and food-service outlets. It is estimated that approximately 60 percent of the price of the product goes to cover the cost of marketing and transporting the product to the end user. Only 40 percent goes to the farmer.

There are also primary and secondary markets. Prices quoted on primary markets influence the pricing on all other markets. The Chicago Livestock Market is a primary market that affects the prices charged in Kansas City and New York. Boston is a primary seafood market, and the prices charged there drive the prices in other cities from Atlanta to Dallas. Buyers learn to watch the activity on the primary markets to forecast what will happen to the price and supply in secondary and local markets. The larger chain operators like McDonald's and Red Lobster purchase in such large quantities that they can bypass the primary markets and buy directly from the producer, grower, or trawler. This allows the chains to save on middleman handling costs.

THE BUYER-SELLER RELATIONSHIP

The operator-supplier interaction is a mutually beneficial relationship. Each party is dependent on the other for its existence; neither can prosper without the other. In nature, this type of relationship is referred to as *symbiosis* and means "consorting together of two dissimilar organisms in a mutually advantageous partnership."

Although some vendors have vertically integrated into the food-service business (e.g., Pepsico, General Mills, Pillsbury are three that come to mind), the majority of vendor-operator relationships are best described as symbiotic where either one can end the relationship at any time.

It seems to work best when both sides view each other in a mutually advantageous partnership. But often, one of the parties, usually the restaurant operator, will approach the negotiation table and present a one-sided unilateral position of demands and conditions the vendor must abide by to get the restaurant's business. The larger the account, the greater the stipulations and the greater the likelihood of the supplier yielding to the buyer's terms. I am not referring to product specifications here, but to the conditions of the agreement, on prices, delivery terms and payment policy.

I am not going to take sides as I have bargained from both sides of the table. Obviously, in such negotiations both parties are attempting to protect their respective interests. But sometimes the attitude of the negotiators is heavily one-sided due to the belief of some operators that you have to be tough on purveyors or they will take advantage of you. Conversely, the attitude of some purveyors is that they cannot let the operator get the upper hand because he or she will take advantage of them.

The food-service operator who is inflexible as to delivery times, days, and payment terms is just as unrealistic as the purveyor who sets the terms for ordering and delivery, returns, and credits without consideration for the needs of the client. This operator seems to be saying, "If you want my business, this is what you must do for me, regardless of how it increases your distribution cost and disrupts your operating procedures." The other side of the coin has the autocratic vendor saying, "If you want to buy from me, this is what you have to do before I will consider serving your account."

The negotiation process can be made more equitable for both parties if each understands the other's situation. Now, I believe that these extreme attitudes are the exception rather than the rule anymore, thanks to allied memberships of national and local restaurant associations and the International Food Service Executives Association (IFSEA), where operators and vendors can meet in a nonthreatening social and professional setting.

From my experience as an operator in a corporate chain capacity and as an individual entrepreneur, I know there are a number of things that determine the vendors I choose to deal with. And from the vendor side, I know that purveyors also analyze the operators to see if it is feasible to do business with them.

HOW PURVEYORS ANALYZE FOOD-SERVICE ACCOUNTS

First, the account is probably analyzed by the distributor for your total purchases over a 12-month period. The percentage of increase or decrease will be noted. If it has decreased, the vendor will seek to learn the reason why—for example, ordering from another supplier, change in specifications to a brand not carried—and try to increase your business.

Once these data have been gathered, the restaurant accounts are put into one of three categories.

A Accounts:	Profitable accounts in sales volume, order size, gross profit, required service level, and payment history. These are their best customers and they do not want to lose them to a competitor.
B Accounts:	These do not meet the minimum A levels but are still profitable.
C Accounts:	These are marginal customers whose order size, profitability, bill paying, or service levels give second thought to maintaining these accounts. In the scheduling of the sales reps' time, more time needs to be devoted to service A accounts and to improve B accounts. Marginal C accounts are time-consuming.

A distributor's sales manager is likely to tell sales reps that if they are calling on a large number of C accounts, they may be costing themselves and the company money. Unless these accounts show potential in terms of sales volume growth and profitability, their time can be better spent with A and B category customers.

HOW PURVEYORS CAN IMPROVE BUYER RELATIONS

1. Be consistent with order taking, deliveries, and product quality; charge a fair price.
2. Look out for the interests of the operators. Keep them in mind when certain products they need are going into short supply or where prices are likely to increase, inform clients of market conditions, protect them from shortages, and/or allow them to benefit from lower prices due to surpluses or special discounts from processors.
3. Maintain adequate stock level of products they need, and in case of emergencies when stocks are low on certain items, make sure they have the first right of refusal to purchase additional quantities before selling stock to new accounts.
4. Give adequate notice of price increases and invoice them at prices quoted at the time the order was taken. Be responsive to their specific needs, and give them the benefit of your superior knowledge about market supply and demand.

The buyer and seller who are aware of each other's interests can work together for their mutual benefit. Although they are "dissimilar organisms," they need each other to prosper and succeed. I love this quotation by the great states-man, John Ruskin: "There is always someone who is willing to make a product a little worse and sell it a little cheaper. Those who consider price only are this man's lawful prey."

THINGS OPERATORS CAN DO TO IMPROVE VENDOR RELATIONS

Don't be a fickle buyer who is "penny-wise and dollar-foolish." Look at the cost of your overall food order and not the prices of specific items. Value is deter-mined by more than just low price. Consider the extra services the purveyor provides; for example, merchandising and marketing assistance, cooperative advertising, order summary reports, handling of credits and returns, special de-liveries, and credit policies. The more business you do with a purveyor, the more important your account becomes and the greater the likelihood the ven-dor will work closely to satisfy your special needs.

Examine your purveyor relationships and determine where you are likely classified as an A account. You should be receiving special consideration in terms of prices, payment terms, and deliveries. Also, understand that you need to be at least a B account with the majority of your suppliers.

Don't make overly restrictive demands on delivery times or demand spe-cial deliveries on items *you overlooked* after the regular delivery has been made. Remember, they probably route their trucks to keep delivery costs down so they can charge more competitive prices. A mutually agreed-upon delivery schedule should be negotiated.

Pay your account on time to agreed-upon terms. The more frequently you pay, the lower prices you should be able to negotiate. The longer you take to pay or the longer the credit period, the higher prices they must charge. There are not too many other businesses who can get merchandise delivered today and not have to pay for it until next week.

Purveyors have the same demands on their cash flow as restaurant oper-ators. Many have to pay their suppliers quickly, and if they are on a 14-day billing period with their suppliers, they cannot give you the lowest price if you take 45 days to pay your invoices. It costs both parties money to extend credit terms.

Don't spread out your orders too thinly between more than two purvey-ors of similar items. Work to make your account an A or B rating; you will get better prices and service. You want to limit your purveyors so each gets a rea-sonable slice of your business. They will tell you that the more you buy from them, the more they can save you on your overall food purchases. The fewer vendors you have to deal with, the more time you can give to your operations, employee training, and customer relations.

When a vendor meets your standards on a consistent basis and charges you a fair price, it deserves your business and loyalty. Switching purveyors over a few cents per pound when they have been reliable and service minded in the past is unwarranted. Operators who have a history of dropping vendors who do not have regard for their standards should also be loyal to the vendors who serve them well. A good purveyor will treat the operators' interests as important as those of his or her own company, for, in fact, they are. Support the vendors who work with you. Be mindful that they are in business to make a profit for their time and expertise. It will all come back to you when product shortages occur or when you need some extra time to pay your bills.

Here is a list of questions that you might ask when you are interviewing suppliers for your operation:

1. Are you willing to stock private label (for chain concepts), or are you willing to add to your line the special brands we specify?
2. Can or will you enter into long-term contracts that will guarantee price and product supply?
3. Will the quality/brands/labels of your products remain consistent?
4. Will you agree to 30- to 60-day notification for price and product changes?
5. What is your policy on returns and credits?
6. What is your policy on deliveries:
   Frequency: number of days and which days?
   Emergency deliveries: extra charges?
   Will you agree to our delivery schedule requirements?
7. Who are your sales representatives in our area that we can call if there is a problem with our account? Or will we be considered a "corporate account" with the regional sales manager as our contact? Will orders be called in or will a sales rep call on the unit manager?
8. Will the delivery drivers put away the delivery or just unload the truck?
9. What are your payment terms?
10. What is your policy on notification of out-of-stock items?
11. Can you provide references of satisfied clients? (Check on their reliability and reputation.)
12. What value-added services can you provide? (For example, point-of-sale pieces, nutritional analysis, product development, recipes, reports of product use levels, and market information about price and supply.)
13. May I visit your distribution center to check on cleanliness and organization of your warehouse?

Sometimes operators and managers try to take advantage of purveyors. I recall a young assistant manager I inherited when I accepted a position of food-service director at a small private college and how he held suppliers in contempt. He would ask them for tickets to football games and Disney World because he felt they could not refuse if they wanted to get our business. On one occasion, a case of frozen product was accidently put into the walk-in refrigerator and not the freezer. He called the supplier and demanded that the company pick it up and give us full credit for the product.

When the sales representative came in with the replacement case, I had a talk with him and told him that it was not the vendor's fault and what actually happened. He had already assessed my assistant and knew it was not his company's fault because it was the only incident reported in his district. If it had been the vendor's fault, others who used the product would have reported the same thing. You are not going to put one over on your supplier for very long. Either the vendor will stop doing business with you or recover the extra costs in the prices you are charged.

The operator has obligations to the purveyor just as the purveyor has obligations to the operator. Developing an honest working relationship of mutual respect will pay off during times of product shortages and questions over billing and spoiled merchandise. Changing purveyors over small price differentials can work against the operator in the long run. There is a fine line between using competitive bidding to one's advantage and being known as a fickle buyer who can be swayed by price alone.

Orders must be coordinated with purveyors' delivery schedules and restaurant production requirements. The ingredients need to be delivered in advance of the day they are required for preparation, or a disruption of production will occur should the needed ingredients not be in stock. Efficient ordering has the product in stock when it is needed.

The purchasing and ordering functions have a significant impact on food costs and are two of the most important activities in any cost control program. An operator who monitors what is purchased and sold can closely monitor the pulse of the business. These critical functions cannot be performed casually or delegated to rank-and-file employees or purveyor representatives. The ordering function can be delegated but purchasing policy is always the domain of the owner or general manager.

Ordering takes place *after* purchasing policy has been set. Using purchase specifications as a guide, competitive bids can be obtained from potential suppliers. Once bids have been returned and purveyors selected, the process of ordering the appropriate quantities can be delegated.

The selection of approved purveyors cannot be made on the basis of price alone as many other factors must be considered. The independent restaurateur will set his or her own purchasing policy and likely consider many factors when making the decision.

While price is certainly a factor, other factors can override a few cents per pound or per case. Very few purveyors will allow an independent operation or chain to "cherry pick" its bids. That term describes purchasing only the items with the lowest prices from a purveyor, leaving the supplier little margin of profit. Keep in mind that, like a restaurant menu, the list of items carried by a supplier are not subject to the same identical markup.

Just as the restaurant operator monitors the sales mix of menu items, noting the food cost and gross profit return, so do vendors. They like to use the example that many supermarkets are using to demonstrate to the public that when you look at a typical shopping cart full of groceries, the total cost of the basket is lower than the competition's. If you examine the individual prices of the goods in the basket, you will find that certain items are higher than at a competitor, but the total market basket price for identical brands, grades, and sizes is less.

FACTORS THAT INFLUENCE PURVEYOR SELECTION

When sending out bids to potential suppliers, here is are a list of other considerations you will need to obtain clarification.

The Extent of Brands, Grades, Varieties, and Sizes Carried

If a standardized recipe calls for a specific brand name product and that brand is carried by only one purveyor, the operator has little choice in purveyors and price. Usually, in such cases, one brand is deemed superior to all others and is considered critical for quality control purposes. If sizable quantities are purchased, the operator has leverage to get another supplier to start handling the item. If the supplier agrees to carry a particular brand because you request it, that is a value-added service that you must take into account.

A purveyor cannot carry every brand and variety of canned good or frozen shrimp. Some purveyors offer low prices but are limited in the number of brands and sizes they carry. Having to purchase items in smaller or larger units than is practical for standardized recipe batches can become a disadvantage in quality and cost control. The greater the varieties and lines carried, the greater will be the prices charged.

The same holds true for certain unit sizes of items e.g., pints, quarts, gallons or 5 gallon buckets. If you want to purchase items in sizes that are best for your standardized recipes instead of bulk packs, that is another factor that may override having to pay a little more. Purveyors do not want to carry items that do not sell well or that they cannot turn over quickly in their inventories. For the same reasons that restaurants try to limit their menu offerings, purveyors try to limit their inventory of brands, varieties, and sizes.

Minimum Order Quantities for Delivery

The cost of making a stop at a restaurant to drop off one case or twenty cases is the same. When the driver's salary, truck lease, maintenance, gas and oil, insurance, and tolls are totaled and divided by the number of deliveries made over a year, the fixed overhead cost for a delivery of 30 cases of product is over $80. That cost needs to be spread over each item ordered. If the order quantity and items ordered (remember the low bid items) do not leave sufficient margin to cover fixed overhead, the vendor may not deliver or may tack on a minimum delivery charge. Therefore, the profit on a small delivery can be very little so the supplier must charge more per case or unit for small deliveries. If you regularly divide up a 30-case order between three different purveyors, the delivery cost per case would be $80/10 = $8.00. But if the order for all 30 cases were placed with a single vendor, the delivery cost per case would be reduced to $80/30 = $2.67, or a total saving of $159.90, which I assume would be reflected in lower prices.

Of course, there will always be purveyors who suspend the minimum order quantity to regular customers when circumstances dictate; that is just good business sense. However, if the customers regularly order below the minimum, the policy will be invoked. There are always competitors who want your business and will not impose minimum order quantities, but if they do not have the brands, sizes, and varieties you request, it becomes a moot point. In addition, expect to pay more per case or per pound when you are regularly ordering less than the minimum orders. You cannot negotiate the lowest price when you are ordering at minimum levels.

Credit Policies

It is not the price but the payment terms that are important. If you are paying COD (cash on delivery) for your food and supplies, you should be negotiating the lowest possible prices with your purveyor regardless of the fact that you are an independent operator. It is when you are extended credit that the price will go up. However, purchasing on credit is critically important to an independent operator trying to manage working capital.

Purveyors have the same cash flow pressures as the independent restaurant operator and corporate chain. They cannot give the buyer any better terms than they are being charged by their brokers or master distributors. If they must pay their invoices within 30 days, they cannot extend you credit for 60 without having to charge you interest or raising their prices. Most purveyors give us one week credit. That is really a fantastic advantage to the cash flow. Consider that what is delivered on Monday is processed and sold that week. We then take the sales to pay for last week's delivery. The longer you take to pay your bill, the higher will be the prices you will pay.

Most retailers must pay for merchandise before it is delivered. Car and appliance dealers must arrange for loans for their floor inventory and pay off the loans as merchandise is sold. In the restaurant business, we get delivery and have a minimum of one week to pay for the merchandise. If a purveyor will extend credit, it is a tremendous consideration to do business with the supplier and again override a slightly higher price than if we paid COD. There are times during the month and year when those workers' compensation premiums and other expenses that cannot be put off must be paid. The credit extended by purveyors is a very low-interest loan, and many restaurant operators, independents and chains alike, have used purveyor credit as a way to finance expansion and get low-interest loans. Bill-paying flexibility is what credit affords the restaurant operator. Purchase on credit allows the operator to spread out the payment of accounts. Having to pay a few cents more per pound to get additional time to pay is more than worth it during periods when cash flow is strained to a dangerously low point.

What is important is the cash-to-cash cycle. Supplies purchased on COD must be sold to *replenish* the cash that was paid out. If this cycle takes too long because excessive amounts were purchased or business was less than anticipated, the cash position of the operation will be strained. This was the case during the 1996 Summer Olympics in Atlanta. Both purveyors and restaurants increased inventories in anticipation of record sales to the tourists and Olympic officials. What occurred was just the opposite. Business activity was lower than would have been the case without the Olympics. Regular customers stayed away, and the out-of-town business did not make up for the loss of local trade. Restaurants expecting to turn over inventories more quickly were burdened with excessive purchases and invoices to pay. Without the anticipated sales, their cash flow was severely strained. Perishable products spoiled and could not be used. Purveyors could not take back much of what went unused because they too increased their inventories and had to pay their suppliers from cash reserves. This is why the credit policies of purveyors is an important factor in the selection of one purveyor over another.

Frequency of Deliveries

Like minimum order quantities, how often a purveyor will deliver is a very important consideration. Purveyors are experiencing the same cost constraints as any business in the economy today. Many are cutting back on the number of trucks used for delivery and that means reducing the number of deliveries per week.

Daily deliveries may become a thing of the past except for some very high-volume operators with good payment histories. Traditionally, bread, produce, and dairy suppliers delivered daily. Those that continue to do so will need to charge more for such services.

The purveyor-operator relationship cannot be a one-sided unilateral arrangement. There must be give-and-take on both sides. For example, the routing of the purveyor's delivery trucks may require that the delivery be made between 11:30 A.M. and 1:30 P.M., traditionally a time restaurants open for lunch will not accept deliveries. The delivery routes are programmed to have the trucks traveling the shortest distances when empty. One of my restaurants in Orlando was only a quarter mile from the John Sexton warehouse, and because we were not able to accept delivery before 8:00 A.M. on Thursdays, we became the last delivery on that truck, which sometimes did not get there until 7:30 P.M. After two of these night deliveries, I changed my schedule to be at the restaurant by 8:00 A.M.

Sales Representative Services

A "professional" purveyor sales representative is more than a simple salesperson or order taker. The sales rep who can provide the independent operator with new product information, market supply and demand reports, and suggestions on product usage can provide tangible services to the independent operator. These types of services are not requested or needed by the large chain and franchise accounts because franchisees and managers do not have the authority to change purchase specifications or menu items. Subsequently, the number of full-service sales reps is shrinking every year.

Chain and franchise operations are usually on national accounts, and orders are either called in or transmitted electronically so there is no need for a sales rep except when problems arise. Many independent operators rely heavily on their sales rep, and it is not uncommon for them to spend upward of thirty minutes to an hour talking with management when taking an order. They get the order and collect the check for last week's delivery. Many sales reps go into the storage areas and write the order for the operator. They maximize their commission this way and reduce the likelihood that they will have to make a personal delivery because of something the operator forgot to order. This scenario occurs in operations where the owner is unorganized and not in control of his purchasing.

One independent operator related how he gets the "best" prices for the items he needs. He said he quit mailing out individual closed bids to his suppliers because every Monday morning all the sales reps he used would come into his restaurant to get an order. He handed each of them a list of what he needed for the week and allowed them to meet together in one of his empty banquet rooms to fill out the bid sheets. When they emerged, the bid sheets were filled out and he seriously thought he had stumbled on the most effective way to assure he was getting the best prices in a competitive bidding process.

After he had finished his remarks and we sat down in my office with a cup of coffee, I explained that what was likely happening was that the sales reps were "taking turns" being low bidder, and they were likely inflating their prices and made the "low" bid look good by comparison.

Sales representatives are your voice with the purveyor. They can help you extend your credit when you are experiencing cash flow stress and protect you if certain products you need are in short supply. When they suggest that you purchase a few extra cases because the price is likely to increase next time or that they are running low on inventory and are not sure when the next truckload will be arriving, you are protected. This is the kind of service you expect from a sales representative who has your business interests first and foremost in mind. He or she wants to continue doing business with you, and in many cases a special bond develops with your sales representative.

Equipment Supplied or Maintained

Some purveyors are able to help an operator defer purchase of certain pieces of equipment by offering to provide what is needed if the operator agrees to purchase certain items from them. Most often provided are coffee makers, soft drink dispensers, ice cream cabinets, milk dispensers, and instant tea and hot chocolate dispensers. If an operator has the needed equipment, it is serviced free by the supplier. The cost of providing the equipment or the maintenance is added to the cost of the product. In the case of the coffee equipment, a few cents per pound is added to the cost of the coffee. Some will lease their equipment like ice makers at a greatly reduced price if the customer purchases their soft drink mix. Again, these benefits may outweigh the additional costs for the coffee, milk, ice cream, and soft drink syrup.

Reliability and Reputation

Regardless of how low prices are, the integrity of the suppliers outweighs most of the factors mentioned. If they do not deliver what they promise, it is no bargain at half the going price. Purveyors will sometimes get into bidding wars when one of their top accounts switches to the competition. The losing purveyor immediately sets out to "get even" by getting clients of the rival to switch to his or her company. I recall being in the middle of a linen rental company war when the rival linen company cut the prices it was charging for napkins, aprons, and swipe towels in half. It was a deal I could not refuse, and the rival knew my current supplier would not outbid it because they could not do it without incurring a loss. Of course after a month when emotions subsided, the new linen company representative came to see me, begging to allow his company to increase the price. I had gotten a six-month term on the prices and technically the company had to honor it. We negotiated a higher price that was still less than I had been paying previously. If I had not allowed the supplier to raise the price, I am sure the product and service it would have provided would have had me terminating the agreement. Eventually, prices returned to normal after a few more months.

Purveyors who want your business often come in and quote very low prices on products they want us to buy from them. This is referred to in the industry as "lowballing." They offer a one-time or short-term price to get you to try their product and then raise the price after you order it on a regular basis. Loyalty to your supplier is important, and if you get a reputation as a price-fickle buyer, you will get exactly what you pay for. When there is a question about a price charged or a credit for returned or spoiled merchandise, a quick and equitable settling of discrepancies makes any additional cost small in terms of the satisfaction that one is being treated fairly and professionally.

HOW MANY PURVEYORS?

When it comes to selecting purveyors to supply the needed items, one must decide on the actual number of companies that will be used. An operator can use as few or as many suppliers as is practical for the volume of product purchased. One option is to use what is called a "total supplier." This is as close to one-stop shopping that an independent operator can come, short of owning and operating its own commissary or distribution center. Rykoff-Sexton (which recently acquired US Foods) and SYSCO are two such companies that can supply everything from kitchen equipment and china to precut steaks and dry goods.

The alternative is to use several small specialty suppliers for specific items like seafood, red meats, poultry, and produce. Certain food items of a specialized type that are purchased in minimal quantities are usually purchased from a single supplier (e.g., coffee and tea, dairy products, and bread). If more than one supplier were used for such items, order amounts would not meet minimum order quantities required for delivery. In addition, the total value of your account would diminish to prospective suppliers.

The minimum order and frequency of delivery policies of suppliers will determine the number of purveyors that the product use levels of the restaurant can support. If a restaurant becomes an unprofitable account due to small orders, slow paying, and returns and credits, purveyors will not want to service the account because the "slice of the business pie" is too small to bother with, given other accounts who deserve their attention and service commitment.

Advantages of a Total Supplier

When deciding between the total supplier and specialty supplier route, consider the following points.

The *total supplier* is the way to go if you have multiple units and can combine their buying power to be able to negotiate the best prices and service. There are fewer deliveries and fewer invoices to process when you use a total supplier. However, the deliveries and invoices are much larger than would be the case with several specialty suppliers. Consequently, some bill-paying flexibility is lost. But perhaps the greatest drawback comes from putting "all your eggs in one basket." With a total supplier you do not have an alternative source of supply to go to in the event of shortages or stock-outs of critical items. Also, you do not have the market information available from multiple suppliers, and no competitive bidding is present to be sure you are getting the best prices. However, there are a number of market reports on supply and price for meat, produce, eggs, and seafood that can keep you informed of market conditions.

Because total suppliers carry a broad line of products, they are forced to cut back on the number of brands, grades, and varieties of canned, fresh, and frozen products. Thus, product specifications may need to reflect allowable substitutions.

Total suppliers claim to offer the lowest overall "food bill." They say, "The more you spend with us, the more we can save you." The only way you can be sure this is true is to obtain prices from rival companies. It is recommended that you have alternative sources of supply for your most critical items so you are not left in a lurch when your supplier is out of stock on an item.

Multi-unit operators like the total supplier concept because it helps control costs and quality. If everyone buys from the same company and pays a corporate negotiated price, managers do not have to spend time on the phone getting price quotations every Monday morning. Standard purchase specifications can be upheld more easily because the supplier is instructed to deliver specified brands and grades.

Because every unit is purchasing the same items at the same price, food cost comparisons between like units can be made (allowing for differences in the menu sales mix). Better service to individual locations is another benefit of the total supplier. Smaller, low-volume units can demand the same service as the high-volume units because they have combined their influence. Unit management is not required to spend time seeking out the best prices. They can use the extra time to train employees, do community service, and interact with customers.

Last, in multi-unit operations total suppliers reduce the likelihood of fraud between the buyer and seller. Only approved purveyors are authorized to sell to restaurants and managers do not have purchasing authority. This is an important aspect in corporately owned units and independent operations with absentee ownership. In order to control cost and assure product consistency, purchasing from total suppliers makes for a more centralized control over ordering.

Quality, service, and price were mentioned by more that half of all operators when asked for the criteria they use when selecting a purveyor. The biggest complaints voiced were sales reps with insufficient product knowledge, lack of responsiveness to problems, and late deliveries. An average of eleven purveyors were used regularly by the operators in the survey. Those that use full-line distributors (75.8%) used an average of four different sources. Those that use specialty suppliers (43.4%) use an average of seven different sources ("An Operator's Guide for Foodservice Distribution," advertising supplement, *Nation's Restaurant News*, August 1982).

The nation's top broad-line distribution giants in 1993—SYSCO Corporation, Rykoff-Sexton, Kraft Foodservice, and White Swan/Watson—control less than 12 percent of the $100 billion+ food distribution market. They have changed the make up of this traditionally fragmented independent operator segment of the food-service industry.

Local Speciality Suppliers

Local specialty suppliers still rule food-service distribution. Forced to reckon with the broad-line giants, distributors everywhere have become increasingly sophisticated, deploying computer technology and expanding the range of services they offer.

During the past two decades, the rise of national food service chains has spawned the need for larger distributors that can provide state, regional, and even national distribution. To combat such development, independent distributors have organized to offset the marketing and distribution clout of the giants. Three of the largest and better known are Comsource, Code, and NIFDA.

The giant distributors have expanded their territories through the acquisition of local independent distributors. Between 1982 and 1987, the aforementioned firms collectively acquired 89 independent distribution companies. Payoffs to the operators of restaurants dealing with these distributors comes in the form of better value-added services because cost efficiencies allow them to charge lower prices.

Operators will still need to deal with the local specialty distributors who are in the position to provide better service to local accounts than the big suppliers. The broad-line suppliers have minimum order quantities and do not seek out the smaller lower-volume independent operations; they typically go after the chain accounts and large hotels and country clubs. This leaves a sizable unserved market for the specialty suppliers.

The value-added services provided by the largest distributors are: one-stop shopping; reduced time spent on ordering and receiving; fewer deliveries and invoices; menu planning services; merchandising assistance; quality control; inventory control; and direct ordering through computers.

In the meantime, chains continue to vertically integrate and operate their own distribution companies. Denny's, Wyatt Cafeterias, Hardee's, and Pepsico are some that have tried this route. They claim that they are saving 1 to 2% of total food cost. Even remote units get excellent service that would otherwise be unavailable from regular purveyors. Some are even into food processing such as cutting steaks, making hamburger patties, sauces, dressings, and pastry dough.

Other companies have abandoned their distribution systems in favor of broad-line suppliers—for example, Collins (Sizzler) and Morrison's (Morco)—conceding that instead of yielding great self-sufficiency, it may have dulled their ability to focus on operations and expansion.

Advantages of Using Local Specialty Suppliers

Many of the disadvantages of a total supplier are the advantages of using multiple specialty suppliers. Since you are dealing with more than one supplier, you have smaller bills and therefore more bill-paying flexibility. You have alternative sources of supply in the event a critical item is out of stock. You have multiple sources for market information and always will have the element of competitive bidding to keep prices in check. In addition, specialty suppliers will carry a greater line of brands, grades, and sizes, which broad-line distributors may not provide.

As for disadvantages, there are more invoices to process and deliveries to check. If you are a multi-unit operation, it is more difficult to monitor cost and quality consistency between units. Management will spend more time with ordering and receiving than with total suppliers. There is also some increased exposure to fraud when you are dealing with more purveyors. Competitive bidding can result in lower prices and better services than can be obtained with total suppliers.

Independent operators will likely prefer the multiple specialty purveyors to the total supplier primarily because of the minimum delivery requirements. Whichever option is preferred is indicative of one's buying philosophy. Motives can be either rational or emotional. The predominant motivators should be quality of products, service, dependability, and price.

DETERMINING THE QUANTITY TO ORDER

How much should you order? This question has important implications on preparation, cash flow, theft, spoilage, and space. Let me relate a story that answers this question. Upon graduation from the master's program in Hotel, Restaurant, and Institutional Management at Michigan State, I interviewed for a position as head of a junior college hotel and restaurant management program in Kansas City, Missouri. The dean of the college brought me to interview the president of the college. After giving me some background on his last job, with as president of a small private women's college that included room and board in its tuition, he told me they fed 500 women three meals a day for a total cost of $5.00 per student.

His question to me was, "How much food inventory should such an operation carry?" I started to do some calculations in my head, multiplying $5 × 500 and assumed a 40 percent food cost as a standard when it came to me that the answer was not a specific dollar amount. I responded with, "*As little as possible.*" It was an answer he liked as he went on to explain that the food-service director had submitted an invoice for $30,000 from a single purveyor that put quite a strain on the cash flow of the small private school. However, as I went on to explain, there can be some very legitimate reasons for such a large order, albeit that with the knowledge of a cash flow problem, such a large order should not have been made without his approval.

The amount to keep on hand must be qualified by a number of factors that influence the quantities ordered at any one time. Perhaps of greatest influence is the frequency of deliveries by the purveyor. In this case, the school was outside the city in a rural area where the purveyor required that the college purchase an entire semi trailer full of product to get the delivery. The order quantity was driven by the purveyor's delivery policy, not the use level of the school cafeteria.

The accurate estimation of order quantities is frequently a problem for many operators. This is easily remedied. An inventory system is presented in Chapter 10 that will allow any manager to interpret what to buy, how much to buy, the price, and which purveyor to use on his or her first day in the unit. It is all possible because proper written records are kept. There will not be runouts or overstocked items for fear of running out. The quantities kept on hand will convert cash into perishable foodstuffs.

Overstocking of food and supplies seems to encourage lax standards, resulting in increased waste and theft. The amounts kept in inventory are inversely related to the frequency of deliveries from suppliers. In a city like Atlanta, Georgia, inventories can be kept relatively small as many purveyors will deliver five days a week and even on weekends. Conversely, if you are located in Opp, Alabama, you may be able to get only one delivery per week on some items. Included here are nine conditions that will influence order quantities and inventory levels. Using the inventory forms shown in this chapter, this information can be quickly and easily assembled.

Frequency of Deliveries

The first condition for determining whether one or two cases should be purchased is how often deliveries can be made to the restaurant. The more frequent the deliveries, the less that needs to be ordered and kept on hand between deliveries. Typically, grocery items like flour, sugar, canned goods, and items not requiring refrigeration are ordered and delivered once a week in most metropolitan markets. Perishable items like produce and fresh fish need to be delivered more frequently unless they are frozen.

Any restaurant located in an area where less than weekly deliveries are made will need to carry a greater supply of nonperishable items. The frequency of delivery may be related to how close the supplier or actual source of the product is to the operation. Restaurants located in Gulf or coastal cities where fishing fleets dock will be able to get fresh fish more readily than a restaurant in Kansas City, Missouri. The quantities ordered and kept on hand are also affected by the distance the product must be shipped. A Kansas City restaurant may order 500 pounds of lobster tails shipped from a distributor in Boston, Massachusetts where a Boston retaurant could order only 50 pounds.

Use Levels between Deliveries

The amount of inventory consumed between deliveries is the next condition that influences order quantities. Since business volume fluctuates from week to week and month to month, so will purchase quantities and inventory levels. When the busy season ends, staff must be reduced and purchases cut back. I recall that every September restaurant sales volumes dropped because the family business dropped significantly as parents outfitted their children for the coming school year.

We monitored labor costs and purchased more closely in September because many managers continued to staff and purchase according to sales levels of the previous month. Subsequently, we ended up with excessive inventories and invoices to be paid in September where business volume dropped almost 50 percent over the previous month. We placed restrictions on managers purchasing multiple cases of expensive food items.

The calculation of the amount of product used between deliveries and the minimum amount needed to get to the next delivery will be covered in Chapter 10. Now inexpensive items are not a concern. An extra case of catsup or mayonnaise is hardly noticeable; but an extra case of breaded shrimp was what you should seek to avoid.

Product Perishability

This is a self-limiting factor that is obvious. Lettuce, for example, cannot be held more than a few days without deterioration. Fresh poultry will spoil if not used in three or four days. Fresh shrimp and fish begin to lose quality after a few days even under ideal refrigerated conditions.

Storage Space and Temperature

I have noted in my consulting that restaurants with limited storage space have much higher inventory turnover levels than restaurants with large storage areas. Therefore, I have concluded that storage space should be designed with frequency of deliveries in mind. When I visited the Buckhead Diner in Atlanta, Georgia, I noted that every square inch of the building was being used and that the storage area was far less than what I would have expected for an operation doing approximately $5 million a year. The Diner is able to function because of daily delivery of foodstuffs by its purveyors.

If you have a large storage area, there may be a tendency to "fill it up." If this occurs, more dollars are converted into food inventory and cash flow can become strained. If food inventory is not turned over at least three times a month in dollar value, you need to reduce your inventory levels. A simple calculation of use levels between deliveries will identify overstocked items.

In addition to the square feet of overall storage space, the amount of refrigerated and freezer space will influence quantities you can keep on hand. If you have only a small reach-in freezer, quantities kept in inventory will be limited to the capacity of the freezer unit. Again, inventories need to be tied to frequency of deliveries and use levels between deliveries, not storage area available. It is much easier to control cash in a bank account than food in your restaurant.

Market Conditions

There will be times when heavier than normal inventories will be needed. Such conditions may arise if there is a likelihood of short supplies or significant price increases. This was the case with tomato products several years ago. If there is a shortage in supply, price will likely increase and product will be harder to find. If you have advance notice and can stock up, you will carry much more than your normal weekly inventory.

Quantity Discounts

I recommend resisting the temptation to purchase more than you will use in a given month just to save a few dollars in quantity discounts. What the supplier is doing is reducing his inventory and replacing it with cash. You, on the other hand, are depleting your cash position and increasing your inventory of perishable foodstuffs. However, there are times when it works to the operator's advantage to purchase enough to qualify for discounts. The operator must have the capital resources to take advantage of discounted quantity purchases. Remember, money tied up in perishable inventory can put a strain on cash flow.

Cash Position

Your cash position will dictate whether you can take advantage of quantity discounts or purchase extra quantities when market conditions call for it. If you do not have the excess capital and the discounts are predicated on quick payment, you may have to continue to purchase on the "spot" market, and pay higher prices.

Credit Terms

When a purveyor offers you favorable credit terms for quantity or bulk purchases, you may wish to take advantage and purchase more than necessary. However, your cash position and the credit terms will keep your purchases at manageable levels.

Proximity to Supply/Supplier

There is a relationship between the quantities purchased and the proximity to supplier or supply. The farther away you are, the more you will likely have to purchase or keep on hand. The distance from the supplier impacts the frequency of deliveries, and the less frequent the deliveries, the greater will be the amounts ordered and kept on hand.

COMPETITIVE BIDDING

Buying competitively requires having a clear understanding of what prices different purveyors can offer. Even the single operation independent operator can exert some purchasing clout on purveyors seeking their business. You need to obtain comparative bid prices from a minimum of two different purveyors of similar product lines to see the range of prices and products available.

However, this is not saying that price is the only or even the most important factor in the bid process. This formal type of buying is a way to survey potential suppliers when one first enters a new market. This is not a process that one does more than two or three times a year. Competitive bidding can be a waste of time unless you utilize the bid process to its fullest advantage. When service and other factors in the purchase decision are equal, you will then turn to the lowest bidder for its products. However, in reality, service can override price considerations more often than not.

Buyers who say they purchase only the highest quality of ingredients need to qualify their statement with the words, "as determined by the intended use." Depending on how an item is incorporated into a recipe, varying levels of quality can be acceptable without lowering the overall quality of the end product. An example would be common Pascal celery used for soup stocks, gravies, and mirepoix. It does not need to be of the size, color, and texture required for decorative relish platters. A can of sliced peaches graded choice because of lack of uniformity in size may be perfectly acceptable for a Jello salad.

Although one would expect that price and quality are always directly related, this is not the case. High prices do not automatically equate to high quality just as low prices do not always mean poor quality. Perhaps the best example of this is fresh produce. When the price of certain produce is high, quality is usually the poorest. The best quality comes when prices are low and supply plentiful because it is in season. It seems that when lettuce is $24.00 a case, it is small and light. When it is $7.50, the heads are heavy and dense.

The prices change due to supply and demand. Fresh products like fresh produce, chicken, fish, and red meats are more likely to fluctuate in price than processed foods. However, there have been times when prices of canned or processed foods have been unstable even after the season's crop have been processed and canned. Several years ago, all products containing tomatoes increased dramatically as California tomato farmers plowed under a season's crop because they could not get enough money for them. This produced a shortage on the market and significantly increased the price.

There are times when you are happy to get any product, whatever the price or brand. A buyer must know what constitutes quality and be able to recognize it to make effective price comparisons when bids are obtained. Having more than one supplier increases your bargaining power.

There are two approaches to commercial food buying: the needs of the operation and the availability of products on the market. The buyer may have to begin with what is available in the local market area. This may mean that adjustments must be made on the menu and preparation methods. Very often, the products purchased are a compromise between need and availability. For example, if you need a prepared meatball for your sandwich shop and there is only one brand being carried by your suppliers, even though you are not completely satisfied with that product, you will buy it until something better can be obtained. This kind of purchase decision must be kept to a minimum or your quality standards will be compromised.

When you have more than two sources of supply for a particular food item and you have multiple units using the same items, it make more sense to pool your purchasing power and negotiate for all locations instead of having each manager hunt for the best price *he or she* can get. In the case of a midwestern family restaurant chain I had the pleasure of working for many years ago, each manager was left to purchase for his restaurant individually. What I discovered was that each manager had his own favorite purveyor and substituted its brands instead of what the president of the company thought they were using. The prices paid were not the same; in fact, different restaurants purchasing the same items from the same purveyors were being charged different prices.

On items in which brand names were specified—for example, Heinz catsup, Cattleman's bbq sauce, Comet Cleanser, Trio hash browns, Coca Cola fountain syrup, and similar items—price was the determining factor in which purveyor was given the order. There were exclusive suppliers of other "custom" items (e.g., dinner rolls, steaks and ground beef, and dairy products). Here, the corporate office negotiated with the supplier or fabricator and required all units to purchase only from these approved sources.

The bid process on grocery items was the first step in enforcing a company purchase policy on *all* items. Even repair and maintenance services were bid out with the condition that the successful plumbing or heating and air conditioning repair company would be given all the company's business. However, even much smaller chains and large-volume single-unit operations can obtain better prices by the bidding process. The smaller operations will not receive the same prices as the larger accounts, but they can move toward being in the top 5 percent of operations their size in getting optimum pricing from their suppliers, especially on high-volume items. A small Italian restaurant may purchase large quantities of canned tomato products. Even a small pizza parlor can be a significant user of mozzarella cheese and therefore be able to negotiate a very good price from its supplier. The quantities it uses may allow the supplier to purchase quantities that qualify for a lower price bracket because of quantity discounts from its cheese supplier.

Being too large of an account by having too many units distributed across a larger part of the state or region may reduce the number of potential suppliers who can handle *all* your units. This is what motivated some larger chains to develop their own distribution companies or commissaries. When they had the processors deliver truckloads of product to their warehouses for their trucks to deliver, they saved on the cost of delivery and eliminated a middleman markup. Smaller chains that do not want to get into the distribution business contracted with certain regional distributors to stock and deliver their custom-packed products to their stores.

Some chains are so large and purchase such large quantities of certain items, they seek to deal directly with the source of the item they need. In some cases they will vertically integrate and own cattle farms and fishing fleets. Red Lobster requires many thousands of pounds of shrimp to supply its restaurants across the country. The company has contracted directly with trawlers on the ocean to supply a certain number of tons of shrimp and get a guaranteed price. Bonds are taken out to insure that if Red Lobster must go to the spot market to get shrimp because of weather or an oil spill reduced the catch, driving up price, it will be indemnified for the difference in price.

Sometimes, smaller operations will try to hedge against price increases, especially if supply is limited and demand is holding constant. One such example in the past involved all tomato products from catsup and barbecue sauce to tomato paste and puree. I was told by my suppliers that not only were prices going to increase but also that supply could not be guaranteed. I was operating an Italian restaurant that used 20 to 30 cases of tomato products per week. If I could not get product, I would be forced to close.

I was offered the opportunity to purchase 400 cases at the current price if I would accept delivery and pay within 30 days. Fortunately, I had some cash reserves and made the purchase. I had no room at the restaurant so they were stored in my garage at home. The market price of heavy tomato paste doubled and we adjusted our recipe to extend the supply of paste. We substituted one can of puree and reduced the paste from two to one can per batch of sauce. I don't know how much I saved on that gamble but it worked out.

The following year, my supplier told me that he was not sure that he could hold the price for six months and wanted to know if I wanted another 400 cases. I checked with other suppliers who told me that price might fluctuate some but not more than $1.00 a case, if at all. I inquired about future supply, and they said there was a significant increase in processed inventories and supply was more than adequate. I decided to purchase just what I needed week to week and take my chances with the price. Prices and supply remained stable that entire year.

The formal bid process also puts into place other standards and procedures that removed the purchasing authority of the unit managers and replaced it with ordering responsibility. Sales reps were told that price increases had to be submitted to the corporate office a minimum of one week prior to going into effect. Telling a unit manager was not considered notification to the corporation. Subsequently, if invoice prices did not match those in the bid, we took a credit on the invoices. Once the vendors saw we meant business, they notified us as requested. This gave us time to shop around for substitutes, for a better price, or to instruct our units to increase their orders before the price increase. Information about prices, purveyors, and specifications now came from the corporate office in the form of official memos, which in turn became part of the unit manager's purchase notebook for future reference.

Standard Purchase Specifications

One of the first "purchasing" decisions that an owner-operator has to make are the specifications for the products the restaurant will use. Specifications are precise statements of quality and other factors required in a commodity to suit production needs. Specifications should be brief but complete enough to assure proper identification of the item. If properly used, purchase specifications will provide suitable buying standards for the food buyers and purveyors.

Specifications allow for purveyor price bids to be compared from item to item. Specifications also give uniformity and consistency to purchasing and receiving that will help maintain consistency in cost and quality. Specifications usually include the following:

1. Trade name or common name of the product (e.g., sliced apples)
2. Quantity in a case, pound, carton (e.g., 6/#10 cans)
3. Trade or federal grade (e.g., USDA Choice)
4. Size of the container (e.g., No. 10 cans)
5. Geographic origin (e.g., Michigan Bing Cherries)
6. Variety (e.g., York Imperial Apples)
7. Style (e.g., solid pack pie apples)
8. Count (size) when applicable (e.g., spiced apple rings 30 count per No. 10 can)
9. Condition upon receipt (e.g., fresh, frozen)
10. Unit size on which price is quoted (e.g., case, 6/#10 cans)
11. Other specific factors such as specific gravity, drained weight, packing medium, degree of ripeness, length of age.

The inclusion of brand names in specifications reduces the amount of written detail in a specification and can sometimes completely eliminate detailed written specifications. However, numerous private label products offer quality products at sizable savings over the branded products. The buyer may then decide on a lesser brand after a can cutting and testing of samples.

When you find a particular brand that meets your specifications, add it to your purchase specifications. There are the well-known national manufacturer brands like Hunts, Heinz, Delmonte, and Kraft, but there are also distributor group brands like Code, Nifda, Nugget, Pocahontas, and Plee-Zing that are comparable in quality and lower in cost than national brands.

Formal bids will also contain the buyer's name and address, closing dates for returned bids, delivery address, payment terms, delivery frequency and location, number of invoice copies required, terms of price change notice, minimum order quantities, and policy on stock-outs and substitutions. Exhibit 9-1 shows a sample of a letter accompanying the bid sheet sent to purveyors.

A sample of the bid sheet is shown in Figure 9-1.

When the bids were returned, a memo, shown in Exhibit 9-2, was sent to restaurant general managers along with the price list and approved purveyors.

Each unit manager had in his or her possession a list of the approved purveyors and the quoted prices for the specified items. They used this list to com-

In these times of increasing costs of both materials and operating expenditures, all of us are even more conscious of our cash outlays. We have received notices of price increases and minimum order quantities for delivery from many of our purveyors who are just as concerned with rising costs as we are.

We, too, have found it necessary to consolidate our buying to counter these cost increases. We have four full-line restaurants and one drive-in requiring the food and supply items listed on the enclosed commodity list. The corporate office, from which all bills are paid, will be directing each unit as to where specific commodities are to be purchased. In effect, all five of our units will then buy specific items only from approved purveyors.

We are already purchasing many of the listed items from you, but prices have been only quoted to each unit individually. We in the corporate office have not been directly involved in the ordering process. We have noticed from our invoices that prices many times vary from unit to unit from the same purveyor on identical products.

We request that you review our product list and quote your prices with the following conditions:

1. In most cases there must be individual unit deliveries (of your minimum amounts). Our locations are: 8031 Metcalf (restaurant and commissary), 6500 N. Oak Trafficway, 9500 Nall, 11121 Holmes, and 2514 Johnson Drive.
2. Certain items, storage space allowing, may be purchased in larger lots and delivered to the commissary.
3. Items listed bearing a double asterisk (**) cannot be substituted.
4. When a brand is specified without asterisks, bid on identical or better quality brands.
5. State can counts and size of net can contents on applicable items, for example, fruits, when quoting house brands or private labels.
6. When a grade is specified, it is the *minimum* grade acceptable for our need. Bid on equal or better grades.
7. State length of time quoted prices will be honored. After stated time, *we will call* to reestablish prices and make necessary changes.
8. If price changes should occur prior to the stated quotation period expiration, *we will require you to notify this office a minimum of seven days prior to the price increase.* Without advance notice, we reserve the right to pay previously quoted prices.

Please return the bid sheet with your terms before February 1. Thank you for your cooperation. Should you have any questions, please direct them to me at 312-555-0000.

EXHIBIT 9-1   Bid letter.

NAME OF PURVEYOR

Sales Manager		Telephone	
Item	Grade or Brand	Size/Count/Weight	Price
Salt Pellets		100 lbs	
Gelatin		case/1.5# boxes	
Toothpicks (round)		case	
Kitchen Cleanser		case/14 oz	
Worcestershire	Lea & Perrins	case/5 oz	
Heinz 57		case/5.5 oz	
Red Beans	Choice	6/10	
Butter Flavored Oil	Koala Gold/Low Melt	35# 5 gal	
Long Spaghetti		20#	
Assorted Cereals (indiv)	Kelloggs	50 or 100/ case	
RG Black Pepper		6#	
Hot Chocolate Mix	Jubilee/Nestlé	case	
Quick Oats	Quaker	42 oz case	
Powdered Sugar	4x	case 1# boxes	
Vinegar	White	4/gal	
	Cider	4/gal	
Paprika		1#	
Granulated Sugar	Cane	100#	
	Beet	100#	
Pancake Syrup		4/gal	
Tartar Sauce	Fancy	4/gal	
Cocktail Sauce	Fancy	6/10 case	
Sliced Dill Pickles	Extra standard	4/gal	
	Choice	4/gal	
Mustard	Heinz	case 6 oz	
	French's	case 6 oz	

FIGURE 9-1   Bid sheet for Regan's Restaurants.

pare to the prices on their invoices. Part of the obligation of restaurants was to use the approved purveyors and not purchase from any others. The purveyors entered into the agreement based on the condition that they would be the exclusive suppliers of all units. When price increases were called into the corporate office, memos were immediately sent to each unit either approving the price increase or instructing the unit to switch to another brand or purveyor.

Enclosed is a copy of the letter sent from our office to the following purveyors: Isis, Lady Baltimore, John J. Meier, Pisciotta, Sun-ra, and Better Foods. Bids were not received back from Sun-ra and Better Foods.

Because we cannot adjust our prices as frequently as our purveyors increase theirs, we are forced to ride out inflation by methods under our direct control. Our last menu price increase has not been able to keep up with our recent cost increases. This is the reason we have consolidated our five-unit buying power. You will no longer be responsible for "shopping the market" for the best prices.

We cannot just consider price if quality is lowered. We will not resort to lowering our quality standards in the face of rising prices. The enclosed bid sheets show the lowest prices *on specified grades and brands.* We believe we can keep cost increases to a minimum if we all purchase the lowest priced items from the purveyors indicated.

We know that you cannot search the market for the best prices as easily as we can do with a formal bid system. In addition, purveyors are required to notify the corporate office of impending prices increases. Telling you when you call in your order *is not considered notice* of price increases. Remind them that they must call the office if prices are going to be changed from those quoted on the bid sheet. Check your invoices for correct prices and circle any that are higher than your official price list.

EXHIBIT 9-2   Bid instructions memo.

This is one way to deal with price increases over the short term or until menu prices can be raised.

Once purchase specifications are written, the bid issued and accepted, the control over perishable inventory begins. The delivery of orders must be checked and stored for eventually use. In Chapter 10, the critical inventory process will be covered.

Chapter Ten

Inventory, Ordering, Receiving, Storage, and Accounts Payable

THE INVENTORY PROCESS

You cannot carry out effective ordering unless you count and control your inventory. Fiscal counts of items in stock should be made before an order is placed with a purveyor. Some computer software programs used by chains are able to determine order quantities directly from sales reports by deducting from inventory the items required for its preparation. However, without such a system, one must inventory what is on hand before ordering. This may mean daily counts on items like produce to weekly counts on canned goods and paper supplies.

I understand that in many restaurants the taking of the month-end inventory is a tedious and dreaded activity. When that is the case, it is because management must remain until the early morning hours counting items. This important activity should not be any more unpleasant than reconciling the sales for the day. Considering that knowledge of what is on hand must be determined before the quantity to order can be determined, inventory is something that must be performed as frequently as one places orders for food items.

If you are buying an existing business and the current owner does not take monthly inventories, the food cost figures shown on the financial statement are not accurate. I would ask to see the balance sheets as well. Look for inventory figures in the current assets section, and if nothing is shown, you know that the business is simply reporting purchases, not cost of food consumed or sold. If there is only one inventory figure, you will need to ask if it contains the total of food, beverage, and supplies, and get individual category amounts. I do not place much reliability on operational results that lack inventory figures. They cannot even be called "cost estimates" because they are based on incomplete information. In such cases, I have delayed making a recommendation until an inventory can be taken and a true cost of food consumed determined.

There must be *written* inventory records listing all goods purchased. The owner or manager who claims to have it all in his or her head and shuns written records leaves the operation open to serious problems. In the event of illness, vacations, dismissal, or transfer, other management personnel can use the written records and continue to order in an efficient manner.

Food cost control requires that regular and accurate inventories of food, beverage, and supplies be kept. Taking inventory prior to placing an order provides management with the "pulse" of the restaurant activity. When you combine the inventory and purchasing information with sales and customer counts, you develop an important perspective on the business activity. As an owner-operator I did not delegate ordering to my assistants. I knew my business so well that I could detect breakage, recipes that were not followed correctly, and errors in deliveries with the knowledge of food production, sales, customer counts, and purchase quantities.

Without taking time to count what you have on hand of prior to placing an order, one of two problems will likely occur. First, you may run out of something before the next delivery and be forced to substitute and disappoint customers who cannot obtain their first choice; or you will have more than is necessary, tying up capital in perishable food products, take up valuable storage space, and increase the likelihood of spoilage and theft.

In order for the monthly income statement to accurately reflect the cost of food consumed and sold, you must take a complete food inventory at the end of the month. This fiscal inventory means counting and extending the prices on all food, beverage, and supply items. There is no substitute or shortcut for taking a fiscal count of all food, beverage, and supply items if you expect your cost ratios and percentages to reflect what is actually taking place in the operation. Without a fiscal inventory and the proper posting of purchase invoices for the month, it is impossible to compute an accurate cost of food consumed or sold.

Every operation needs to take inventory at least once a month for accounting purposes. However, the number of operations that do not take monthly inventories is alarmingly high, and some of these operations are doing over $3 million dollars per year in sales. Not only do they not take monthly inventories; they do not prepare monthly income statements and balance sheets. A consultant colleague told of a client with five hotels and sales in excess of $24 million that prepared only annual financial statements. The income statement should not be viewed as only an IRS report. Chapter 7 is devoted to the income statement and how it can become a management tool for cost analysis.

The inventory system described in this chapter is a basic manual system (vis-à-vis a computer system) that can quickly and inexpensively be started in any operation. The computer programs for inventory were developed from this manual system. The inventory forms are available from most office supply stores (see Figure 10-1). With this system in place, a record of purveyors, product specifications, prices, and usage levels can be interpreted by any management employee. This is especially important in the restaurant industry because of management turnover from year to year.

The following information is true of an inventory book:

1. Provides a record of what is needed
2. Provides a record of product specifications
3. Provides a record of the purveyors
4. Provides a record of prices and unit of purchase
5. Provides a record of product use levels
6. Makes it easy to interpret for efficient ordering
7. Increases the accuracy of inventory
8. Makes the inventory process easier and faster
9. Makes it easier to detect variance in inventory levels

Monthly fiscal inventories of bulk foods in the walk-ins and storeroom can be taken on the same form. The current prices are indicated for ease of extension of inventory values at the end of the month. In addition, a separate page/section should be for *food in process*, which should also be inventoried. Food in process is all the foods on the serving line or salad bar, sugar, salt, pepper, and condiments in the dining room and food in line refrigerators. Inventory should also include food prepared for service but not yet used, such as prepped vegetables and meats, pasta, and rice. If these items are not counted, your food cost will be overstated (because you will show a lower inventory value and therefore a higher cost of food consumed).

The column "Stock No." can be used to indicate the purveyor from which the item is ordered. If there is an alternative or secondary supplier, it should be also indicated. Buyers know that the purveyor listed first is the primary supplier. The "Description" column is used for detailed product specifications. This is necessary to be sure the proper items are ordered and received. Examples of entries are shown in Figure 10-2.

The column "Average Monthly Consumption" is used to indicate the price and unit of purchase. The price should be written in pencil so it can be easily changed when price increases occur. The "Date," "On Hand," and "Ordered" columns are used as they are shown. Before an order can be given, an inventory must be taken. The date the count is taken is indicated and the amount on hand

	STOCK NO.	DESCRIPTION	AVERAGE MONTHLY CONSUMP-TION	DATE		DATE		DATE		DATE		DATE		DATE		
				ON HAND	ORDERED	ON HAND	ORDERED	ON HAND	ORDERED	ON HAND	ORDERED	ON HAND	ORDERED	ON HAND	ORDERED	
1																1
2																2
3																3
4																4
5																5
6																6
7																7
8																8
9																9
10																10
11																11
12																12
13																13
14																14
15																15
16																16
17																17
18																18
19																19
20																20
21																21
22																22
23																23
24																24
25																25
26																26
27																27
28																28
29																29
30																30
31																31
32																32
33																33
34																34
35																35
36																36
37																37
38																38

FIGURE 10-1   National form no. 15-006, "Count of Stock" inventory.

NATIONAL 15-006 MADE IN U.S.A.

"COUNT OF STOCK" INVENTORY

Purveyors*	Item Description	$/Unit	Date 12-1		Date 12-8		Date 12-15		Date
			OH	Ord.	OH	Ord.	OH	Ord.	
Sexton CFS	Cut Gr Beans, 4 sieve, BL, Ex Stand	$9.86 6/10	0	1 cs	2	1 cs	3	1 cs	
Sexton CFS	Gabonzo Beans Fancy	$11.50 6/10	0	1 cs	2	1 cs	3	1 cs	
Sysco Sexton	Tomato Sauce Hunts	$17.50 6/10	0	4 cs	1+3	3 cs	2	4 cs	
Manco Bari	Crushed Tomatoes Fancy	$14.60 6/10	0	3 cs	2+2	2 cs	3 cs	1 cs	
*Primary and alternative suppliers									

FIGURE 10-2   Inventory book page format.

is recorded. The amount needed to meet forecasted business volume and include a small safety factor, is reflected in the *ordered* column. The *use levels between deliveries* will become apparent after several week of taking inventory. For example, in Figure 10-2, if there was one case (six no. 10 cans) of green beans on 12-1 and only two cans on 12-8, the use level is four cans. Therefore, another case must be ordered to have enough to get through to 12-15. Since cases are not broken by vendors, there will be a built-in safety margin of four cans.

Every item that is purchased, from perishables to paper supplies and china, can be listed on this form. It allows inventories to be taken as often as ordering requires. The information provided allows management to set par stock quantities if it so chooses. The inventory can be reduced to as small as conditions will allow without fear of running short in the middle of the week. Slow moving expensive items can be given special reorder points so to limit the dollars tied up in inventory.

The value of this inventory record is extensive. It provides a record of what is purchased, the product specifications, the primary and alternative purveyors, the price, and the unit in which the item is purchased. In addition, and equally important, it indicates the use levels between deliveries. It is easily interpreted by other management personnel, increases the accuracy in taking inventory, and expedites the counting process. Regular inventory taking also helps detect shortages and overages. It allows for comparisons to be made from month to month and between units in a multi-unit operation.

TAKING INVENTORY

The process of taking inventory can be accomplished quickly and efficiently by following some very basic practices. First, organize the pages of the inventory book to correspond to specific products and/or storage areas. For example, the items kept in the freezer should be put on one page to keep from having to turn pages or move back and forth between storage locations. Group like items (e.g., seafood, vegetables) on consecutive lines on the page. Like items should also be stored together so counts can be quickly taken. If items are stored on shelves in the order they are listed on the inventory record, the counting can proceed more quickly and with less chance of omitting an item.

The month-end inventory can be taken right on this form. Since the current prices are indicated, there is no time lost checking old invoices that have been paid and filed away. Remember to indicate food in process on a separate page. In some operations, backup stocks of prepared foods can account for a significant dollar amount of food cost.

Inventory should be taken on the same day(s) each week. Making up orders on a specific day, regardless of when the delivery is made, will determine the proper amounts that should be kept on hand between deliveries. Items ordered once a week (e.g., canned goods and supplies) can be counted all at once, even when several purveyors are used and their order days are different. In this way, the operator is organized to give orders on certain days and receive deliveries on others.

Don't forget to also include all the spices and condiments that are on the shelves by the cooks' station. This can be a sizable amount so it must be inventoried. Since food in process stays relatively constant over time, a weighted average value can be applied to the inventory after six months. The only thing that will impact the value of food in process is the day of the week that the last day of the month falls on. Another variance will occur when business volume reaches its maximum due to seasonal or special event reasons.

The food cost percentage should reflect only the cost of food consumed or sold. Supplies (nonfood items like plastic wrap, plastic gloves, paper towels, pan liners, carryout containers, paper napkins, cocktail napkins, etc.) need to be inventoried separately from food. Some fast-food operators count paper food containers against food cost because every food item served must be either wrapped or in a cardboard or styrofoam clamshell. If supplies are counted as food inventory, your cost of food consumed will be understated (because you will show an inflated food inventory, thus lowering your cost of food consumed).

THE MONTH-END INVENTORY PROCESS

The end-of-the-month inventory process is absolutely essential for accurate food cost calculation and the preparation of the income statement. A set procedure needs to be established and followed month after month. Since the inventory book contains all the items that are to be counted, copies of the pages can be used for accounting purposes. Since the prices paid are part of the information contained in the inventory book, all units need only provide the actual counts of items on hand.

Invoices for the month are tallied to arrive at total purchases. If an inventory book is not being used, separate sheets will need to be prepared for ease of comparing figures from unit to unit and from month to month. Separate sheets should be provided for produce, meat, frozen foods, groceries, fountain, paper items, dairy products, fish and seafood, and miscellaneous. Inventory sheets should already contain the names of the common items purchased but space should be left for specific brands, grades, and units of purchase and price to be added. You may even leave a space for the name of the purveyor the product was purchased from. This is especially important if you do not have a centralized purchasing system and unit managers can purchase a variety of brands from different purveyors. Prices shown should be those on the most current invoices.

An example of an inventory entry might contain the following under the description column; *Long Spaghetti, Lee, Isis, 20 lb box @ $8.50.* The extension would include the quantity on hand and the value of the inventory, for example, *35 lb @ $14.88.* The value of the inventory can be computed based on either *LIFO (last-in, first-out)* or *FIFO (first-in, first-out).* Under LIFO, inventory is valued on the basis of the cost of the first items placed in stock. The last items purchased, usually at higher prices, are assumed to be the first sold. By using LIFO, inflation is removed from your inventory value. This eliminates phantom profits, reduces taxable income and income tax, and increases cash flow.

Accountants will tell you that LIFO is a tax planning tool. LIFO does its job best when you are having a good year. In general, the more LIFO inventory you have on hand at year-end, the lower your profit will be. No other day in your year counts; only the last day of the year. Tax laws will allow you to use FIFO to value your inventory for balance sheet purposes, where you want to increase your assets, and LIFO for income statement and tax purposes. Check with your accountant before valuing your inventory to see which is best for your tax bracket and purposes.

ORGANIZATION OF THE INVENTORY BOOK

The order and sequence of the inventory book allows one to see the quantity and dollar value of various food classifications. The Uniform System of Accounts for Restaurants (USAFR) identifies 20 such categories but typical classifications might include: Meats, Dairy, Poultry, Fruits and Vegetables, Fish and Seafood, and Canned Goods. You may further define certain classifications such as Meat by having separate sections for beef, pork, veal, lamb; and Poultry by chicken, turkey, duck, and so forth. The more detailed the breakdown of your inventory, the easier it is to locate the exact cause of problems.

You may find it useful to calculate the percentage of your total food cost dollar or inventory value for each of the separate food categories. You will probably find that over 50 percent of your inventory value is tied up in fresh meats and seafood. This knowledge will help you set controls and procedures to monitor more closely those food items that have the biggest impact on your overall food cost. The more expensive the food item, the more control management must place over that item.

For example, if the monthly food purchases amounted to $16,800 and the total amount of fresh meat purchased totaled $9875, approximately 59 percent of your food dollar was spend on meat. When this is tracked over several months, management can see a trend or discover variances that will signal where costs may be out of line.

By comparing monthly inventory totals by food categories to the total value of food inventory, another view of food cost is provided. This kind of detailed analysis is very easy to accomplish at basically no cost. In general, the percentage of the food dollar that is spent on various food categories will show that only 12 to 15 percent is tied up in canned and dry goods. It is somewhat ironic to see the dry goods storeroom locked up tight while the walk-in refrigerators and freezers remain open. The incidents of a case of cut green beans disappearing from the storeroom is practically nil while just a few pounds of shrimp or beef tenderloin could easily exceed to $25. The control needs to be placed where the loss is likely to be the greatest.

In the cost control process *total control* is the objective. It is impossible to monitor every item equally and management should never let the employees know that they are practicing cost control in a "selective" manner. If management cannot monitor all costs they must prioritize their attention; in other words, shrimp and steaks are closely watched while green beans are for the most part ignored. The largest or the most frequently occurring costs are those that are most closely monitored.

Many chain operations monitor weekly purchases by having each of their operations summarize their delivery invoices when they are turned in for payment. See Figure 10-1 (Inventory Form). The purpose of the sheet is to uniformly summarize all food, supplies, laundry, and repair invoices received during the week. This allows the corporate office to have a "snapshot" of what occurred in each of its operations. Each unit is required to turn in all invoices, deposit slips, time cards, and other internal paperwork to the corporate office for processing. The Weekly Invoice Summary Report, shown in Figure 10-3, summarizes all invoices received that week on a single page.

The form is broken down into sections that separate food, nonfood supplies, pay-outs for food and supplies, miscellaneous and commissary, returns and credits. There is a spot for weekly sales so percentages can be calculated for food purchases, laundry, and suppliers. This form is useful in keeping managers mindful of their purchases relative to their sales.

Purveyors who deliver three or more times per week post the *total* of the invoices for the week. Purveyors having one or two deliveries per week have their invoices posted separately but consecutively. The total of food invoices is placed at the bottom right of the form.

Week of: 2-4

	Food Purveyors				Supplies/Nonfood				
Date	Invoice	Vendor	Amount	Date	Invoice	Vendor	Linen	R & M	Supply
2-4	1090013	Sunshine	127.94	2-5		St. John		128.50	
2-3	09763	A Reich	124.20	2/1 - 2/7		Faultless	450.00		
2-5	12960	Presto	40.50	2-3	7900	KC Air filters			25.00
2-6	94122	Pisciotta	160.80						
2-7	40716	Overland	480.30						
2-5	40762	"	123.75						
2-3	06761	JJ Meier	180.60						
2-6	20063	Kelly	53.76						
2-3	5621	Henkle	149.50						
2/1 - 2/7	–	Manor	488.30						
2-5	067112	Laoy Balt	553.60						
2/1 -2/7	–	Foremost	236.70						
Totals			2719.95				450.00	128.50	25.00

	Pay-outs			Miscellaneous and Commissary		
Date	Description	Amount	Date	Description		Amount
2-4	Red Beans	10.89	2-2	Commissary		318.00
2-6	Band aids	2.50	2-5	"		393.73
			2-7	"		229.48
			2-3	Eli Witt		88.50
Total		13.39	Total			

	Returns and Credits				Summary			
Date	Invoice	Vendor	Item	Amount		Sales	Cost	Percent
2-5		Commis.	16 Filets	21.70	Food	8742.85	3672.02	42 %
					Linen		450.00	5.1 %
					Supplies		27.50	.03 %
					Miscell.		88.50	1.0 %

FIGURE 10-3 Weeky invoice summary report.

Under the section titled "Supplies/Nonfood," all laundry, repairs, and nonfood supplies are recorded. Managers are instructed to adjust food invoices if supplies are delivered by broad-line suppliers or they will overstate their food cost. In the "Pay-outs" section they list all food and supplies purchased with petty cash. Limits are placed on the total amount of any single pay-out, with approval required from the corporate office if a pay-out exceeds the maximum allowed. In the section on "Miscellaneous and Commissary," invoices from the commissary are listed. Miscellaneous includes deliveries of cigarettes, cigars, candy, and gum. In the section "Returns and Credits," credits due for returned goods or merchandise billed for but shorted on deliveries are indicated.

ORDER QUANTITIES

Once product specifications have been determined and the purveyors have been selected, the next step is to establish order quantities and inventory levels. A number of factors will influence the quantities purchased and kept on hand (see Chapter 9). Generally, the amounts purchased and kept in stock should be as small as conditions will allow. It is impossible to set a dollar amount or a quantity that will apply to every operation or even to a single operation over the entire year. If one were to base inventory levels on the busiest week of the year, it might mean tying up space and dollars over the other 51 weeks.

WRITING THE ORDER

Now that the quantities needed have been determined, an order can be prepared. Because the inventory book is not organized by purveyors, it is not easy to use when giving your orders to the sales rep or calling them in over the phone. You do not order every item you stock each time an order is made. In addition, a record of what was ordered from each purveyor is needed to check deliveries against purveyor invoices.

This is the purpose of the purchase order shown in Figure 10-4. It is basically a retrofitted bid sheet where the purveyors and their prices were recorded and the purveyor getting the order was circled. The names of the purveyors are written in at the top of each column. To the left are three columns containing the item purchased, the unit, and the amount. It is filled out by going down the inventory book pages, with an entry being made for each item that needs to be ordered.

The circle placed in the cell opposite an item description and in a purveyor's column indicates that the order will be placed with that supplier. The checkmark (✔) placed inside the circle means that the order has been placed. An X in the circle means one of two things: Either the purveyor was out-of-stock, or the minimum order was not met so the order was given to the secondary vendor.

Item Description	Unit	Quan.	Sexton	CFS	SYSCO	PYA	Kraft	Wilson	
The Week Of: 12-1					Purveyors				
Cut Green Beans	6/10	1 cs	⊗	⊘					
Garbonzo Beans	6/10	1 cs	O						
Tomato Sauce	6/10	4 cs		⊘					
Crushed Tomatoes	6/10	3 cs		⊘					
Provolone	15#	6 ea					O		
Tomato Puree	6/10	2 cs		⊘					
Chopped Clams	12/52 oz	1 cs	O						

FIGURE 10-4 Purchase order sheet.

When the sales rep comes in or calls, all the operator has to do is check the order sheet and read down the column of the company for the order. There is no need for the salesperson even to come to the operation as the order can be placed over the telephone. If the owner or manager is not available when the sales rep calls, the assistant manager or lead cook can read off the order. Deliveries can also be double-checked against this purchase order when the person doing the receiving is different from the one who placed the order.

RECEIVING

Now that the ordering function has been completed, the next step is to assure the proper items are received at the restaurant. Receiving is the *quality assurance* part of the buying function. A well thought-out receiving system can catch errors, verify vendor billing, and often signal supplier problems before they become crippling to the operation. A receiving system does not have to be elaborate and overdocumented; the most important element is responsibility.

Although it seems that the examples dwell on food items, the same care must be given to checking deliveries of such products as linens, chemicals and detergents, paper supplies, small wares, printed menus, and placemats. Since these items are all "consumed" in the operation of a food-service establishment, they should be as rigidly accounted for as the larger volumes of food and beverages that are delivered to the operation.

The time to detect errors in orders is when they arrive. In the vast majority of restaurants, the delivery is checked against the invoice that the driver hands the person checking the order. Let it be clear, the invoice is not necessarily an accurate record of what has been *ordered*; it is a record of what has been *delivered*. The invoice may be accurate most of the time, but unless the person checking in deliveries was the one who called in the order, mistakes will likely go undetected at the time of delivery. Consequently, the order form becomes a backup record to refer to when discrepancies arise about the quantity and quality of delivered items.

With the new electronic ordering systems, where numbers are entered over a telephone line or computer terminal, a simple transposition of a number on an order can change olive oil into graham cracker crumbs. This kind of error is more likely to happen with electronic order taking than with manual systems so it is even more important to have something to compare to the delivery invoice at the time of delivery.

What about price extensions? Well, that is another item that must be checked, but it is usually caught before the payment is made. In the section on accounts payable, the role of credit memos will address this occurrence. However, should a pricing error be discovered at the time of delivery, it needs to be noted on the invoice. Circling the error and writing in the correct price will alert the accounts payable clerk prior to writing a check.

There may be times when an item ordered is left off the delivery invoice. This is impossible to detect unless the person receiving can check the invoice against the purchase order. In other instances the invoice will list an ordered item as "back-ordered." The receiving person must notify the manager so the latter can contact another purveyor to get the needed product. If this is discovered when the order is being given, the sales rep will notify the manager and get authorization for a substitute item.

Many regional and local distributors will never back order an item and always ship a substitute brand. They leave it up to the operator to accept or return the item; it cannot be accepted if it would compromise quality or cost standards. This should be worked out with your purveyor beforehand. Chains cannot accept substitutes whereas independent operators can. This is a frequent occurrence with country clubs, hospitals, and contract feeders.

Products sold by the pound must be weighed for correct weight. Items like fresh whole or cut fryers packed in ice need to be checked for total weight and for the average size of the chickens supplied. If the total weight is correct, but the purveyor shipped 2.5-pound fryers when the specifications called for 2-pound fryers, the delivery must be returned. Precut steaks must be similarly weighed. A quality scale is an essential piece of receiving equipment. I recommend a digital scale with 150-pound capacity as it should handle the vast majority of quantities delivered by weight. Digital portion scales with a 5-pound capacity would also be helpful.

Not every single item needs to be weighed each delivery. Random weighing will expose problems. However, if you become predictable as to whether or not you will check weights, you become vulnerable to fraud. If you do not have scales to weigh product sold by weight, you are also vulnerable. Each random weighed item should be compared to the weight shown on the box, label, or invoice. If the item is in a cardboard box, the tare weight of the box should be deducted. The scale weight should be written down on the invoice beside the figure supplied by the purveyor, even if the two weights are the same. By accepting this marked invoice, the driver agrees to the weights recorded.

The vast majority of purveyors will be accurate and fair and will not risk your business for a few dollars. However, the delivery personnel are most aware of your receiving vulnerability. Sometimes a driver will purposely leave something on the truck to see if you catch if it's missing. Don't compromise your receiving security because the driver is running behind on his route and is in a hurry.

The person receiving the deliveries must also check the condition of the product when it is received. For example, if frozen product is partially thawed, it should be refused. The ripeness of fresh vegetables must also be verified. Freshness is extremely critical when checking fresh fish. Sometimes it is difficult to tell the variety of the fish that is delivered if it is already cut into fillets. The product identification of what can be sold as "snapper," for instance, does not mean you are getting "red" snapper.

Once discrepancies are discovered, the responsibility for rectifying the mistakes must be clear. A note left for the relief shift manager that an important item was not delivered may not be enough. The note should more properly notify the manager that the missing item has been ordered from another purveyor and when to expect delivery. The sooner an error is discovered, the sooner the remedy can be administered. Remember, the objective of ordering is to have the right product and quantity in the right place at the time it is needed. Sometimes price is secondary to these objectives.

The problems encountered with purveyors on deliveries, back orders, and shortages will impact the amount of business given that purveyor. If problems occur frequently, it is likely that the operator will look for a new supplier or substantially reduce the amount of business done with that particular supplier.

When items are returned or not accepted, the procedure is to fill out a *credit memorandum,* attach it to the invoice, or check when payment is made. Either the delivery driver or the operator can issue the credit. When it comes from the operator, it is a *request for credit memo.* It is a simple form containing the following information: name of purveyor, name of restaurant, amount of credit requested/taken, the reason for the credit, and the date and number of the delivery invoice (see Figure 10-5). Two copies are made: one for the restaurant records and one for the purveyor.

The delivery invoices are often signed by a dishwasher or cook. Some purveyors have delivery policies that state once the invoice is signed, shortages are the responsibility of the operator. Consequently, each and every item on the invoice must be verified by the person signing the invoice. I remember how this

Request for Credit Memo		
Regan's Restaurants, Inc.		

Restaurant Location:

Purveyor	Date	
Invoice Number	Please Credit Our Account For:	
Unit/Quantity	Description	Credit Amount

Reason for Credit: Wrong Mdse. _____ Shorted Order _____ Wrong Price _____

Requested By: _____ Spoiled/Damaged _____

Prepared in duplicate: One copy to Purveyor; One copy attached to original invoice.

FIGURE 10-5 Request of credit memo.

was indelibly imprinted in my mind from my teenage years when I went to my stepfather's restaurant. A delivery came in and I was told to check it in. The driver told me he was behind on his route and was double-parked. I signed the invoice without checking it against the items. When I handed the invoice to my stepfather he asked me if I had checked the delivery for accuracy and I told him what had happened. Well, I learned that the delivery driver should not dictate that receiving procedures be compromised. My stepfather told me, "Next time he makes a delivery and says that, you tell him to put everything back on the truck and come back later so you can properly check it."

Deliveries should be arranged to arrive at least one day before supplies will be needed, especially prior to heavy preparation days. Nothing is more disruptive than being unable to complete preparation for lack of a key ingredient; production schedules are disrupted and substitutions that impact quality and cost occur.

Purveyors will make their deliveries on set days of the week and generally at the same time of the day, give or take an hour or so. Some establishments make a hard and fast rule that deliveries will not be accepted between the hours of 11 A.M. and 2:00 P.M. if they are open for lunch. Most purveyors honor this request and route their trucks to locations without this limitation.

STORAGE

Few restaurants can afford the luxury of a full-time storeroom attendant, even those doing $2 million to $3 million in sales. It is impractical because the bulk of food cost is most likely in the walk-in refrigerators and freezers, not the dry storeroom. In addition, these areas are not located in a central area where a single door provides access to all areas.

One key to taking a quick and accurate inventory is to have a set place in the storeroom, freezer, walk-in, and the like for each item purchased. Many times an item thought to be out-of-stock has been stored in the wrong bin or shelf where no one thought to look for it. If the storage area is not organized, moving from one area to another, flipping pages, and skipping lines will increase the time it takes to complete the inventory and raises the possibility of mistakes being made.

To simplify the inventory-taking process, the following practices will make a difference:

1. Group items on shelves to correspond to listings on pages.
2. Organize pages by storage location or major food classifications.
3. Have set storage space for every item.
4. Do not store goods in more than one place.
5. Keep storage areas neat and orderly.

Too often, the storeroom in a restaurant is a hodgepodge of supplies and foodstuffs and a convenient place for old or broken equipment, chairs, and utensils. The condition and layout of the storage facilities can actually hinder the efficiency of the inventory and cost control function. The size and type of storage area needs to fit the menu, your standardized recipes, and the frequency of deliveries. Unused storage space is a waste of valuable building space, and excessive inventory is a waste of financial resources.

You can tell a lot about the owner or manager of a restaurant by the condition of the storeroom and walk-ins. By looking on the shelves you can ascertain whether those in charge have purchase specifications, are diligently following standardized recipes, and if their food costs are stable or fluctuating. If you see more than one brand of mustard, mayonnaise, or Italian salad dressing on the shelf, it indicates stock is not being rotated so that the oldest is used first; the operation's food costs will probably fluctuate because those ordering are likely buying from different purveyors with different prices; they have no purchase specifications or are not following them; and there will likely be inconsistency in the taste of products using those ingredients.

Control over inventory and storage areas can take place without full- or part-time storeroom personnel. Control is greatly enhanced when inventory is taken on a regular basis and storage areas are kept clean and organized. An operator relying exclusively on what he or she can see with the naked eye, hear with his or her ears, or remember in his or her head to control costs will be far less aware of what is taking place than the operator who supplements this intuitive information with written records. Written records reveal what cannot be seen, heard, or remembered.

Limit access to storage areas to authorized personnel only. Storage areas should be off-limits to certain employee job categories such that their presence in those areas would be questioned. The only employees allowed to remove food from storage areas are the kitchen preparation staff or a member of management. The only personnel allowed in the liquor storeroom would be the bar manager or head bartender. When a dishwasher or waiter is in either of these areas without direct supervision of a member of management, one would immediately question the person's reason for being there.

The best way to increase control is to limit access to restricted areas with locked storage areas. The use of bin cards or requisitions are not practical except for liquor and certain meats and seafood. By being able to detect shortages, even though you cannot determine individual responsibility, you will slow down your losses. Being aware of a problem is the first step in finding a solution. It may take a while, but the person or persons responsible will be discovered through the process of elimination and investigative activity.

Limiting access to only certain employees narrows down the number of individuals who could be the cause of any discrepancies. The following ideas also help:

1. Have all employees enter and depart through one door that is monitored by management.
2. Check all packages and backpacks.
3. Do not leave the back door unlocked. Keep it locked, and when trash is emptied, have a member of management stand next to the door and check the garbage and linen that go out.
4. Keep expensive inventory under lock and key.

Walk-ins should be locked when all preparation has been completed. Items should be given date stamps and rotated to the front whenever fresh inventory arrives. When storing items, you may find keeping items in their original packages provides greater control and counting efficiency. Multiple case purchases of canned goods need only have a weekly supply on the shelves. Floor pallets are better suited than shelves for cases of products.

Recipes are likely to call for case quantities of ingredients, and it is more efficient to remove a single case than try to handle six loose number 10 cans. If your par stock never exceeds two cases, always remove items from their shipping containers before placing them on the shelf. The boxes are breeding and hiding places for roaches and other vermin.

In most restaurants' operations, the storage area cannot be secured and requires management to control inventory on a selective basis. One places the greatest control on items that will result in the greatest loss. Therefore, more control is placed over 10 pounds of steaks or shrimp that 100 pounds of flour. Expensive items like saffron, truffles, caviar, and other items in small containers are usually kept in locked cabinets or cages. Remove items in set lots, (e.g., of three, six, nine). Keep perpetual inventory records of expensive items that are likely targets of theft.

The biggest deterrent to theft is letting the word get out to the employees that management is aware something is missing. Also, make it clear that those caught stealing will be prosecuted to the full extent of the law. The more quickly shortages can be detected, the less likely they are to occur. Management is naive to think that employees will inform them of dishonest employees freely. The only time they may is when the dishonesty reflects back upon them personally. They are doing it in either case for *their own* protection, not for the operators' sake.

Don't think it is just the hourly employees and the delivery people who are the perpetrators of all the fraud and dishonesty. The biggest losses probably occur between the sale reps and managers or the employees entrusted to handle cash and pay bills. Kickbacks to managers, which are actually discounts and credits that should be given to the company, are ways that the manager and the purveyor steal from the operator. This is why chain operations have national accounts set up with virtually all suppliers and have very strict guidelines if one of their unit managers wants to purchase from a purveyor not on the approved list.

Offers of tickets to basketball, baseball, and football games, junkets to topless bars, and even dates have been arranged by purveyors for clients. If you are purchasing from these companies because of such considerations, you are compromising your professional credibility.

Don't ever risk compromising your professional integrity that you have worked long and hard to get. That is why many companies do not allow managers or employees to accept gifts or favors from purveyors. We are seeing governmental agencies drafting codes of ethics regulating such activities in political fund-raising and lobbying activities. There will always be someone willing to test you in this regard.

ACCOUNTS PAYABLE PROCEDURES

Once the deliveries have been received, invoices checked for correct pricing extensions, and returns and allowances deducted, the invoices are sent in for payment. Each month, the purveyor will mail a statement of account listing all the invoices and amounts due. One very important rule to remember is, *pay from invoices, not the statement.* The invoices we have in our possession are current and reflect all returns and allowances. Sometimes it takes weeks for credits to show up on statements. One sales representative instructed me to go ahead and pay the full amount and a credit memo would be forthcoming. This was the only time I followed this procedure. Since I was owed money, I had to remember to watch for the forthcoming credit on my next statement. The more I thought about what I had done, the more determined I was not to let it happen again.

I had overpaid my account so the purveyor had my money. It was money I needed more than the purveyor did. I had to keep checking to see if the credit was applied to my account. In addition, I inconvenienced my business to accommodate the purveyor's bookkeeping procedures. From that time on, I paid my bills from the invoices I had signed, less any credits I had coming. My record-keeping system was in control, and it made my job a lot less stressful to pay only what I owed.

Another reason to pay from invoices and not statements is the accounting cycle for restaurants and for purveyors are not the same. Purveyors may close their books one week before the last day of the month to get their statements out by the first. Most restaurants, on the other hand, will use the full month for their accounting period. This means that invoices from two different months are shown on a single statement. This makes monthly income statements inaccurate in terms of food cost. If you deal with as few as 15 different purveyors, there could be different statement dates for every one of them. Consider that some operations have twice that number of suppliers they regularly deal with every month. Such variances in billing periods complicates your bill-paying routine. Being able to determine accurate accounts payable information would be difficult and time-consuming to assemble.

If you are a multi-unit operation and pay bills from a corporate office, never have the statements mailed to the unit; have the statements mailed to the corporate office. The statements can be compared to the invoices turned in by the units. Remember, since most operators pay from invoices, there have been instances where unit managers have withheld invoices for payment to make their purchases look lower than they actually are to get bonuses or bring their monthly food cost into line.

One absentee restaurant owner who was having problems with cash flow went to his minority partner, who was manager of the restaurant, and told him he needed to bring the food cost in line. The next month he saw a sizable turn-around and thought that they were now on the road to profitability. He liquidated some personal assets to pay the restaurant bills and even changed the menu in an effort to turn business around. The finances reached a point where he had to manage the restaurant himself and when he went through the manager's desk he found statements and invoices totaling more than $25,000 that were never turned in for payment. The same ploy was used by a manager of a very successful restaurant chain. By withholding invoices, his food cost was such that he was paid several thousand dollars in bonuses that he did not earn or deserve. So the moral is, have the statements mailed to the corporate office, not the individual unit.

> *Set up two checking accounts; one general account into which your sales are deposited and from which you write the checks to pay the bills. The second checking account is for payroll. Special checks are used there also. Transfer funds from general checking account to payroll account only as needed to cover checks written.*

Many managers of chain operations doing $2 million to $5 million annually, will never experience the cash flow pressures that an independent operator deals with every day. That is why bill-paying flexibility is such an important element in selecting purveyors. While it is true that chains experience similar cash flow problems from time to time, the independent operator deals with it every day of the year.

Invoices received at the time of delivery should be filed alphabetically by company. Invoices are collected on a weekly or monthly basis for payment. Prices charged should be checked along with price extensions, especially on handwritten invoices. I recommend stapling the adding machine tape to the bundle of invoices being paid. This speeds up the check writing step.

Earlier in this chapter I said that the time to catch errors in deliveries and on invoices was at the time of delivery. The truth is that often errors are found long after the driver has left, sometimes even days later. You open a case to find a broken bottle of mayonnaise; a price extension error is discovered when you are getting ready to pay your bills. In both cases, the credits from these errors will lower your outstanding balance. What do you do?

If you write your check for an amount less than what is showing on the statement, the purveyor's accounts receivable clerk will call to ask why you did not pay your account in full. One thing you can do is attach a *request for credit memo* to your check with an explanation of the credit taken. I recommend that you order checks that have a space on them for you to list the invoice dates, numbers, and amounts right on the check (see Figure 10-6). The check is your proof of payment, and the check lists the specific invoices you paid and the amount of each.

You can expect a call from one of your purveyors telling you that its record keeping does not show payment of an invoice from six months ago. Since you pay from invoices, the only way you would not have paid it would be because you misfiled or lost the invoice. Given the invoice number and month in which it was delivered, you go back to your paid invoice file for that particular company. You find the invoices for each week stapled together with the adding machine tape. On each bundle of paid invoices you have listed the number of the check used to pay those invoices. You retrieve your canceled check to verify that it cleared. If the number of the missing invoice is on the check, you have proof that it has been paid and the error is likely due to a posting error of the purveyor.

Date	Invoice	Amount		
			Angelo's Restaurants, Inc.	Check 100
			6233 S. Orange Blossom Tr.	
			Orlando, FL 32810	
			Tele: 912-555-6223	
				_____ 19 ____
Total				

Pay to the order of _____

_____ Dollars

_____

Memo _____

⑈‖000019‖⑈ ⑊:001113326⑊:⑈‖1336⑈⑈⑈00132⑈⑈⑈9‖⑈

FIGURE 10-6 Check design for bill paying.

The canceled check is proof of payment and this system, which is simple and inexpensive to install, will be used many times to verify payment of invoices and taxes. On another occasion, I was unable to locate the invoice the purveyor said remained outstanding so I asked the company to mail me a copy. When it arrived I noted that the signature on the invoice was not one of my employees. The invoice was for a dock pickup, not a unit delivery. Since we had not had any previous billing problems with this purveyor, the supplier removed the invoice from our account when it was realized that either some unauthorized person used our name to get a dock pickup or the person writing the invoice put down the wrong account name.

Another time I used this system to prove that we had paid was when I received a notice of delinquent beverage license fees from the Bureau of Alcohol and Firearms. I knew that I had paid for that license four months before it was actually due. When I found my canceled check and mailed a photocopy to the bureau, our files were corrected.

If all your bills are paid by check, your ledger and journal records can all be done with a computer software program. All you have to do is provide your accountant with your check register, list of deposits, payroll records, and invoices for the month. Inventory figures and pay-outs complete the accounting information needed to completely prepare your monthly income statement, balance sheet, as well as your sales tax, payroll tax, and income tax withholding.

Chapter Eleven

Labor Productivity Analysis

When restaurant executives are asked to indicate the most strategic issues facing the industry in the immediate future, in almost all surveys labor costs and turnover will very likely be mentioned. Increasing costs cannot continue to be passed on in the form of higher prices without impacting customer counts and market share.

Top management must recognize the need to improve on operating efficiencies or run the risk of being displaced by more efficient operators. The challenge is to improve efficiencies and increase worker productivity so fewer can do more. The initial steps are to establish standards for employee productivity and control labor costs.

You cannot control labor cost until you realize that you are not hiring people but rather purchasing a potential to do work. The only conceivable reason for hiring or scheduling an additional employee is that certain work needs to be done and that person will be able to do the required job .

In the United States, employee benefits are approaching 50 percent of an employee's "real wage cost." The federal and state government have supported efforts to pass legislation requiring operators to offer medical insurance and paid maternity leave, on top of unemployment insurance, workers' compensation insurance, and Social Security. When voluntary vacation pay, sick leave, bereavement, life insurance, and disability benefits are added to administrative payroll costs, this percentage will continue to increase.

Hourly wage, weekly salary, holiday pay, bonus pay, sick leave, vacation, bereavement leave, meals, uniforms, shift and holiday differential, insurance (all), retirement plans, severance pay, training costs, recruiting costs, employee development programs, educational expense reimbursement, travel expenses, moving allowances and expenses, loans, Social Security, discounts on meals, recreational or social activities, and sponsorships

FIGURE 11-1   Costs of employing a worker.

An employee's "real wage" is far greater than his or her total net pay, whether computed on a hourly rate or as straight salary. You can estimate that an employee's total enumeration, deferred or otherwise, is at least double his or her earnings before taxes. Added benefits and fringes are becoming a necessity to attract and retain qualified employees. Therefore, *total labor cost* is defined as *any cost incurred as a result of employing a worker*. A list of labor-related expenses are shown in Figure 11-1.

LABOR SUPPLY AND DEMAND

Labor costs have always been a significant concern of both independent and chain restaurant operators. The supply of potential employees who are willing to work at low starting wages is diminishing every year. The industry is not attracting young people as a long-term career choice. Employment in food service continues to be an entry level to the work force for unskilled, uneducated individuals of all ages.

The industry continues to report that there are an insufficient number of "qualified" applicants. This may be due in part to the low entry-level pay and low quality of life associated with the food-service industry. To make matters worse for ourselves, we do not do an adequate job in selecting applicants for jobs. After running an ad in the newspaper and hardly getting a call, we rationalize that we are not going to get a qualified applicant so we hire the "best of the lot" from those who did apply.

When demand exceeds the supply of qualified applicants, management often resorts to adopting a rationale of selecting the "best applicants" even when they do not meet their original minimal qualifications for the position. When we are operating shorthanded and need some relief, we are forced to lower our standards to fill the open position. However, in the long run, we create a self-fulfilling prophecy of high labor turnover and poor productivity. Then we exacerbate our labor woes by not adequately training the unskilled employees. We complain that employees today have poor work habits and a bad attitude about working in food-service operations. I guess we expect them to come already trained and motivated. Another fatal error we make is failing to provide adequate supervision while on the job.

Basic management principles tell us that unskilled workers need more direct supervision than skilled workers. Without adequate training or supervision, is it any wonder that we get poor productivity, bad service, waste, and inefficiency in our operations? When management and workers are unhappy, the result is high turnover and low retention rates. It is a self-fulfilling prophecy without an end in sight.

When demand for labor exceeds supply, we begin to treat good employees with more respect and appreciation. We want to keep them and not surprisingly, wage rates go up. We begin to understand that a manager or cook needs to have "quality time" away from the stress and pressures of the business. We develop more of a human relations attitude toward our employees.

However, when business is down and labor in excess supply, we abandon the human relations approach and return to the "bottom line mentality." We stop increasing wages, eliminate the higher paid hourly and salaried workers, and work the remaining employees six and seven days a week without adequate time off. The quality of life issues are thrown out the window. We continue to expect employees to "adapt" to a "workaholic" environment and lifestyle.

QUALITY OF LIFE ISSUES

Today, men and women do not feel it is right to have to make a choice between their family and professional career; they want both. When 25-year-old college graduates who had a full social life are suddenly given a schedule that takes their social life away from them, it is not surprising that they leave the industry for other careers after just four to five years. Research has shown that there is no correlation between work ethic or previous experience and industry burnout. Even the employee with a workaholic mentality eventually gets burned out, albeit a little later than some of the others (Pavesic and Brymer, 1990 and Brymer and Pavesic, 1990).

We seem to be saying to employees that they have to "adapt to the industry environment" rather than changing the conditions in the industry that are contributing to the attrition rate of many good people. The industry environment is "killing off" many potential employees. There are still some of us around who can deal with the long hours, low pay, and high stress. However, as the industry grows, there are fewer of those kinds of employees in existence. The industry needs to address this before its too late.

It is not the intention of this chapter to get into the factors that create turnover and lower worker productivity. I will defer on this to my colleagues in the human resources area. Yet other reasons for high labor costs and low productivity include poor layout and design of operation, lack of labor-saving equipment, poor scheduling, and no regular detailed system to collect and analyze payroll data.

LABOR COST STANDARDS

A continuing dialogue exists between top management and operations management concerning labor cost standards with top management inclined to give priority to low labor cost percentages and to monitoring the ratio of payroll to sales. Unit managers tend to rationalize higher labor cost percentages on a qualitative as well as quantitative basis. They reason that the level of service provided to the customer is equally important to income and profits.

During periods when labor cost percentages are low and service is at its best, both top and unit management are in harmony on labor cost. However, when labor costs are high and service has not been improved in proportion to the additional costs incurred, top management will demand a reduction in labor cost.

Both levels of management need to have a common benchmark to analyze labor productivity effectively. The traditional measure of labor cost—the ratio of payroll to total sales revenue—is poor measure of labor productivity. The Uniform System of Accounts for Restaurants (USAR) groups management salaries with hourly payroll when reporting industry labor cost figures. While this is an acceptable accounting practice, it is better to separate management and hourly payroll for cost and productivity analysis.

Salaries for management are really "fixed" labor costs, and in multi-unit chain operations, starting salaries are negotiated by corporate administrators, not unit managers. Salaries of managers should be included in administrative overhead on the income statement. The payroll shown in examples in this chapter reflects only hourly employees hired, trained, and scheduled by unit management.

As stated earlier, labor cost can be defined as any cost incurred as a result of employing a worker, but labor cost analysis focuses primarily on hourly wages and employment taxes when examining labor cost. According to the latest figures in the Restaurant Industry Operations Report for 1996, the average labor cost percentage, including benefits, for all types of restaurants ranged from a low of 22.6 percent to a high of 42.2 percent.

If you were asked to give a "good" labor cost percent goal, it would be difficult to quote a single percentage applicable to all types of operations. One must look at the *combined* food and labor cost percentage, referred to as *prime* cost. Table 11-1 shows some possible cost ratios for different types of restaurant operations. Note how the labor cost percentage varies.

Generally speaking, each operation's financial idiosyncracies make its food, beverage, labor, and prime cost unique, so it is impractical to arrive at a useful and valid industry average. Since labor cost is calculated based on *total* sales revenue, those operations serving liquor will run a lower payroll ratio than operations without liquor. This is because the gross profit return on every dollar of beverage revenue is much higher than that on each dollar of food revenue.

Table 11-1 PRIME COST EXAMPLES

	Local Steak House	Fast Food	Hotel Dining	Units Earning Profits	Units Incurring Losses
Food Cost %	49	41	34***	41	41
Beverage Cost %	25	0	18	28	29
Total Cost %*	42	41	28.5	37	39
Payroll Cost %	24	19**	34****	31	37
Prime Cost %	66	60	62.5	68	76

*% of total food and beverage sales
**Automation, training, labor-saving equipment keep it low
***Higher overhead of downtown locations requires lower food cost
****Union wages

DEFICIENCIES OF THE TRADITIONAL LABOR COST RATIO

The traditional labor cost ratio calls management's attention to higher payroll percentages, but it has some definite deficiencies. First, it is an *aggregate* labor cost ratio and therefore too generalized to interpret. Typically, we report the entire weekly or monthly payroll as a single figure. Since the figure is compiled from employees in all job categories (i.e., wait staff, cooks, bartenders, busboys, dishwashers, etc.), it is impossible to tell from the percentage which employee or employee group, and which day or meal period may have caused the variance.

Second, percentages calculated for weekly or monthly periods are historical, after-the-fact figures. The information comes too late to do anything about it. To be effectively controlled, variations in labor cost must be monitored at least weekly and preferably daily. In some cases, hour-by-hour labor scheduling is conducted.

Third, since labor cost has a large "fixed cost" element as well as a variable element, it is subject to showing percentage increases or decreases that vary inversely with sales levels. When business is good, the ratio of payroll to sales is low. Exactly the opposite occurs when sales are low. This decline or increase in the percentage of sales is in no way an indication that labor productivity is higher or lower; it is partially due to the fixed cost component of labor cost. As sales increase, the payroll percentage will usually decrease without any direct managerial action.

In addition, the ratio can be further distorted by menu price increases and wage rate increases. This too is caused by the fact that labor cost has both fixed and variable cost components. The fixed cost portion is not just salaries, but the cost of scheduling the employees needed at the slowest time, day, or meal period of the week. The minimum staff needed to start a meal period, whether there are customers being served or not, is the lowest payroll can be if the restaurant opens for business. Fixed cost labor is the bare bones or skeleton crew. Even when sales revenues fall to their lowest levels, a minimum staff must still be scheduled. During these periods, further reduction in labor hours is not feasible. Cost can only be reduced so far and then only increases in sales can lower the labor cost percentage. If management is required to act as host, cook, and bartender to cut payroll costs, the restaurant will likely be close to closing its doors. Eventually, you have to increase your sales.

The variable portion of labor cost are those employees added to the schedule as business volume warrants. Few restaurants bring in the entire crew at the same time. They arrive on staggered schedules corresponding to the customers in the restaurant. On busy nights, more servers and bus help are scheduled to handle the increased volume of business. It is the overscheduling of variable cost labor that puts payroll figures over standard costs.

Labor cost does not increase proportionally with sales increases; therefore, changes in sales levels will cause the traditional labor cost ratio to fluctuate. Table 11-2 shows three different sales levels of a restaurant and the resulting impact on labor cost. In this case, it is assumed that minimum or fixed labor is adequate to handle the volume of business. Only certain employee classifications are increased when customer counts increase. Eventually, no additional employees can be added to a particular shift regardless of business level because they become counterproductive; for example, putting three bartenders on two stations, adding additional servers, and reducing the station size.

While in Table 11-2 the productivity of the employees definitely improved from period I to III as the same number of employees had to handle 40 more customers, it is no reflection of poor productivity in period I. The operation could not reduce labor, and the only thing that improved the labor cost ratio was the increase in sales.

To prove that reliance on the traditional ratio of labor cost to sales can result in some incorrect conclusions about labor productivity and scheduling efficiency, consider the following figures in Table 11-3 from two identical restaurants in different locations. In addition to the traditional labor cost percentage, four other ratios are offered to assess productivity more discriminately.

From the information in Table 11-3, which unit is using labor more productively? The majority of us would look at the traditional labor cost ratio and feel very confident that Unit B, with the lower labor cost percentage, would be the one. It has a higher sales level and a higher average check than Unit A.

Table 11-2 IMPACT OF SALES ON LABOR COST RATIO

	I	II	III
Customer Count	80	100	120
Sales @ $10 Average Check	$800	$1000	$1200
Fixed Labor	$200	$200	$200
Labor Cost %	25%	20%	16.6%

Table 11-3 LABOR COST ANALYSIS

	Unit A	Unit B
Sales	$28,636	$32,593
Payroll	$8,856	$8,856
Payroll %	30.9%	27.2%
Labor Hours	2360	2360
Cost per Labor Hour	$3.75	$3.75
Sales per Labor Hour	$12.13	$13.81
Average Check	$5.50	$7.30
Covers	5206	4465
Covers/Labor Hour	2.2	1.9
Labor Cost/Cover	$1.70	$1.98

The sales are greater for Unit B but sales alone do not indicate better employee productivity. What if you discovered that Unit B was located in a tourist area of the city and Unit A in a residential area? Do you think the spending habits of the restaurant clientele would be affected by location?

The payroll is identical for both locations since they are the same size with identical layouts. The next figure is *labor hours* worked and that, too, is identical for both locations. Thus the average *cost per labor hour* is also the same at both locations. The only differences to this point are the sales and labor cost percentages.

While *sales per labor hour* and *average check* are higher at Unit B, neither are indicators that labor is being utilized more productively. Tourists are more likely to purchase appetizers, wine, and desserts than local residents. It is a classic example of the spending habits of clientele "dining out" and "eating out" discussed in Chapter 6. Most would still feel comfortable with their decision that Unit B is doing a better job with labor cost.

The number of covers (customers or meals) served is higher at Unit A, which seems somewhat contradictory to the previous information. Ask yourself, "What criteria does management use when making up employee schedules and determining how many employees are needed? Most will respond with *the number of customers we expect to serve*. Thus customer count must be included in any labor productivity analysis.

The number of *covers per labor hour* was greater at Unit A, and the *labor cost per cover* was also lower. Although Unit A had a higher labor cost percentage, it is getting more productivity out of its employees than Unit B's. In fact, if Unit B had been as productive as Unit A, its payroll should have been only $7590.50 ($1.70 × 4465), which would have meant a labor cost ratio of 23.3 percent instead of the 27.2 percent.

Using such nonproductive indicators as the traditional labor cost ratio, sales per labor hour, and average check to assess labor productivity, we would end up criticizing the manager of Unit A and praising the manager in Unit B. Criteria such as covers per labor hour and labor cost per cover are needed to get the complete picture of payroll management and productivity. This same information is used to establish employee schedules and hold payroll costs in check.

Much of the necessary data needed for this analysis is already collected and reported elsewhere in the cost control system. It is part of the daily sales reports and weekly payroll reports. All that needs to be done is to put this information into a format conducive for analysis.

Management must have an accurate index of labor productivity. Simply stated, productivity is the relationship between output of goods or services and the input of manpower, money, or materials. When output grows faster than input, goods and services are being produced more efficiently and at a lower per unit cost, thereby generating a rise in productivity,

No single measure can be used to evaluate labor productivity efficiently; therefore, management must employ multiple measures collectively. The five additional measures that need to be included with the traditional labor cost ratio are:

1. Total labor hours
2. Sales per labor hour
3. Covers per labor hour
4. Labor cost per labor hour
5. Labor cost per cover

Total Labor Hours

Each time payroll is processed, total labor hours worked is tallied. When there is a variance in the total hours actually worked compared to those scheduled, management must investigate to discover the reason for the overage. If labor hours are further broken down by job categories (e.g., busboys, cooks, dishwashers, etc.), the employee category causing the overage can be discovered. See Table 11-4.

Sales per Labor Hour

This index is only marginally better than the aggregate labor cost percentage and has some weaknesses that must be carefully noted. It is calculated by dividing sales by the total labor hours worked. Many fast-food operators have used this figure to schedule labor hours to this value. For example, if the standard were sales of $25 per labor hour, one employee is scheduled based on the hourly sales divided by $25. Thus if sales of $125 per hour were forecasted, up to five labor hours could be scheduled during that hour.

If the operation's sales per labor hour met or exceeded the standard, the manager is thought to be scheduling his labor productively. This conclusion has proven to be inadequate for several reasons. First, with menu price increases, this index will appear to improve without scheduling changes. Secondly, many

Table 11-4 TOTAL LABOR HOURS BY JOB CATEGORIES

Job Category	Labor Hours	% Labor Hours	Payroll $	% Payroll	LC/LH	Sales/LH	Covers/LH	LC/Cover
Servers	850	36	1912.50	22	$2.24	$33.69	6	$.37
Busboys	500	21	1875.00	21	$3.75	$57.27	10	$.36
Dishwashers	85	4	318.75	3.5	$3.75	$336.89	61	$.06
Hostesses	80	3	383.50	4.3	$4.80	$357.95	65	$.07
Cashiers	40	2	190.00	2	$4.75	$715.90	130	$.04
Cooks	605	26	3176.25	36	$5.25	$47.33	9	$.61
Bartenders	200	8	1000.00	11.2	$5.00	$118.18	26	$.19
Totals	2360	100	8856.00	100	$3.75 (avg)	$12.13 (avg)	2.2 (avg)	$1.70

LC/LH = Labor Cost per Labor Hour
Sales/LH = Sales per Labor Hour
Covers/LH = Covers per Labor Hour
LC/Cover = Labor Cost per Cover

fast-food operations with drive-through windows found that labor hours scheduled according to a sales per labor hour standard were sometimes inadequate to provide the level of service needed to satisfy customers. The drive-through window resulted in a significant increase in the number of transactions (the fast-food equivalent of customer counts and average check). In addition, fast-food operations soon discovered that breakfast and lunch required more transactions to achieve the sales per labor hour standard because of a lower average transaction amount than lunch and dinner.

In some operations, sales per labor hour are decreasing even with rising prices. This may indicate poor worker productivity, but it can at least be partially explained by the fact that many operations are opening earlier and staying open longer in an attempt to maximize the use of their physical facilities. In 24-hour operations, a skeleton crew must be on hand during the early morning hours when business is so slow that even the minimum number of employees cannot be kept productive. It can also be attributed in part to the high percentage of part-time workers who are inexperienced. Until these workers are trained and gain experience, their productivity is generally lower than more seasoned workers.

Covers per Labor Hour

Because of the inefficiencies of the sales per labor hour index, operators switched to what is perhaps the most "inflation-proof" indicator of productivity, *covers per labor hour*. Here the customer count or meals served is divided by the total number of labor hours worked. The covers per labor hour is also calculated for each job category.

Covers or customer counts are not distorted the way sales are affected by price increases. Although operations typically experience declines in customer counts after price increases, covers per labor hour remains the most effective indicator of employee productivity from month to month.

Labor Cost per Labor Hour

This index is calculated by dividing total payroll by total labor hours. One can readily see the wage differential between employee job classifications when labor cost per labor hour is calculated for each job category. This information can assist management in establishing wage ranges for the various job categories. In both food only operations and operations serving both food and beverage, the category of service employees (e.g., servers, hostess, cashier, bus help, etc.) accounts for the greatest percentage of total payroll. In food only operations, preparation labor is next in percentage of total payroll while in food and beverage operations, the management and administrative employee category is the second greatest percentage of total payroll.

An aggregate labor cost percentage of 27.5 percent does not indicate how much each employee category contributes to the total percentage. By calculating the percentage of total payroll for each employee category, areas where payroll costs are concentrated can be isolated to show where the greatest savings can be obtained.

Labor Cost per Cover

This index is calculated by dividing payroll by the number of covers served during the period the payroll covers. Analysis of this index by job category will reveal the employee group with the highest and lowest cost per cover. This index is affected by the wages paid and will show distinct differences because of the usual wage differentials between bus help, cooks, hostesses, bartenders, and the like and the number of employees scheduled for the meal period. There will be more servers than cooks and more busboys than bartenders.

PRODUCTIVITY STANDARDS

Before productivity standards can be established, relevant data must be assembled and analyzed. The following steps are necessary to establish the information base required to develop productivity standards for any given restaurant.

The determination of realistic productivity standards, those that are attainable, involves careful planning. In order to accomplish this, standards must be developed from and be representative of actual on-the-job conditions. A standard of productivity must be general enough to compensate for different employees and the actual circumstances of the task and work environment. It also must be specific enough to be used repeatedly without capriciousness on the part of the evaluator.

Realistic minimum activity levels must be established for each job classification. An efficient measurement must be made of both *the amount of work that must be accomplished within a time frame* and *the qualitative level of performance required*. These activity levels are then used as the standard of performance for scheduling employees in each job category.

Before attempting to develop any standard of employee performance, an operator must first have a clear and detailed image of the restaurant. This includes an understanding of the quality standards for food and beverage offered, the level of service, and the nature of the clientele. Only then can productivity standards be set realistically and practically.

Once the products and service to be offered have been determined and what jobs will exist as a result, it becomes possible to determine the regular assignment of work. The first jobs filled are the *fixed labor* positions that must be staffed regardless of sales volume.

Do not expect overall industry standards or those of a competitor to work for your operation. Develop standards that reflect the uniqueness of your operation. No sound automatic rules of thumb can apply to any given restaurant and be accurate. Review labor hours worked by job categories. Break the payroll information down by days and meal periods. Observe employees at work and judge their productive effort throughout their shift.

You will quickly identify the employees and shifts with the best and poorest productive efforts. Use the most productive employees as the minimum standard for that job category. Keep in mind that employees cannot be expected to perform at 100 percent efficiency all shift-long; they are not machines. Many do feel, however, that productivity can be immensely improved if the work effort expended averages 75 percent over the workday. An average of 90 percent for a shift would be close to optimum productivity.

Ask questions like: What makes an efficient dishwasher? What is it that makes Tom a more productive dishwasher than Bill? How many covers can be served before it is necessary to schedule a second dishwasher? What you are doing is conducting a form of *work analysis* utilized by industrial engineers in designing assembly lines and workstations. Your observations help ascertain whether quality as well as quantity standards are being met in the performance of the job at various levels of business activity.

The information gathered will serve as a basis for job descriptions as well as setting staffing guidelines. It may also reveal inefficiencies and the opportunity for improving operations with labor-saving equipment, a more efficient layout of the equipment, and changes in the ingredients to eliminate certain steps completely.

Setting Up a Reporting and Evaluation System

The measurement criteria used to analyze labor productivity must be held constant over time. If the criteria change, interpretation against historical records is clouded. For example, customers or covers must be counted by the meal period. It must be perfectly clear as to who is to be counted as *one cover*. Do you count small children? Do you count adults ordering only coffee? How do you count children in high chairs or boosters seats? These management decisions can be different from one operation to another. The important thing is to do it one way consistently.

A restaurant that had been operating for about seven years kept track of customer counts through counting the number in the party listed on the guest check. Then for some reason, it stopped including customers who ordered only coffee. The restaurant had a counter where these coffee drinkers would regularly come on a daily basis. Although it is management's prerogative as to how to "count customers," the problem with this change in policy made comparisons to past records impossible. If the customer count was down, it was usually explained with the coffee customers. However, there was no way to tell what was really happening. Average check increased and covers per labor hour decreased by simply eliminating the coffee only customers. The variances that were showing up were at least partially influenced by the changing of the criteria, not employee productivity.

A stable database is necessary if one expects to pre-control labor cost. Pre-control implies advance planning vis-à-vis after-the-fact corrective action. You wish to maximize profits first as opposed to reducing the losses after the damage has occurred. Scheduling too much labor is an expense that can never be recovered. The comparison of data from past periods to current figures is very important in pre-controlling labor cost. The essence of pre-controlling costs is knowing where you are going as opposed to using the information to discover where you've been.

The point-of-sale computer systems being used today make gathering of productivity information easy, accurate, and timely. In fact, several systems have employees using the system like a time clock to time in and out. The programs can calculate all the productivity indicators automatically and print them out at any time.

The information is collected, summarized, and printed out in a comparative analysis against previous periods and budget standards, showing positive or negative variances. Breaking the payroll data down by job categories will show management where scheduling needs to be adjusted. The faster management is made aware of negative variances and trends, the faster they can take preventive measures to keep them from reoccurring.

Preparing Forecasts from the Information

Data must be gathered regularly, treated as critically as opening and closing readings of the cash register, and assembled at least every pay period. Many operations, especially when labor costs are excessive, accumulate data daily and even by meal periods to keep on top of the problem.

A minimum test period of five to ten weeks is recommended before forecasting labor hour requirements can be reasonably representative. As time goes by and the historical database increases, the easier it is to predict customer counts. Any external factors that may influence the volume of business should be noted. The initial test period should include periods of both high and low volume. You need both to arrive at the standards you will require for a minimum and maximum staff schedule. Over a period of time a pattern will evolve revealing trends that enable an operator to forecast quantities to purchase and prepare as well as set labor hour schedules.

Forecasts must be constantly adjusted when actual data are gathered. The comparison of actual data to forecasts is the critical step in locating trouble areas. It does not necessarily tell you what or why it is happening; that must be ascertained by closely examining the conditions. But the first step in correcting a problem is being able to detect something is out of the ordinary.

These three steps have been referred as a "systems" approach to labor cost. The system is that it combines customer count predictions with labor hour scheduling. By combining these two criteria, productivity standards can be established allowing management to prepare daily and weekly schedules that will optimize the use of labor while providing the quality and quantity of service expectations to the customers.

SCHEDULING TECHNIQUES

Labor cost control involves proper hiring, training, and supervision. The assumption is made that these are being done to the optimum, and therefore your biggest concern is to schedule your employees so they will be on the job when you need them and off the clock when they are not needed. The key to controlling labor cost is not by having a low average hourly wage but by proper scheduling of productive employees.

The restaurant industry is characterized by periods of idleness followed by periods of intense rushing. This "hurried" activity should be avoided as it causes mistakes and service flaws. When operating shorthanded, your labor problems take on a different nature than when you are overstaffed. If your valued employees are the ones who must "cover" for the slackers, eventually they will become discouraged, burn out, and quit.

Everything must be done to facilitate the flow of materials and manpower to minimize the hectic "lost it" or "in-the-weeds" pace where qualitative standards are disregarded in an effort to get caught up. Customers notice disorganization and poor service, which will eventually cause them to not return to your establishment. Scheduling becomes complicated and restrictive when you try to factor in all employee requests when making them out. You have to arrange for adequate coverage with the employees available for that day and time period.

Like a baseball manager or basketball coach, you want to start your best athletes when you have an important game. Such is the case when a restaurant manager makes up the schedule. He or she wants to place the best servers, cooks, bartenders, and dishwashers strategically to optimize productivity and customer service. Scheduling is complicated by the fact that it must reflect the variations in business volume that occur daily and within meal periods. The goal is to accomplish the necessary qualitative and quantitative productivity standards with a minimum number of labor hours.

If the forecasted customer count for the period is 350, the number of employees scheduled will be determined by such factors as the length of the meal period, the number of tables and seats in the dining room, the number of tables assigned per station, the maximum number that can be served at one time, and table turnover rates.

The staffing requirements for each and every job category will reflect the forecasted customer count. Using waiters as an example, the meal period is six hours long, the dining room has 40 tables and 160 seats, and an average of 130 seats are occupied. Each waiter will be assigned a 5 to 6 table station and will serve 40 to 50 covers over the course of the shift. Seven *experienced* waiters will likely need to be scheduled. If one of the seven is a trainee, service may not be up to standard. Subsequently, even with seven waiters scheduled, management may consider they are still "understaffed" to handle the business effectively. An additional trainee may be added to the schedule, thus raising the labor cost without appreciably increasing the level of service.

Scheduling is not just a mathematical numbers game. When scheduling employees, the manager must put the *right* employee in the right time slot. This implies that in order to schedule effectively, a manager must know the strengths and weaknesses of each employee. Most operators and managers can recall a day when they struggled through a meal period with a weak cook, dishwasher, or bartender. They were not "shorthanded" in terms of the number of employees but were "understaffed" because standards of service and preparation could not be sustained without considerable assistance. The skills and capabilities of each employee must be examined when making up schedules for maximum productivity. The most productive and efficient employees need to be scheduled on the busiest days while trainees are broken in on slower volume days.

In addition to customer counts and employee capabilities, physical conditions of the facility itself pose additional considerations that need to be factored into the scheduling of employees. Two factors that can affect scheduling of servers, for example, are the number of tables in the dining room and the distance of stations to the kitchen and/or bar. Regardless of the total covers served during a meal period, a restaurant can serve only what the table turnover will allow. The physical limitations caused by the number of tables, seats, and the length of time it takes to be seated, order, be served, eat, pay, clear the table, and set it for the next party will all influence scheduling.

Other factors influence scheduling, such as the duties and responsibilities of the employee. Using the service staff as an example, do they serve both food and beverage? Do the customers serve themselves at a salad bar? Are there busboys to bring water, clear, and set tables? The same holds true for dishwashers, busboys, and cooks. The more they are required to do, the fewer customers they will be able to handle. This is why it is impractical to use scheduling guidelines from another operation for your business.

Table 11-5 is a chart of labor hour guidelines based on forecasted covers for three meal periods by job categories. Note that the number of covers per labor hour (C/LH) is different for each job category and that the number of scheduled labor hours does not increase in incremental increases of customer counts.

The labor hours scheduled for 0 to 50 covers represents the minimum or fixed labor hours. Labor hours added as customer counts increase are the variable employee labor hours. Each meal period has different guidelines reflecting the varied demands brought on by the menu, preparation, and service requirements.

Management must first prepare a forecast of expected covers and required (standard) labor hours. The actual labor hours worked and covers served must be compared to the forecast. In so doing, management can determine the meal periods and employee job categories that are performing up to standard.

Variance from the standards must be examined closely to detect causes unrelated to scheduling and employee productivity; for example, equipment breakdowns, poor forecasting, training new employees. Also, the covers per labor hour actually served may show an increase, which may have been

Table 11-5 COVERS PER LABOR HOUR CHART

Forecasted Covers	Cooks: LH and C/LH	Dishwashers: LH and C/LH	Busboys: LH and C/LH	Servers: LH and C/LH	Total LH and C/LH
Breakfast 7–11 A.M.					
0–50	4.5 and 11.0	4.0 and 12.5	4.5 and 11.0	4.5 and 11.0	17.5 and 2.8*
51–100	4.5 and 22.0	4.0 and 25.0	4.5 and 22.0	8.0 and 12.5	21.0 and 4.7
101–150	5.5 and 27.0	4.0 and 37.5	4.5 and 33.3	10.0 and 15.0	24.0 and 6.25
Lunch 11 A.M.–4 P.M.					
0–50	5.0 and 10.0	5.0 and 10.0	5.0 and 10.0	8.0 and 6.25	23.0 and 2.1*
51–100	8.0 and 12.5	5.0 and 20.0	5.0 and 20.0	8.0 and 12.5	26.0 and 3.8
101–150	10.0 and 15.0	7.0 and 21.4	7.0 and 21.0	10.0 and 15.0	34.0 and 6.7
151–300	10.0 and 30.0	7.0 and 42.8	10.0 and 30.0	15.0 and 20.0	42.0 and 7.7
301–400	13.0 and 30.7	9.0 and 44.4	12.0 and 33.0	20.0 and 20.0	54.0 and 7.4
Dinner 4–10 P.M.					
0–50	6.5 and 7.6	6.5 and 7.6	6.5 and 7.6	13.0 and 3.8	32.5 and 1.5*
51–100	10.0 and 10.0	6.5 and 15.2	6.5 and 15.2	19.0 and 5.2	42.0 and 2.3
101–200	13.0 and 15.4	9.5 and 21.0	13.0 and 15.4	24.0 and 8.3	59.5 and 3.4
201–300	15.0 and 20.0	9.5 and 31.5	16.0 and 18.8	29.0 and 10.3	69.5 and 4.3
301–400	15.0 and 26.6	11.5 and 34.7	19.0 and 21.0	33.0 and 12.1	78.5 and 5.0

LH = Labor Hours
C/LH = Covers per Labor Hour
*Fixed Labor Hours (Minimum Labor)

brought about by absenteeism and working shorthanded. Although labor cost will be lower and productivity higher when we work understaffed, quality standards may have been adversely affected. If allowed to continue, sales may decline due to customer dissatisfaction with service quality.

Scheduling would be fixed if customers arrived at a steady pace all day long. Some restaurants enjoy this kind of steady traffic (e.g., Houston's and the Cheesecake Factory), but most find their business volume fluctuating between very slow and frantically busy. The length of an employee's shift depends on the operating hours of the restaurant. Ideally, the operation sets its hours according to customer patterns. This is not always the case in restaurants located in hotels and motels. It may be their policy to provide both dining-room and room service during very slow periods.

The times of day customers enter your operation needs to be monitored if you expect to schedule effectively. This kind of information can be obtained in a number of ways. One way would be for the server or hostess to note the time each party is seated. The point-of-sale programs in use in most restaurants note the time an order is entered into the system. Another way would be to note the time an order is placed in the kitchen by the server. The ticket is usually timed in and out to check the ticket times. If the timer is set at the correct time, it can be used to gauge the customer count in the dining room.

Note: You may recall that the date and time of the credit card machine and cash register at the Mezzaluna Restaurant where Nicole Brown dined and Ron Goldman worked on the night they were slain, were off by hours and days. This was an indication of lax management controls.

The information about customer counts can be plotted on a chart by hours of operation (see Figure 11-1). Cover per labor hour guidelines can be used to develop the optimum schedule shown in Figure 11-2. (Adapted from Dittmer and Griffin, 1976)

The schedule shown is for the service staff and made with the following standards: maximum number of covers that can be properly served by each service employee is 25 covers per hour; company policy requires a minimum of two (2) service personnel be scheduled at all times; the company pays employees for a minimum of four hours each time they report to work; no employee can work more than eight hours per shift; and a 30-minute break is given to all employees working over 4.5 hours. By computing the number of labor hours for each hour of operation, the exact time of day labor productivity can be improved may be determined.

Staggered Arrivals and Departures

The arrival and departure of the employees should correspond to the volume of customers expected so maximum labor hours are scheduled during peak periods and minimum labor hours during slack times. This is referred to as

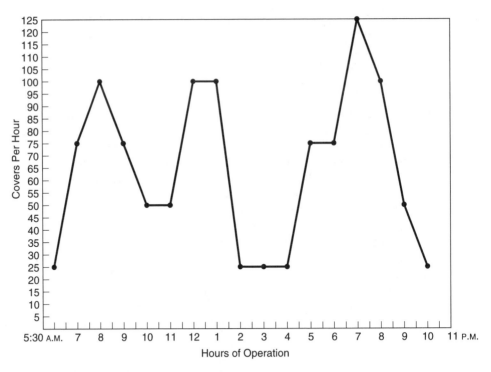

FIGURE 11-2   Customer counts by hours of operation.

staggered arrival and departure scheduling. The number of employees gradually increases to its maximum during the peak volume periods and is gradually reduced as the restaurant approaches closing time.

Spanner Shifts

When an operation is open for two or more consecutive meal periods, employees should arrive and leave without inconvenience to customers and allow departing employees to complete their side work and time out at scheduled times. Many times employees remain on the clock past their scheduled departure time because they are still cleaning up, doing side work, or waiting for a table they are serving to pay up and leave.

Staying past scheduled departure time can be minimized through another scheduling technique called *spanner shifts*. Note the overlapping schedules in Figure 11-3. For example, if the lunch shift ends at 4:00 P.M., there will be an employee scheduled to come in from 30 minutes to one hour earlier, depending on the duties that need to be completed and the table turnover rate. The departing server(s) will cease to take new parties after the spanner shift employee arrives. They will be able to complete side work and be through with all customers by 4:00 P.M. This helps reduce the amount of overtime employees work.

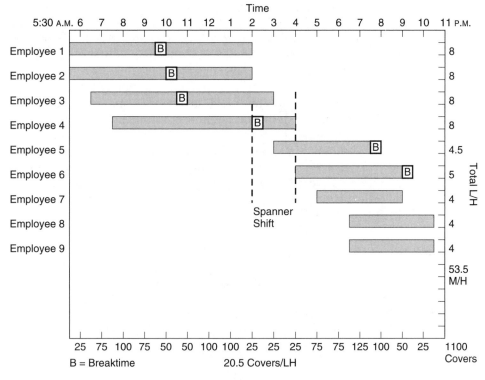

FIGURE 11-3   Spanner shift schedule.

On-Call Scheduling

When forecasts of customer counts are not accurate, scheduled labor hours must be adjusted down or up as necessary for productivity standards. For those unpredictable periods of time, management can utilize *on-call scheduling* and *send home early* scheduling. What is meant by on-call is that employees remain at home where they wait for a call to come in to work. If the call does not come in by a certain time, they know they are not needed. This is preferred to driving in and then having to be sent home. It was the waiters in my restaurant who came up with this system when it seemed that we were overstaffed more often than understaffed. Tipped employees do not want to work when there is little business.

In order to be fair to all employees, different individuals are placed on-call each shift. This is strictly a short-term solution to uncertain business volumes. If you never call in the employee on-call, then there is no need to use it. If you are regularly calling the waiting employee, he or she should be placed on the regular schedule.

There are those who use on-call as a emergency backup to cover for employees who call in sick or simply do not show up. This is not the purpose of on-call and its use for this is actually counterproductive and shows disregard for formal scheduling. It should be the responsibility of an employee scheduled to fill a shift to get someone to cover if he or she needs the shift off or if anything short of an emergency occurs. Employees who are absent without cause will not be on the schedule for long.

On-call is also a way to increase the hours of newly hired employees who have not been given a full schedule. It is a good probationary period scheduling technique to test the dedication of new employees before giving them a permanent shift. Of course, local wage practices, union, and corporate policy will determine whether this technique is used and its effectiveness. Remember, these techniques are used for scheduling "variable cost" employees. If neither of these methods can be employed to help scheduling efficiency, then marketing and advertising will need to be used to increase customer traffic; that is, early bird specials, happy hours, and so forth.

Send Home Early

As for *send home early*, no restriction under the Federal Wage and Hour Law says that if you discover you have too many employees scheduled that you have to keep them on the clock and pay them. Union contracts, corporate policy, and local wage practices may require minimum "show-up" pay to be provided, especially in the case of banquet servers at hotels. In the case that weather conditions deteriorate (e.g., blizzard, tornado, or hurricane watches), keeping most of your anticipated business away, your employees will volunteer to leave.

Also, if you have overscheduled and are having to send someone home every night, you will need to find a way to fairly determine who goes home. If it is the same employee every shift, that employee will find that his or her paycheck is greatly reduced. When it comes to hourly employees keeping them on the clock will increase your payroll costs if they are variable cost employees on the schedule when they are not needed. Drawing straws from a broom or asking for volunteers are two fair ways to select the employee to leave early.

In addition to the spanner shift, staggered arrival and departure, the on call, and send home early scheduling techniques, four more are worth mentioning. These scheduling techniques may be known by other names and you may already be using them and never thought of them as scheduling techniques.

Part-Time Scheduling

Another way to keep payroll to the minimum in times of uncertain business activity is the use of *part-time employees*. Part-time in the scheduling sense does not mean "fewer than 40 hours a week"; that is a Department of Labor term that does not apply here. What I mean by part-time employees are those former employees in good standing who are no longer on the permanent schedule. If you have college students working for you, you know what I mean. They may have to drop off the permanent schedule for a semester because they are taking a difficult load of classes or have other school-related obligations.

They go on a list to call in an emergency to fill a shift where an employee wants off or is sick or injured. Part-time employees' names and telephone numbers are posted for full-time employees to call if no one on the permanent schedule wants the extra work. I have found that part-time employees will either come back to work after six months or will take their name off the call list. It is a source of trained employees you can call on with short notice.

Split Shifts

Split shifts are another scheduling technique with limited application but excellent results if you can find people to work them. Split shift entails scheduling employees to work a short shift, usually a peak period, and then clocking out. It works especially well on residential college campuses. Students can work a few hours in the dining hall between classes and during peak meal periods when you need more employees to handle the rush. Contrast this to having to schedule employees for a full eight-hour shift because they cannot be sent home.

On Break Schedules

When you cannot send people home, put them *on break*. When you give an employee a 30-minute break and provide a meal, you can deduct the 30 minutes off his or her time card and take a credit for the reasonable cost of the meal provided against the minimum wage. Here is an example that shows the savings that can result from break and meal deductions being taken.

Assume that the average hourly wage is $6.00. Your policy is to give all employees who work more than 4.5 hours a meal and a 30-minute break. Further assume that the reasonable cost of the food provided is $2.00. That converts to approximately $.25 an hour based on an 8-hour shift. That amount can be credited against the hourly wage, whereby you will not pay $6.00/hour but $5.75/hour. In addition, the 30 minutes of break time is not paid, resulting in an additional savings of $3.00 per shift over 4.5 hours. Assuming a 40-hour/5-day workweek, the savings in payroll costs from providing meals is $10.00 ($.25 × 40 hr) and $15.00 in breaks ($3.00 × 5 days). That totals to $25.00 a week and $107.50 per month. When you add up the savings over a 12-month period for several employees, the average cost reduction is almost $1300 per employee!

Short-Run Use of Overtime

Although *overtime* is forbidden in many companies, it can be used to reduce labor costs *in the short run*. With temporary emergencies that occur due to injury, illness, vacations, and termination for cause, overtime paid another experienced employee can be less expensive than hiring and training of a temporary employee. However, overtime becomes counterproductive when allowed to go on for too long. Not only are labor costs increased, you run the risk of burning out an employee who has not had a day off in several weeks.

THE CONSEQUENCES OF THE PRODUCTIVITY PUSH

The effects of understaffing are immediately detectable. However, overstaffing is more difficult to detect unless your staffing standards are in place. If you assign two employees one hour to do a job that one could have finished in the same time, they will divide the work between them and take one hour to finish it. This is referred to as Parkinson's Law—work expands to the time allowed.

Once employees have been used to dividing up work because you have been overstaffed, they are not receptive to increasing their output when the labor hours have been cut back and the output or time in which they have to accomplish the work remains the same. Some employees develop what I call an "overstaffing bias." They have adjusted their productivity to a lower standard and have difficulty stepping up their efforts, especially for their "old" boss. When management changes, they are more responsive to changes of this nature.

Even when the upgraded output level is only 70 to 80 percent of the individual's capability, the employee may still complain. Once employees have adjusted their work habits to slow down in service or production, they are rarely receptive to speed up unless closely supervised and have sanctions placed on performance. They develop poor work techniques and habits that prevent them from becoming productive on their own.

In addition, unneeded personnel on the schedule creates idle time that contributes to inefficiencies in productivity. The staff is inclined to become too relaxed when business is slow; this is not the case when it is busy. It also seems to me that more complaints about service and food occur during slow periods than in the heat of a rush. Most of the complaints could have been eliminated if the employees kept on their toes.

Physical and mental fatigue develop as does an attitude of "no need to hurry." Extra steps and motions become habitual; like employees who go to the dishroom for stock and bring out only what they need instead of the tray of cups or rack of silverware. I find that they procrastinate doing their side work and the housekeeping standards slip. Morale drops, too, because management is always on their case and tips are low.

When changes are constantly being made, as often occurs in a developing company, many times it is the employees with the longest tenure who have difficulty taking on increased job responsibilities. Contrast this attitude to that of the newer hires who accept whatever job responsibilities you give them without question.

I recall an incident in my own restaurant when I decided to change the cleanup assignments at closing by having the waiters vacuum the dining room at the end of the day. Heretofore, it was the busboys that vacuumed. I was approached by my two most senior waiters who voiced their displeasure with the new work assignments. I overheard them complaining to the new waiters about this change. They wanted to have a meeting after closing to discuss the matter. I took them aside and told them that this was necessary for our company to reduce costs and that I expected their support for this new side duty. The newer waiters had no problem with the duty, it was only the most senior employees.

Let me just say that there was no waiters meeting and the two senior waiters supported the new changes. The story got around to all the employees through the grapevine and later that same month when the duties of the cooks were expanded to sweeping and mopping the food line, there was not one comment about the addition of the new duties from the senior cooks. Because it is a natural occurrence that senior employees exert some informal influence over the newer employees, care must be taken to be sure their reluctant attitudes are not passed on to new hires. The old adage "A few bad apples can spoil the barrel" is very true with employee attitudes.

You are always better off to begin somewhat understaffed than overstaffed. Employees rarely complain when you give them additional help (unless they are tipped employees and it takes money out of their pockets). They are less receptive when they are asked to do what more than one person in the past was asked to do. In the late 1980s and early 1990s, the hotel industry went through a major downsizing. Many positions were eliminated and combined. One hotel food and beverage manager told me he was now doing the work that just three months earlier was assigned to six other people. He was getting it all done too, an indication of earlier overstaffing.

Many times, an increase in wage or salary provides an incentive to take on the added duties enthusiastically. It is not that you have added a burden to employees' job responsibilities that they cannot do; it is just that overstaffing was recognized and eliminated. Sometimes the only way to get employees to increase their productivity is by replacing the employee or manager of a particular department or unit. If these employees transfer their bad attitude to new hires, the problem will continue.

Controlling labor cost is the biggest challenge you will face as a restaurant manager. You will leave for another company more often for reasons related to the way you were treated as an individual than for monetary reasons. Managers are terminated more for their inability to deal with employees than for their inability to control food cost or beverage cost.

Understaffing can cause problems with efficiency and morale as well. Good hardworking employees can become burned out because they are frequently asked to fill in when short-handed or during busy periods. They are usually the most loyal and productive employees on the schedule. If their efforts are not recognized by management, they will soon lose incentive to remain more productive.

Would you agree that if you pay employees a premium wage they will be more productive than if they were paid just the minimum wage? Or put another way, you have a worker who is not performing to your level of qualitative and quantitative standards. You tell him that you are increasing his wages by 25 percent. Can you be assured that his productivity will improve? If it were true, higher wages would guarantee higher productivity, and the National Restaurant Association would not be against raising the minimum wage. The truth is that it just doesn't work that way.

It is said that over one third of all employees leave a job voluntarily for better pay. However, this is relative to the working conditions and their job satisfaction. You may believe more money cannot be a motivator for increasing productivity. While it is true that high wages and high productivity do not always go hand-in-hand, money can be used as an effective reward for outstanding performance and loyalty. When it accompanies outstanding performance, it can be an effective productivity motivator.

Now when it comes to raises and bonuses, if they are doled out on seniority and not performance, they are not effective motivators. In fact, they become sources of dissatisfaction and negative reinforcement. If everyone receives the same bonus, it devalues the bonus in the minds of the employees who have gone the extra mile and put out extra effort. You need to rank order your employees and pay and reward them accordingly. The fact that employees come to work on time and do their job is not sufficient grounds for raises and promotions. Think about that. That's what they are hired to do. It is like customers praising your restaurant because you serve hot food and have a clean operation. These are minimum expectations that all restaurants are expected to meet, and you should not reward employees for doing what is expected. Those who go beyond the normal scope of their duties are the exceptional ones who should be duly compensated and rewarded.

You cannot turn an unproductive employee around by simply paying him or her more money. Consider the employee who approaches management and says, "If you pay me $1.00 more per hour, I will work twice as hard for you." When you think about it, we are all somewhat underpaid for our jobs. If everyone who felt that way lowered his or her productivity to a level commensurate with his or her pay, there would be a drastic reduction in the output of goods and services. The American way is to first prove your worth to your employer and then be rewarded monetarily. Make you boss feel guilty about not paying you enough by identifying with ownership interests. Management will realize that they have a valuable asset that they want to keep. If they do not treat you any differently, leave and go to work for someone who will appreciate your work ethic.

It is not unusual to find low productivity and inefficiency in establishments paying below average wages to their employees and management personnel. It is likely that businesses that pay below the market average will not attract the more productive workers. Such places attract marginally productive employees who cannot qualify for the higher paying positions at the better restaurants or who were let go because they did not perform well enough to earn their pay. If you consider yourself a exceptional manager, would you work for someone who paid you wages far below what you are currently making?

The same holds true when you are hiring servers, bartenders, cooks, and dishwashers. If you want to attract the best employees, you better pay premium wages because you will not attract them without it. Therefore, the places that pay above the going wage rate in the area will likely get the more productive applicants.

SUPERVISION AND PRODUCTIVITY

The importance of management supervision in labor cost control and productivity cannot be overstated. Much of the attitude, ability, and professionalism of a manager is reflected in the type of employees attracted to a restaurant and the staff a manager eventually hires, trains, and retains.

The manager remains the key element in improving labor productivity. It is imperative that management inform the employees right from the start what is expected of them in terms of attitude and performance. They must explain the "why" behind the procedures to keep employees from taking shortcuts that compromise quality for the sake of quantity. A conscious effort must be made to implement standards and monitor performance. Employees need objective measurements to guide them while management acts as the scorekeeper.

If management allows the standards to slip or accepts less than the accepted standards, it will become more difficult to set standards in the future. Remember, employees will deviate from standards only as far as management allows. Follow-up and constant appraisal are necessary to permanently implant standards in the minds of the employees.

Like a coach, the manager sets the team spirit. As management goes, so goes the restaurant. Systematic evaluation of an employee's job performance is essential to measure progress in developing job skills, to identify substandard performance and correct it, and to provide a basis for recognition, promotion, and merit wage increases.

To illustrate how payroll data can be organized into a format conducive to in-depth analysis, the following payroll worksheets are offered (see Tables 11-6 and 11-7).

Organizing weekly payroll data into a format that will allow the operator to see exactly how payroll costs are allocated to individual job categories as well as the aggregate figures, will greatly improve labor cost data analysis. The comparison of current figures with past periods will show where variances are occurring. The *total* payroll figure by itself does not provide enough detail that depth analysis demands. Staffing and scheduling guidelines can be developed

Table 11-6 WEEKLY PAYROLL ANALYSIS WORKSHEET
FOOD SALES: $12,000   CUSTOMER COUNT: 1600

	Servers	Bus Help	Dishers	Cooks	Host/Cash	Totals
Payroll	$455.10	$338.10	$196.00	$882.00	$168.00	$2039.20
Labor Hours	222	98	56	168	42	586
% of LH	37.9%	16.7%	9.5%	28.7%	7.2%	100.00%
Labor Cost %	3.8%	2.8%	1.6%	7.4%	1.4%	17.0%
% of Payroll	22.3%	16.6%	9.6%	43.3%	8.2%	100.0%
Cost/LH	$2.05	$3.45	$3.50	$5.25	$4.00	$3.48
Sales/LH	$54.05	$122.45	$214.29	$71.43	$285.71	$20.48
Covers/LH	7.2	16.3	28.6	9.5	38.1	2.7
Labor Cost/ Cover	$.284	$.211	$.1225	$.551	$.105	$1.275

Table 11-7 WEEKLY PAYROLL ANALYSIS WORKSHEET
BEVERAGE SALES: $4500   CUSTOMER COUNT: 850

	Bartenders	Servers	Totals
Payroll	$280.00	$245.00	$525.00
Labor Hours	56	98	154
% of Labor Hours	36.4%	63.6%	100.0%
Labor Cost %	6.2%	5.4%	11.6%
% of Payroll	53.3%	46.7%	100.0%
Labor Cost/Labor Hour	$5.00	$2.50	$3.41
Sales/Labor Hour	$80.36	$45.92	$29.22
Covers/Labor Hour	15.2	8.7	5.5
Labor Cost/Cover	$.33	$.29	$.62

from monitoring the sales and covers per labor hour. By closely monitoring the labor cost per cover, the job categories where overscheduling has occurred can be quickly detected.

The information that is recorded over a period of weeks and months will provide management with information to set and assess productivity and cost standards. The criterion used to determine the number of labor hours needed to be scheduled will be the forecasted customer counts by separate meal periods. Separate standards will be set for each respective job category. To illustrate, assume the server schedule for the evening meal is being prepared. The projected number of covers will be indicated for each day of the week as shown in Table 11-8.

After the customer counts have been estimated, divide them by the standard covers per labor hour to determine the optimum number of labor hours that should be scheduled. This is converted to the number of actual servers that needs to be scheduled. The most efficient form of scheduling would examine customer counts by the hour and schedule accordingly.

Table 11-8 SCHEDULE WORKSHEET
JOB CATEGORY: SERVERS MEAL PERIOD: DINNER (5–11 P.M.)

Day of Week	Projected Customer Count	Covers/Labor Hour Standard	Total Labor Hours to Schedule
Saturday	300	7.2	41.7
Sunday	280	7.2	38.9
Monday	180	7.2	25
Tuesday	150	7.2	20.8
Wednesday	160	7.2	22.2
Thursday	170	7.2	23.6
Friday	320	7.2	44.4

Comparison of actual labor hours and customer counts to forecasted numbers must be done to fine-tune scheduling. A comparison of actual to forecasted labor hours in shown on the Weekly Payroll Summary, Table 11-9.

The format of the schedule provides management with a breakdown of labor hours by job categories so variances can be readily seen. If totals are monitored daily, management can send employees home early or adjust schedules to meet the weekly labor hour standards. However, it would be impractical and impossible to have every day and shift exactly within standard. Consequently, it is the weekly average that management will look at as the overall indication of how well labor scheduling is being conducted. A day or shift where standards were not met will be canceled out when forecasted customer counts exceeded expectations and actual productivity exceeded the standard.

The actual labor hours worked were +7 and thus exceeded the standard number of labor hours for the period. The cause of the variance can be seen in the bus help and dishwasher job categories. This small variance would be considered within a tolerable range and not be seen as a problem. Justification of the extra labor hours may be explained by reasons not related to scheduling.

The type of specific conclusions that can be drawn from review of payroll-related data containing multiple measures cannot be made from review of payroll ratios and sales per labor hour figures. The key to controlling labor is scheduling and the use of covers per labor hour as the standard for determining labor requirements. Accurate forecasting of customer counts is also critical to effective labor cost analysis. The cost information must be compiled and reviewed at least on a weekly basis so schedules can reflect actual business activity.

The U.S. Congress approved an increase in the minimum wage to $5.15. The following is a list of things to do that will help reduce the impact of rising wage rates.

1. Employees should be cross-trained to do more than one job. This allows them to fill in during slow periods and keeps you from having to schedule additional workers. When employees distinguish themselves by

Table 11-9 WEEKLY PAYROLL SUMMARY
DINNER LABOR HOURS SCHEDULE: STANDARD VERSUS ACTUAL

	Servers	Busboys	Dishwashers	Cooks	Hostess-Cashier	Daily Total
	*Standard/ Actual	Standard/ Actual	Standard/ Actual	Standard/ Actual	Standard/ Actual	Standard/ Actual
Saturday	42/47	18.5/19.5	10.5/11.5	32/30	6**/6	109/114
Variance	+5	+1	+1	-2	+.5	-4.5
Sunday	40/37	17.5/18.0	10.0/11.0	29.5/27	6/5.5	103/98.5
Variance	-3	+.5	+1	-2.5	-.5	-4.5
Monday	25/27	11/10.5	6.5**/6.5	19/20	6/6.5	67.5/70.5
Variance	+2	-.5	0	+1	+.5	+3
Tuesday	21**/21	9.5/9.5	6.5/6.5	16/20	6/6	59/63
Variance	0	0	0	+4	0	+4
Wednesday	22.5/20	10/10	6.5/6.5	17/19	6/6	62/61.5
Variance	-2.5	0	0	+2	0	-.5
Thursday	24/24	10.5/11	6.5/7	18/18	6/6	65/66
Variance	0	+.5	+.5	0	0	+1
Friday	44.5/43	20/21	11.5/12.5	34/32	6/6.5	116/115
Variance	-1.5	+1	+1	-2	-.5	-1
Totals	219/219	97/99.5	58/61.5	165.5/166	42/42.5	581.5/588.5
Variance	0	+2.5	+3.5	+.5	+.5	+7.0

*Standard LH based on forecasted customer counts divided by standard covers per labor hour as shown on Weekly Payroll Analysis Worksheet, Tables 11-6 and 11-7.
**Minimum LH; equivalent of Fixed Labor Cost.

being able to perform several jobs, they need to be appropriately compensated.

2. Use time clocks and time cards. Set up procedures for breaks and meal allowances. Have time-in and time-out rules; for example, manager's OK needed if more than 12 minutes early or late timing in or out.

3. Eliminate the need for a worker whenever feasible. Try to get the work done with the least number of people. Invest in labor saving equipment or purchase in a form that eliminates the need for the worker. Increase your inventory of glassware and china so you lower the turnover of flatware and china. It may allow you to reduce the dishwashing crew.

4. Go to self-service where feasible.

5. Hire and train skilled employees. Two lesser skilled and lower paid employees are far more expensive than one skilled, well-compensated employee.

6. Place emphasis on marketing and ways to increase overall sales. Remember, labor has a significant fixed cost component and increasing sales will lower labor cost percentage. The old adage is still true, "Volume hides a multitude of sins."

7. You could always raise your prices as a last resort.

8. Cut back on overhead by closing during unprofitable times of the day.

9. Schedule more closely using the techniques given in this chapter.

10. Look into rearranging your layout if it would improve productivity without increasing labor cost.

BIBLIOGRAPHY

Brymer, Robert A. and Pavesic, David V., "Personality Characteristics and Profiles of Hospitality Management Graduates," *Hospitality Research Journal*, Vol. 14, No. 1, 1990, pp. 77–86.

Dittmer, Paul R. and Griffin, Gerald G., *Principles of Food, Beverage, and Labor Cost Controls*, Boston: Cahners Books, Inc., 1976.

Pavesic, David V., "Myth of Labor Cost Percentages," *Cornell Quarterly*, Vol. 24, No. 3, Nov. 1983, pp. 26–38.

Pavesic, David V. and Brymer, Robert A., "Why Young Managers are Quitting," *Cornell Quarterly*, Vol. 30, No. 4, Feb. 1990, pp. 90–96.

Restaurant Industry Operations Report 1996, National Restaurant Association, Deloitte & Touche Ltd., pp. 68–69.

Chapter Twelve

Beverage Cost Controls

FACTORS IMPACTING BEVERAGE COST

If you were asked what is an average bar cost or liquor cost percentage, how would you respond? Why is the beverage cost percentage more likely to be higher in a restaurant than in a lounge with live entertainment not serving food? How does the sales mix of beer, wine, and spirits affect the overall beverage cost percentage?

The answer to the first question is that there is not a single pat answer. The response would have to be, "It all depends." First determine what type of operation the questioner has in mind. A lounge with live entertainment will have a higher drink price structure because it and will sell more mixed drinks than beer and wine. These conditions will result in a lower cost of beverage sold there than in a restaurant where the opposite occurs.

MARKUP OF ALCOHOLIC BEVERAGES

Beer and wine, the beverages commonly consumed with food, do not have the markup of mixed drinks. Beer and wine are marked up two or three times their cost, resulting in 33 to 50 percent cost to price. Think about it; If domestic beer costs $14.50 for a case of twenty-four 12-ounce bottles, the cost per bottle is $.60. To return a 33 percent cost, it would be priced at $1.80. Knowing this, what is the customers' perceived price-value when it is priced at $2.50 or $2.95? That is a 20–24 percent cost to price.

This is another example that demonstrates that pricing decisions on food or beverage are not simply a cost markup exercise. The subjective and indirect cost factors that must be taken into account will sometimes allow an operator to charge far more (or less) than originally considered. When Mexican beers were first marketed in the United States and they were uniquely served with a wedge of lime that is squeezed and dropped into the bottle. Demand skyrocketed and allowed restaurants and bars to price them as premium imported beers like Heiniken and Amstel. Even the prices that beer distributors charged was demand driven.

The markup on beer, wine, and mixed drinks in restaurants is still lower than the markup in operations where liquor makes up the majority of sales and where live entertainment and/or state-of-the-art sound systems play recorded music. The prices reflect the uniqueness of the operation and the overhead costs of equipment and entertainers. If the restaurant or lounge becomes a leader in the market, more aggressive pricing strategies can be used. It gets back to either charging the highest price the customer is willing to pay or the lowest price at which you can make your profit.

A bottle of domestic white wine that costs $6 a bottle would have to be priced at $24 to return a 25 percent beverage cost and may not sell because of the price. If it is a popular wine sold in grocery or liquor stores, the customers will know the retail price and refuse to pay more than $4 to $5 more than retail. Therefore, it will be marked up only 50 percent to $11.95. The lower price stimulates sales.

Contrast this to the prices of mixed drinks with a portion of 1.5 ounces. A quart of premium scotch, with a cost to the operation of $17.50, should yield twenty-one 1.5 ounce shots. That leaves a slight allowance of 1/3 ounce for spillage and over-pouring. That makes the cost approximately $.84 each. If we poured 1-3/4 ounce we would get a yield of approximately 18 drinks at $.97. A scotch and water could be priced anywhere from $1.95 up to $4.95. If a 1.5-ounce shot is used and priced at $2.95, the beverage cost percentage would be just over 28 percent. At $4.95 for a 1.75-ounce pour, the cost is just over 19.5 percent.

Typically mixed drinks produce beverage cost percentages in the low to high teens. The double and triple liquor drinks are in the low to mid twenties. Most patrons of all ages are curbing the quantity of what they drink when they go out. When people order a drink, they are more likely to request a premium brand and have only one or two drinks. We are seeing an emergence of wine and beer bars that carry hundreds of varieties. The single malt scotches and premium bourbons, vodkas, and tequilas are the choice today. You can see that the ratio of beer, wine, and liquor sold can impact the overall liquor cost.

MONITORING BEVERAGE COST

In order to monitor your liquor costs accurately, you need to separately record the sales of each type of alcoholic beverage. A single "beverage" key on the cash register is not sufficient. To report "total" beverage sales is not enough for proper analysis. Separate keys for beer, wine, and liquor should be used. Obtaining a representative sales mix of liquor sold has traditionally been much more difficult to accomplish than it has with food sold.

When the back bar inventory of bourbon, scotch, rum, gin, vodka, tequila, beer, and wine contains dozens of brands of each type, the pricing structure recognizes only "classes" of drink and not specific brands. For example, the price structure at a typical bar or restaurant lounge would show three price levels for mixed drinks: house brands, call brands, and premium call brands. A house brand of vodka might be Smirnof 80; a call brand Stolichaya 80; and a premium call Absolut 100.

Further, mixed drinks like Long Island Ice Tea, and Margarita made with Grand Mariner instead of house Triple Sec and with premium tequila like Jose Cuervo Gold complicate getting a true sales mix with the manually written bar checks that typically do not fully describe the drink that was served. Usually, the order is verbally called in to the bartender and the price charged is the only indication of the "class of drink"; whether it was vodka, gin, or bourbon is sometimes difficult to tell as well.

The same trade-off of pricing for specific brand identification occurs with beer and wine. When restaurants or bars inventory 40 or 50 different brands of bottled beer, they also compromise with three pricing structures for domestic, imported, and microbrews. Microbrewed beers are enjoying a demand-driven pricing period as they are the trendy new choice of many baby boomer customers.

Unless an electronic point-of-sale system is used, a detailed beverage sales mix (i.e., brands and type of drink) is extremely difficult and time-consuming to obtain. Several "touch screen" systems allow the server to quickly and completely identify the drink, brand, and even special preparation variances of the mixes and presentation.

LIQUOR, BEER, AND WINE ORDERING

The function of the purchasing agent or buyer of alcoholic beverages is simply to insure that an adequate supply of the required wines, beers, and spirits is available. There is no need to "shop around" for the best deal as is done when purchasing food and supplies because:

1. Specific brands are sold by specific dealers only.
2. Wholesaling of alcoholic beverages is state regulated and controlled.
3. Prices are published in monthly journals and there is little change from month to month.

4. Only quantity discounts are available.
5. Purchase is done by brand name.

Factors that determine the number of brands to be stocked are:

1. Customer preferences in the area of the country.
2. Class of clientele and operation; that is, country clubs will carry more brands than a chain restaurant.
3. What is used as the "well" or "house" brands. Well and house brands are poured when a customer requests a drink like gin and tonic or bourbon and seven and does not specify a particular "call" brand. For example: well bourbon—Cabin Stills; call bourbon—Jack Daniels Green; premium call bourbon—Makers Mark.
4. Drink price structure: cheaper prices, fewer brands. This strategy is not used in hotels and restaurants.
5. Volume of the operation: the greater volume, the greater variety that can be stocked. Convention hotels like the Hyatt Regency in Chicago carry over 1100 different bottles of spirits and wines.

INVENTORY

Liquor, beer, and wine need to be inventoried just like food. In fact, greater security is given to alcoholic beverages because of the cost and abuses that can take place if they are not watched closely.

Liquor inventory is kept under lock and key in separate storerooms, locked cages, or cabinets in storerooms and walk-ins. Only authorized individuals have access to such areas, and requisitions must be filled out to record any withdrawals.

It is also recommended that you establish par stock levels for all remote and service bars and replenish stock from stamped empty bottles. Bottle stamping is used to prevent bartenders from bringing in their own bottle and selling it. If they do, even with close inventory controls, shortages are not detectible because there are none. The receipts are kept for each sale made with this phantom liquor. Drops in sales levels of $50 to $100 a night are the signs of phantom bottles in the inventory.

Inventories must be audited to verify that the liquor is actually in the storeroom. If phantom inventory is reported and/or a purchase invoice is not turned in, the cost of liquor consumed will be understated and show a lower beverage cost than actually exists. This is why monthly statements from vendors should be mailed to the corporate office and not the individual unit. Bills are paid from invoices, not statements. However, statements let the comptroller know that all invoices have been submitted for payment.

Deliveries need to be checked for completeness and accuracy. Again, too often, the driver's delivery invoice is used to check the delivery. It is recommended that a purchase order be available to verify the invoice, for correct brands, units, quantities, and prices.

Perpetual Inventory

The most common method for controlling and recording beverage inventories is the *perpetual inventory system*. A constant count is kept of all merchandise ordered and requisitioned such that a running count is kept for every brand in inventory. A master record (Figure 12-1) is maintained by the accounting department that records all deliveries and subtracts all requisitions. There would be a similar record kept by management in the liquor storeroom. A separate bin card may be used in place of a record book (Figure 12-2), but a book is recommended over the bin cards. Duplicates of liquor requisitions (Figure 12-3) are made, one going to that accounting department and one kept by management to update their inventory book.

At the end of the month, a complete fiscal inventory is taken and compared to the perpetual inventory amounts. The two should be the same. If not, the discrepancy needs to be investigated. No merchandise should be taken from the liquor storeroom without recording it on the requisition form containing the proper authorization signature. The information contained on the requisition is the brand, size, number of bottles, date, name of person filling out the requisition, and the authorized signature. If the *par stock–empty bottle requisition system* is used, an empty one must be returned with the requisition for every full bottle issued.

CONTROLLING SALES OF BEVERAGES

Controls for determining dispensing costs, recording sales, and accounting for beverage consumed is accomplished by use of three different systems.

BIN NUMBER 34   BRAND: CHIVAS REGAL   UNIT: QUARTS
DISTRIBUTOR: AMERICAN BEVERAGE

Date	Quantity on Hand	Quantity Delivered	Total	Quantity Issued	Balance in Stock	Issued To:	Issued By:
7-22-98	18	12	30	6	24	RRF	DVP
7-23-98	24	na	na	4	20	DDR	DVP
7-24-98	20	na	na	2	18	RRF	DVP

FIGURE 12-1   Perpetual inventory control record.

BIN NO. 34   BRAND: CHIVAS REGAL   UNIT: QUARTS
DISTRIBUTOR: AMERICAN BEVERAGE

Date	Amount on Hand	Amount Delivered	Amount Issued	Balance in Stock
7-22-98	18	12	6	24
7-23-98	24	na	4	20
7-24-98	20	na	2	18

FIGURE 12-2   Bin card.

DATE: *7-22-98*   BAR STATION: *MAIN BAR*   REQUESTED BY: *RRF*

Quantity	Brand	Unit Size	Empties Returned
6	Chivas Regal	Quarts	6
3	Dewars	Quarts	3
1	Glenlivet 12 yr	Fifth	1
3	Jim Beam	Quarts	2
2	Skyy Vodka	Quarts	3
1	Cuervo 1800	Quarts	1
1	Amaretto Di Saronno	Quarts	1

Filled By: *DVP*

FIGURE 12-3   Liquor, wine, and beer requisition.

1. Automated: systems that dispense and count
2. Ounce or drink controls
3. Par stock or bottle control

Automated Dispensing Systems

Automated systems are being installed in many of the chain operations. The better-known ABC Computerbar and the Berg system are just a few of dozens of systems on the market. They range from mechanical dispensers attached to individual bottles, magnetic pourers that can be activated only when an electronic scanner is placed around a magnetic pourer that can be activated only when the cash register records the sale. These systems dispense the exact amount every time, allow for more consistent drinks, reduce spillage, cannot give free drinks, and allow no over- or under-pouring. With some systems the bottles are never touched by the bartender. Liquor cannot be dispensed without being recorded in the system.

The suppliers of these systems will tell you that you will need to dispense at least 80 percent of all alcohol through the system to receive the optimum benefits. Since each magnetic pourer or dispensing head is not cheap, it requires that you reduce the number of brands offered. More than likely, a premium well program would be used. Cordials and liqueurs have a high sugar content and will clog up the sensitive moving parts that control the amount dispensed. Such items may be left off the system or require frequent maintenance of pouring heads to keep them freeflowing.

Dispensing systems that measure and count portions are available for draft beer and draft wines. Their use allows servers to dispense their own orders and not require a bartender. This is highly useful in restaurants without full liquor licenses. The systems have portion meters that count each glass, pitcher, or carafe served. At the end of the shift, the readings are taken and the number of servings at the different sizes can be quickly tallied and compared to point-of-sale records.

Bottled beer and wine can be controlled by a perpetual inventory system that counts what is on hand at the beginning and end of the meal period and compares the difference to the sales records or guest checks. One server is given the responsibility of taking inventory and replenishing the par stock of beer and wine. Management should spot check and sign off on the count when the server has completed the restocking. This provides the operator with virtually 100 percent control.

Advantages of dispensing systems

1. Systems provide measured pouring, which eliminates problems of under- and over-pouring.
2. Drinks are more consistent.
3. Systems can utilize 1.75-liter bottles, which reduce the cost per ounce of the liquor. In this instance, the bartender does not handle any bottles behind the bar.
4. Liquor is counted every time it is dispensed and, therefore, can be tracked.
5. They provide sales mix information for use in sales analysis.
6. They speed up the service in high-volume bars and increase productivity.
7. No requisitions need to be used since the liquor is dispensed from the secure liquor storeroom.

Ounce or Drink Controls

Prior to the development of automatic dispensing systems, the most common method for determining the sales mix of liquor sold was through counting the drinks sold. This was extremely difficult because of the manual recording of beverages and the multi-tiered price structure to identify the house, call, and premium call brands used in the drinks. It was further complicated by the fact that there were numerous ways the liquor could be sold and combined with other wines and spirits that significantly impacted the price and cost percentages. Note the information contained on the beverage check produced with a point-of-sale system shown in Figure 12-4 and the additional printouts it produces providing management with detailed information for beverage cost analysis in Figures 12-5 and 12-6. In the absence of a point-of-sale system, the drink control system can be used for a period of time to determine the drink sales mix so a potential, standard, and actual beverage cost percentage can be estimated.

The ounce or drink control requires that the following be established:

1. Standardize glassware and recipes
2. Record each drink sold for sales analysis
3. Determine the cost of beverage consumed
4. Compare actual use levels to "potential" consumption base on the sales mix
5. Compare actual beverage cost percent to the "potential" beverage cost percent

Par Stock—Empty Bottle Control

Par stock or bottle control is the third method of control used for alcoholic beverages. The steps are:

1. Determine the maximum consumption/usage for each type of liquor and add a small safety factor; state in terms of number of bottles to keep behind the bar. This becomes the "par stock" that is maintained.
2. All empty bottles are turned in for full ones; no full bottles are issued without an empty turned in.
3. A standard sales value per bottle is determined based on the types of drinks made from each liquor.
4. A sales value is determined from consumption and compared to actual sales for variances. If more was consumed than sold, investigate.

Standardized Drink Recipes, Glassware, and Ice

Like food, all drinks must be prepared according to standards. If dispensers are not used, measures like jiggers or "Posi-Pourers" are used. When first learning

THE ABC GUEST CHECK
AND PAPER RECEIPT

ABC provides complete order information on either guest checks or paper reciepts. Here is a facsimile of each:

GUEST CHECK

```
Ck  0902 Prev. Total        .00
    CndnClub GingerAl      3.15
    WildTrky               3.55
         Manhattan         3.15
         PerfManh          3.15
  2  Budweiser             4.50
         WhtRussn          3.50
    Check Total           21.00
Ck  0902-01-95  09:16PM 10/25/98

TOTAL            21.00

Ck  0902 Prev. Total      21.00
    CndnClub GingerAl      3.15
    WildTrky               3.55
         Manhattan         3.15
    Check Total           30.85
Ck  0902-01-95  09:22PM 10/25/98

TOTAL            30.85

Ck  0902 Prev. Total      30.88
    Check Total           30.85
    Tax                    2.47
    Tip                    3.00
    Paid Amer ExPress     36.32
Ck  0902-01-95  09:26PM 10/25/98

TOTAL            36.32
```

DATE	SERVER	TABLE NO.	PERSONS	CHECK NO.
				508902

532 W. MARKET ST.
AKRON, OHIO

TYPE OF DRINKS

BRAND OF DRINKS

ComputerBar STATION NUMBER

PAYMENT METHOD

SERVER IDENTIFICATION NUMBER

DATE AND TIME OF DAY

CHECK NUMBER

PAPER RECEIPT

```
Chivas      Water     3.30
SeagrmVO    Soda      3.15
Vodka       Tonic     2.90
Vodka       Tonic     2.90
            BldyMary  2.90
            LI Ice T  3.50
Kahlua                3.60
Drambuie              3.60
RemyMrtn              3.65
RemyMrtn              3.65
Check Total          33.15
Tax                   2.65
Paid  Cash           35.80
     02-55  11:06PM 10/25/98

TOTAL           35.80
```

**ABC
Dispensing
Technologies, Inc.**
Technology for the
hospitality industry

✿ Makers of the ABC ComputerBar™

451 Kennedy Road
Akron, Ohio 44305
330/733-2841

FIGURE 12.4   ABC Computebar Management Report (Courtesy of ABC Dispensing Technologies, Akron, Ohio 44305).

ABC COMPUTERBAR MANAGEMENT REPORT

X-Read Ringoff #02	- 01:33 p.m.	06/08/92	
Accumulators Cleared	- 01:00 a.m.	06/07/92	

REPORT #1 – SALES BY MAJOR CATEGORY

Sales by Major Category	STATION 1 SALES	STATION 2 SALES	TOTAL SALES
Liquor	334.10	668.20	1002.30
Draft Beer	48.85	97.70	146.55
Bottled Beer	60.30	120.60	180.90
Wine	.00	.00	.00
Soft Drinks	32.30	64.60	96.90
Misc A	.00	.00	.00
Misc B	.00	.00	.00
Misc C	.00	.00	.00
PLU	.00	.00	.00
Non-Taxable Food	.00	.00	.00
Taxable Food	82.00	164.00	246.00
Special	.00	.00	.00
Beverages	475.55	951.10	1426.65
Non-Taxable Food	.00	.00	.00
Taxable Food	82.00	164.00	246.00
Special #1	.00	.00	.00
Special #2	.00	.00	.00
Price Mode 1	562.55	1125.10	1687.65
Mode 2	.00	.00	.00
Mode 3	.00	.00	.00
Tax Rate #1	.00	.00	.00
Rate #2	.00	.00	.00
Rate #3	.00	.00	.00
G.S.T. Rate #4	.00	.00	.00
Extracted Rate #5	.00	.00	.00
Reported Tips	5.00	10.00	15.00
Void Total	4.50	.00	4.50
Void Count	02	00	02
Transactions	36	72	108
Non-Clearing Sale	585.80	1171.60	1757.40
Gross Sales	562.55	1125.10	1687.65
Net Sales	557.55	1115.10	1672.65

MONITORS UP TO FOUR SEPARATE STATIONS

ABC Version JOT4B3   ⊕ *ABC ComputerBar*™

FIGURE 12.5   ABC Computerbar Management Report (Courtesy of ABC Dispensing Technologies, Akron, Ohio 44305).

ABC COMPUTERBAR MANAGEMENT REPORT

REPORT #3 – SALES BY SERVER

Reported Server	Total Tip-ES	Sales	Cash	Visa	MC	Amex	Dine	Voids
			[All Sales Include Tax and Tips]					
02	7.38	92.40	73.35	19.05	.00	.00	.00	.00
04	16.62	208.05	129.15	78.90	.00	.00	.00	.00
05	16.65	105.00	20.70	84.30	.00	.00	.00	.00
08	1.92	24.30	24.30	.00	.00	.00	.00	.00
09	2.16	27.00	27.00	.00	.00	.00	.00	.00
22	98.46	1230.90	916.35	223.80	10.50	80.25	.00	4.50
Totals	135.01	1687.65	1190.85	406.05	10.50	80.25	.00	4.50

REPORT #4 – SALES BY SETTLEMENT METHOD

Settlement Methods	STATION 01 SALES	STATION 02 SALES	TOTAL SALES
Cash	396.95	793.90	1190.85
VISA	135.35	270.70	406.15
MasterCard	3.50	7.00	10.50
AmericanExpr	26.75	53.50	80.25
Discover	.00	.00	.00
Total Settlements	562.55	1125.10	1687.65

ABC Version JOT4B3

 ABC ComputerBar™

FIGURE 12-6   ABC Computerbar Management Report (Courtesy of ABL Dispensing Technologies, Akron, Ohio 44305).

to mix drinks, measures should be used. You should not learn by "eye" or "count."

A drink recipe is much the same as one for a menu item. It lists ingredients, portions, and method of preparation.

Cost of Liquor	1 1/2 ounces @ $8 qt	$.375
Cost of Mix	4 oz @ $.025 oz	.10
Cost of Garnish	@ $.02	.02
Total		$.495

Prices charged are influenced by the same factors used in pricing menu items. Divide the beverage cost by the desired beverage cost percentage and adjust up or down according to indirect cost factors.

Cost	Price	Beverage Cost %
$.50	$1.95	25.4
$.50	$2.50	19.8
$.50	$2.95	16.8

Happy Hour with two-for-one would double each of the above percentages.

Operations that do not have elaborate point-of-sale units to record beverage sales usually classify their drinks into one of the following categories with a separate price for each category.

Highballs: vodka tonics, scotch and soda, 7 & 7

Cocktails: martini, manhattans

Collins/sours: whiskey sour, tom collins

Frozen drinks: frozen daiquiris and margaritas

Double liquor drinks: harvey wallbangers, tequila sunrise, rusty nails, godfather

Cream drinks: grasshoppers, pink squirrels

Cordials and liqueurs: amaretto, grand mariner

Specialty drinks: Zombies, Long Island Tea

In addition, prices are increased in each category when the customer requests a call or premium call brand be used (i.e., Stoli vodka and tonic; Tanqueray martini).

Glassware must be standardized and so must the size and quantity of ice used. Larger cubes are harder, melt slowly, and are best for making cocktails. However, they do not displace much liquid when used for on-the-rocks drinks where "mini-cubes" are recommended. When making cocktails, always start with fresh ice. See Figure 12-7.

All transactions need to be entered into the system. If you do not possess a point-of-sale system, each order needs to be written on a check similar to a food order so you can go back and determine the sales mix of alcoholic bever-

STEMMED COCKTAIL GLASS: (Martini, Manhattan, etc.) ranges in capacity from 3-to 4½-ounces.

ALL-PURPOSE WINE: 4-to 8-ounces; stemmed glass.

WHISKEY SOUR: 3½-to 4½-ounces.

STANDARD WINE: from 3-to 4-ounces; stemmed glass.

OLD-FASHIONED: 6-to 9-ounces; average size is 8-ounces. Used for "on the rocks."

CORDIAL: sometimes called a Pony; 1-ounce capacity is normal.

ROLY POLY: adaptable for many drinks; ranges from 5-ounces to 13-ounces in size. May be used for "on the rocks."

BRANDY SNIFTER: designed to enhance aroma; 6-to 12-ounce capacity.

STANDARD HIGHBALL OR TUMBLER: 8-to 12-ounce capacity; straight sided shell or sham.

Sherry: 2-ounce capacity is normal.

COOLER: tall, slim glass for summer beverages, (Zombie, Collins, etc.), varied capacity, 14-to 16-ounces are popular. Often frosted.

SHOT GLASS: lined or unlined; 1-ounce capacity with ¾-to 1½-ounce line.

PILSNER: 8-to 12-ounces; 10-ounce size is most popular.

SHAM PILSNER: 8-to 12-ounce capacity.

STEIN OR BEER MUG: 8-to 12-ounce capacity.

TAPERED CONE PILSNER: 8-to 12-ounce capacity.

TULIP CHAMPAGNE: 6-to 8-ounce capacity; sometimes hollow-stemmed.

STEM PILSNER: 8-to 12-ounce capacity.

SAUCER CHAMPAGNE: ranges from 4½-to 7½-ounces.

GOBLET: 6-to 10-ounce capacity.

FIGURE 12-7 Common sizes and shapes of liquor glasses.

ages. No drinks should be issued without a written requisition. In some bars and lounges, servers carry their own banks and pay for every drink they serve. Such a system guarantees that the house is paid first.

BEVERAGE FRAUDS

Only a few of the most common beverage frauds perpetrated on restaurant and lounge owners are discussed here. Whenever the bartender has access to the cash drawer, such frauds can occur. If bartenders do not handle cash, as with service bars and banquet bars, or the operation utilizes liquor dispensing systems that measure each drink dispensed or the actual bottles are never touched by the bartender, the likelihood of fraud diminishes. When the servers carry their own banks, occasionally collusion between a server and a bartender can occur. But this happens less frequently than the employee who can act alone. This list is by no means exhaustive and is offered only to show the most common kinds of fraud and how they can be detected and prevented.

Short Pouring

Realistically, not every transaction can be monitored. Short pouring is where the drink is under-portioned and the amount "stockpiled" until a full drink can be made and sold without showing a deduction from inventory. This can be done even with automatic dispensing systems.

1. Watch for bartenders keeping a glass under the bar with liquor in it. This is not a frequent occurrence since it takes so much time and can be easily observed.

2. Require bartenders to use a jigger to measure all drinks. The opportunity for this to occur would be with free pouring where bartenders will "short pour" and after four or five drinks have enough for a free drink.

Customers especially vulnerable to short-pour fraud are those requesting doubles. Happy hour is another time when free-pouring bartenders can make a lot of money with short pouring because of the two-for-one or doubles-for-one price structure.

Substituting House Brands for Call Brands

Because there is a price differential between house brands and call brands, a bartender can substitute a house brand and charge for a call brand. This is a difficult one to control. Many restaurants have limited the number of brands of liquor served and are using a call brand as their house brand. For example, they may use Jack Daniels Green as their well bourbon. They will subsequently reduce the number of premium call brands on the back bar.

Only a few customers will be able to detect that their Black Jack and Coke has been substituted with Old Library. The substitution will not likely be made when bourbon and water or soda is ordered. If you suspect that this is being done, a secret shopper may be able to detect it.

Dilution of Liquor

This occurs typically at inventory time to cover up missing liquor. The white spirits like your gins and vodkas are the most vulnerable to be diluted with water. However, if this is taking place you will likely be receiving a lot of complaints about weak drinks. Look for more than one bottle of a particular brand open behind the bar. The diluted bottle can be used in drinks like Screwdriver, Bloody Marys, and Long Island Tea because the mix overpowers the taste of the white liquor.

Bringing in Own Bottle

Bartenders can easily bring in their own bottle of stock liquor and pour from their own bottle and never record the usage or sale. With 30 shots per bottle at $2.95 per drink, a bartender can steal close to $90 a shift, and the inventory will never show that the sales ever took place. There are several things an operator can do to prevent this occurrence or increase the likelihood that it will be detected.

1. Use an indelible stamp on all bottles leaving the liquor storeroom. A black ultraviolet light reveals the stamp on authorized bottles. Periodically check the bottles at the bar. Also, the tax stamp on liquor sold by the wholesale distributor or state liquor store is a different color than the stamp of bottles sold in retail outlets. Look for the different stamp color.

2. Keep a par stock number of each type of liquor behind the bar. If you notice that there is an extra bottle of bourbon, get out the black light and look for the bottle stamp.

3. Inspect all empty bottles before breaking and discarding. If you use the empty bottles to determine the issues from the storeroom to replenish the stock, you have another check point for foreign bottles.

4. Do not let employees bring backpacks or large handbags behind the bar. Have employees enter and leave through one entrance and check all packages large enough to hide a bottle.

5. If you have an automatic dispensing system, the bartenders may never touch the bottle so it eliminates free pouring completely. However, it is an expensive mechanical cost control system.

Giving Away Free Drinks

This is a ploy for bartenders to increase their tips or simply pocket the money from the customer without ringing the transaction. It is usually used with over-pouring as a strong drink is considered better than a weak one. This is used when the restaurant has a lounge with stools and customers come in just to drink and socialize.

Require a cash register receipt to be printed for each drink and placed down with the drink when served. Require a tab be run with the check placed in front of the customer or in a rack with slots corresponding to seats at the bar. If the problem is excessive, some have initiated a procedure that in prominently posted, "Your drink is free if we fail to give you a receipt." Some even use a tape with randomly printed "stars" that qualify the patron for a free drink. The object is to get the transaction recorded and entered into the system.

The sale of nonalcoholic beverages including virgin Bloody Marys, Piña Coladas, and soft drinks from the bar are virtually untraceable, even with a point-of-sale system unless the sale is entered into the register. The policy that a check or receipt must be printed on each sale is still the only way to control this fraud, but management must routinely check for compliance. In some instances, these virgin drinks and mocktails could be charged as alcohol drinks and rung in as nonalcoholic.

Money can be taken directly from the cash register and be undetectable until the drawer is reconciled at the end of the night. If more than one bartender is working out of a cash drawer, one could steal knowing that they will have to make it up. But if $60 is taken and each bartender has to ante up $20, the guilty one still comes out $40 ahead. Limit access to cash drawers to one bartender so each is responsible for his or her own cash.

There are only three places where bartenders can keep their "extra earnings": in the register, in their pockets, or in their tip jars. Putting money into their pockets would be risky and likely questioned by management. If a tip jar is used, "extra" money will be placed into it immediately. Without the tip jar, the only other place the money could be is in the register.

Extra funds placed in the tip jar are usually divided among all the bartenders working. Consequently, the bartender who took the extra will likely retrieve it before it is divided, a difficult task to go undetected by the other bartenders. If the cash drawer is the location of the extra earnings, and management, not the bartender counts the drawer at the end of the night, the money will have to be removed from the register before the closing reading. If management suspects that this might be occurring, a random change of the drawer in the middle of the shift will result in cash over in the drawer.

Collusion between Server and Bartender

Again, the greatest likelihood of this type of fraud occurs because management cannot obtain an accurate sales mix of drinks served. If your operation does not have a point-of-sale system, you are vulnerable. With a point-of-sale system, you reduce the likelihood of fraud because your records will reveal that you have a problem.

The most important element of control is getting the transaction recorded and entered into the system *before* the drink is made and served. You can still have control without a point-of-sale system, and restaurant and lounges have used these controls for many years. Steak & Ale restaurants had a very effective system that still works well today in operations with written guest and bar checks. They issued servers separate checks for food and liquor. They did not allow the server to *verbally* transmit the beverage order to the bartender. This simple rule required them to write the order on the beverage check. The bar check was placed in a check rack at the service bar. A system of abbreviations and descriptions was used to identify what was ordered.

The bartender filled the order and placed a grease pencil line under the last drink prepared to indicate it was completed. He did not accept cash but could not make a drink without that check being submitted. The server attached the beverage check to the food check when presenting the bill to the guest for payment.

This system, however, can be beaten as related to me by one of my former students who worked in a hotel lounge. It requires the bartender to be lax about marking the ticket with the grease pencil. This allows the server to "resubmit" the same check when a second round of the same drinks are ordered. Since the server also collects the money, she can collect for all the drinks served but show that only one round is written on the check. She splits her earnings with the bartender at the end of the night. This student related that cocktail waitresses were stealing up to $100 per shift in a very busy downtown commercial hotel lounge.

No system is foolproof. You need to check for compliance and make it very clear that noncompliance will result in dismissal and prosecution.

Inventory Fraud

Inventory fraud occurs with both beverage as well as food. In operations where month-end inventories are taken to compute cost of food or beverage consumed and sold, verification of inventory is a critically important element of this calculation. In chain-owned corporate restaurants, the corporate or district supervisor or vice president will likely make only a few physical visits to the locations each year unless there are problems with food, labor, or beverage cost.

Each manager is given certain cost standards that they are expected to meet to earn bonuses, raises, and promotions. Some managers have learned how to "manipulate" the numbers to get the results that corporate management expects. One way they always achieve their food and beverage cost percentages is by falsifying their inventory amounts. By overstating their liquor inventories, they will *reduce* the cost of beverage consumed. Thus when that amount is divided by the beverage sales, the smaller cost of beverage consumed produces a lower beverage cost percentage.

Whenever a manager is transferred from one store to another, or when a new bar manager takes over a different store, you must verify the inventory amounts. This is especially important if the previous manager had been at that location for an extended period of time. Since the general manager approves all the reports sent to corporate, he or she will have the opportunity to "adjust" the figures to make costs come out.

I have been told of auditors discovering as much as $15,000 in missing liquor inventory when a new manager took control. Corporate management and ownership must physically certify inventory and petty cash at least once a year to detect this kind of fraud.

In all these cases, the use of *secret shopper* services can help find fraud if you expect it. You instruct the company to send in shoppers to observe bartenders, servers, and management and specifically tell them what you want them to look for.

Index